The Anthropocene: Politik—Economics—Society—Science

Volume 5

Series editor

Hans Günter Brauch, Mosbach, Germany

More information about this series at http://www.springer.com/series/15232
http://www.afes-press-books.de/html/APESS.htm
http://www.afes-press-books.de/html/APESS_04-05.htm

Úrsula Oswald Spring · Hans Günter Brauch
Serena Eréndira Serrano Oswald
Juliet Bennett
Editors

Regional Ecological Challenges for Peace in Africa, the Middle East, Latin America and Asia Pacific

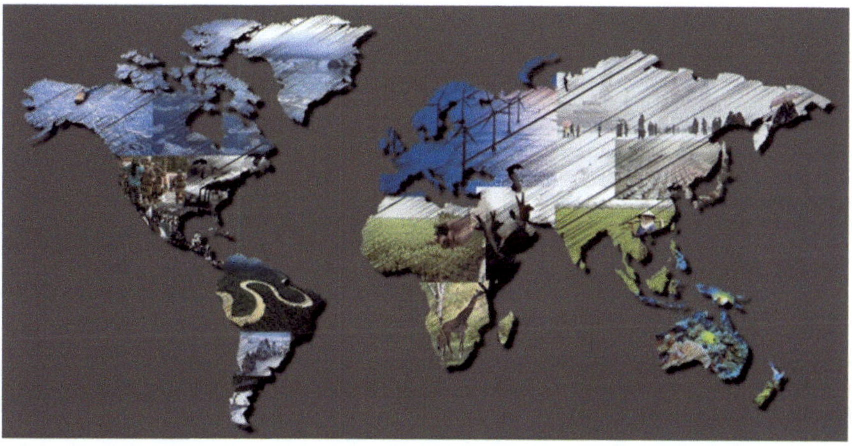

Springer

IPRA2014

Editors
Úrsula Oswald Spring
Centre for Regional Multidisciplinary Studies (CRIM)
National Autonomous University of Mexico (UNAM)
Cuernavaca, Morelos
Mexico

Serena Eréndira Serrano Oswald
Centre for Regional Multidisciplinary Studies (CRIM)
National Autonomous University of Mexico (UNAM)
Cuernavaca, Morelos
Mexico

Hans Günter Brauch
Peace Research and European Security Studies (AFES-PRESS)
Mosbach, Baden-Württemberg
Germany

Juliet Bennett
Centre for Peace and Conflict Studies
University of Sydney
Sydney, New South Wales
Australia

ISSN 2367-4024 ISSN 2367-4032 (electronic)
The Anthropocene: Politik—Economics—Society—Science
ISBN 978-3-319-30559-2 ISBN 978-3-319-30560-8 (eBook)
DOI 10.1007/978-3-319-30560-8

Library of Congress Control Number: 2016946019

Copyediting: PD Dr. Hans Günter Brauch, AFES-PRESS e.V., Mosbach, Germany
Language Editing: Juliet Bennett, University of Sydney, Sydney, Australia and Mike Headon, Colwyn Bay, Wales, Great Britain (Chapters 4, 8)

The photo on the book cover was taken on 26 December 2013 in Vientiane, the capital of Laos, by © Hans Günter Brauch who also granted the permission to use it here. The image on the internal title page was designed by Angel Paredes Rivera, Cuernavaca, Mexico. More on this book is at: http://www.afes-press-books.de/html/APESS_04-05.htm.

Printed on acid-free paper

This Springer imprint is published by Springer Nature
The registered company is Springer International Publishing AG Switzerland

Foreword

When Pope Francis declared in the wake of the 13 November 2015 shootings in Paris that left over 120 people dead that we have entered the 'Third World War', not many people took him seriously. What is more, I suspect that most people would want to see the Pope's declaration as simply referring to acts of extremism and terrorism such as these random shootings and killings and many others like them earlier in 2014 and 2015 in Paris, Sydney, Copenhagen, etc.

However, a more complex reading of this declaration, given the Pope's recent calls on the rich world to do more to end global poverty, is likely to include other equally or more threatening global conflicts and crises, such as global warming and its immediate consequences (e.g. hurricanes, tsunamis, floods, earthquakes), growing inequality, poverty, forced migration, human trafficking and so on. All these challenges are simply dismissed as 'invisible crises of everyday life'.

As the essays in this collection argue, these 'invisible' forms of violence, what Johann Galtung, one of the founders of peace studies, called 'structural violence', are at the centre of the increasing imbalances in global society created by the 'processes of globalization and global environment'. What makes this volume an exceptional collective effort is its multidisciplinary approach, grounded in just peace theory. It analyses the negative impact of the hegemonic global power structure, fed and sustained by corporate global capitalism, on the livelihood, well-being and health of the vast majority of people in global society, especially in the global South. All the essays are rich in research and analysis, and provide a holistic appreciation of a human-centred approach to addressing, or preventing, the challenges of globalization and its ecological transformations. As the book argues in its introduction, "The processes of globalization and global environmental change have created increasing socio-economic imbalances among continents, nations and social classes within the countries."

The other strength of this collection is the inclusion of global perspectives and case studies from almost all corners of the world on how the 'fierce' structures of global capitalism are unleashing havoc on vulnerable societies. Amartya Sen, the 1998 Nobel Laureate for Economics, describes this form of violence as being created "by the imposition of singular and belligerent identities on gullible people, championed by proficient artisans of terror" (Sen 2006: 2). This point is underscored by Shaw (2012), who argues that for a solution to be found in the eradication of global poverty, "the obstacles standing in the way of the realization of the Right to Development as fully adopted in Vienna in 1993 must be resolved or removed".

The volume also analyses how countries in the global South, despite all the gains made by the emerging BRICS countries (Brazil, Russia, India, China, and South Africa) in serving as a global counterweight in a still largely unipolar world order since the demise of the Soviet Union in 1989, "are still in a lower level of regional development and complexity, due to the colonial and postcolonial processes of domination, exploitation of natural resources, terrorist attacks and power inequalities". Moreover, all this despite their apparent 'social resilience', as is evident in the coping mechanisms of Palestinians denied access to clean water; Columbians using cultural networks and relations to resolve conflicts and build peace; the Japanese developing strategies to overcome air pollution; the Vietnamese using human rights approaches to win the right to have nuclear energy; the DDR programme to rehabilitate former combatants in the Niger Delta conflict in Nigeria, and so on.

The contributions in this volume have implications for the human rights approach to development and have the potential to enrich research and policy in the broad field of human development, and they serve as an important resource for students and scholars of peace and conflict studies, development studies, geography, human rights, and global political economy. I commend the editors, Úrsula Oswald Spring, Hans Günter Brauch, Serena Eréndira Serrano Oswald and Juliet Bennett, for their hard work in putting together such a very useful and relevant volume.[1]

Newcastle upon Tyne Ibrahim Seaga Shaw, Ph.D.
26 January 2016

[1]Dr. Ibrahim Seaga Shaw is Senior Lecturer in Media and Politics and Programme Leader for the MA in Media Cultures at Northumbria University in Newcastle upon Tyne, UK. He holds a PhD from the Sorbonne and is Secretary General of the International Peace Research Association (IPRA). His research interests include media and human rights; media, conflict and development; democracy and media agenda-setting; business and journalism, political economy of media and journalism, peace journalism; history of journalism; global journalism; and media representations of conflict and humanitarian intervention. His work has been published in highly respected journals and he is the author of the groundbreaking book Human Rights Journalism (2012) and co-editor of Expanding Peace Journalism (2012). He is also the author of Business Journalism: A Critical Political Economy Approach (2015) and co-editor of Communicating Differences (2016). He has a background in journalism spanning 20 years, having worked in Sierra Leone, Britain and France.

Acknowledgements

This book and another volume on *Addressing Global Environmental Challenges from a Peace Ecology Perspective* emerged from written papers that were orally presented in the several sessions of the *Ecology and Peace Commission* (EPC) during the 25th Conference of the *International Peace Research Association* (IPRA) in Istanbul in August 10–15, 2014, on the occasion of the 50th anniversary of IPRA and 100 years after the start of World War I on July 28, 1914.

The editors are grateful to Dr. Nesrin Kenar—with Dr. Ibrahim Shaw, co-secretary-general of IPRA (2012–2016)—who organized the Istanbul conference with her able team from Sakarya University at the Bosporus where Europe and Asia meet. We also thank all the sponsors—including the IPRA Foundation—who supported the participation of a few colleagues from developing and low-income countries who had submitted written papers that were assessed with regard to their scientific quality by the two EPC co-organizers as a precondition for their grant.

The four co-editors of these two books would like to thank all authors who passed the double-blind anonymous peer review process and subsequently revised their papers taking many critical comments and suggestions of these reviewers into account. Each chapter was at least reviewed by three external reviewers who are unrelated to the editors and the authors and in most cases also came from different countries.

We would like to thank all reviewers who spent much time to read and comment on the submitted texts and made detailed perceptive and critical remarks and suggestions for improvements—even for texts that could not be included in both volumes. The texts by the editors had to pass the same review process based on the same criteria. The goal of the editors has been thus to enhance the quality of the submitted texts. The editors were bound by these reviewers' reports, even if they did not necessarily agree with all their comments and decisions on acceptance or rejection.

The following colleagues (in alphabetical order) contributed anonymous reviews:

- Dr. Kwesi Aning, Kofi Annan Centre, Accra, Ghana
- Ms. Juliet Bennett, University of Sydney, Australia
- Prof. Dr. Sigurd Bergmann, Norwegian National Technical University Trondheim (NRNU), Norway
- Dr. Katherina Bitzker, University of Manitoba, Canada
- Dr. Lynda-Ann Blanchard, University of Sydney, Australia
- Prof. Dr. Michael Bothe, emeritus, Johann Wolfgang Goethe University, Frankfurt on Main, Germany
- PD Dr. Hans Günter Brauch, ret., Free University of Berlin, Germany
- Mr. Christopher Brown, University of Sydney, Australia
- Dr. Carl Bruch, Environmental Law Institute, Washington., D.C., USA
- Prof. Dr. Halvard Buhaug, Norwegian National Technical University Trondheim and Peace Research Institute Oslo, Norway
- Prof. Dr. Ken Conca, American University, Washington., D.C., USA
- Prof. Dr. Hendrix Cullen, University of Denver, Colorado, USA
- Prof. Dr. Paul Custler, Lenoir Rhyne University, North Carolina, USA
- Prof. Dr. Simon Dalby, CIGI Chair, Political Economy of Climate Change, Balsillie School of International Affairs; Professor of Geography and Environmental Studies, Wilfrid Laurier University, Waterloo, Ontario, Canada
- Dr. Paul Duffill, University of Sydney, Australia
- Dr. Josh Fisher, Columbia University, USA
- Dr. Giovanna Gioli, Hamburg University, Germany
- Mr. Karlson Hargroves, Adelaide University, Australia
- Fredrik S. Heffermehl, Nobel Peace Prize Watch, Oslo, Norway
- Dr. Francis Hutchinson, University of Sydney, Australia
- Dr. Tobias Ide, Georg Eckert Institute for School Book Research, Braunschweig, Germany
- Dr. Anders Jägerskop, Stockholm International Water Institute, Stockholm, Sweden
- Dr. Peter King, University of Sydney, Australia
- Jesús Antonio Machuca R., Faculty of Political and Social Sciences, UNAM, Mexico
- Dr. Eyal Mayroz, University of Sydney, Australia
- Dr. Annabel McGoldrick, University of Sydney, Australia
- Prof. Dr. Syed Sikander Mehdi, University of Karachi, Pakistan
- Dr. Bonaventure Mkandawire, Director of Research and Training at Church and Society Programme, CCAP Livingstonia Synod, Mzuzu, Malawi
- Prof. Dr. Michael Northcott, University of Edinburgh, Scotland, UK
- Prof. Dr. Úrsula Oswald Spring, UNAM, CRIM
- Dr. John Pokoo, Kofi Annan Centre, Accra, Ghana
- Prof. Dr. Mary Louise Pratt, New York University, New York, USA
- Abe Quadan, University of Sydney, Australia

- Prof. Dr. Daniel Reichman, University of Rochester, New Jersey, USA
- Prof. Dr. Luc Reychler, Emeritus, University of Leuven, Belgium; former Secretary-General of IPRA
- Dr. Vivianna Rodriguez Carreon, University of Sydney, Australia
- Dr. Hilmi Salem, Bethlehem, Palestine
- Prof. Dr. Salvany Santiago, Federal University of Sao Francisco Valley, Brazil
- Dr. Janpeter Schilling, Hamburg University, Germany
- Dr. Klaus Schlichtmann, Nihon University, Japan
- Dr. Ayesha Siddiqi, King's College London, London, UK
- Dr. Sunil Tankha, Institute for Social Studies (ISS), The Hague, The Netherlands
- Andres Macias Tolosa, Universidad Externado de Colombia, Colombia
- Em. Prof. Garry Trompf, University of Sydney, Australia
- Prof. Dr. Thanh-Dam Truong, Emerita, Institute for Social Studies (ISS), The Hague, The Netherlands
- Prof. Dr. Catherine M. Tucker, Indiana University, Indiana, USA
- Prof. Dr. Arthur H. Westing, Westing Associates, Vermont, USA; ret., SIPRI, PRIO
- Prof. Dr. Kazuyo Yamane, Ritsumeikan University, Kyoto, Japan

These two books are the result of an international teamwork among the editors and convenors of IPRA's EPC. As co-convenors, *Prof. Dr. Úrsula Oswald Spring* and *PD Dr. Hans Günter Brauch* organized several sessions of IPRA's EPC in Istanbul and are also the two lead authors of the introductory chapters of both books. Hans Günter Brauch prepared both volumes, managed the peer review process, and did the copyediting. As a native English speaker, *Ms. Juliet Bennett* (Sydney University, Australia)—who was elected in Istanbul as the third EPC co-convenor—language-edited the contributions of the second book and also authored the concluding chapter of this second volume.

The publication and production of this book was handled by an able female team of editors and producers at Springer's office in Heidelberg coordinated by *Dr. Johanna Schwarz*, senior publishing editor, focused on earth system sciences, marine geosciences, paleoclimatology, polar sciences, and volcanology, and *Janet Sterritt-Brunner* (producer and project coordinator) both working at Springer's editorial office in Heidelberg, Germany, and *Ms. Divya Selvaraj*, *Ms. Vinoth Selvamani* and *Mr. Arulmurugan V.* who coordinated the typesetting and production of the book in Chennai, Tamil Nadu, India. Thus, this book is the result of a close cooperation among authors, reviewers, and producers from all five continents.

The editors are looking forward to see new readers, speakers, and authors at IPRA's next conference in Freetown (Sierra Leone) in November/December 2016.

Cuernavaca, Mexico — Úrsula Oswald Spring
Mosbach, Germany — Hans Günter Brauch
Cuernavaca, Mexico — Serena Eréndira Serrano Oswald
Sydney, Australia — Juliet Bennett
December 2015

Contents

Abbreviations

AEC	Atomic Energy Commission
AIES	Arava Institute of Environmental Studies
APEC	Asian Pacific Economic Cooperation
ASEAN	Association of Southeast Asian Nations
AU	African Union
BRICS	Brazil, Russia, India, China, and South Africa
CEN-SAD	Community of Sahel-Saharan State
COMESA	Common Market for Eastern and Southern Africa
CONACULTA	National Council for Culture and Arts, Mexico
CRIM	Regional Multidisciplinary Research Centre
CTWM	Center for Transboundary Water Management
DNA	US Defense Nuclear Agency
DRAE	Dictionary of the Royal Spanish Academy
DRR	Disarmament, demobilization and reintegration
EAC	East African Community
ECCAS	Economic Community of Central African States
ECOWAS	Economic Community of West African States
EPC	Ecology and Peace Commission
EU	European Union
EZLN	Zapatista Army of National Liberation
FCR	Frontier Crimes Regulation (FCR)
GNP	Gross national product
ICH	Intangible Cultural Heritage
IGAD	Intergovernmental Authority on Development
IMF	International Monetary Fund
INAFED	National Institute for Federalism and Municipal Development, Mexico
INEGI	National Institute of Statistics and Geography, Mexico
IPRA	International Peace Research Association
km	Kilometer

M-19	April 19th Movement (in Columbia)
NCA	National Constituent Assembly
NDB	New Development Bank
NPP	Nuclear power plant
ODA	Official development assistance
ODA	Japanese Official Development Assistance
PAP	Presidential Amnesty Programme
PECC	Pacific Economic Cooperation Council
PWEG	The Palestinian Wastewater Engineers Group
SADC	South African Development Community
SCO	Shanghai Cooperation Organization
UMA	Arab Maghreb Union
UN	United Nations
UNAM	National Autonomous University of Mexico
UNESCO	United Nations Educational, Scientific and Cultural Organization
US	United States
WTO	World Trade Organization

Chapter 1
Introduction: Regional Ecological Challenges for Peace in Africa, the Middle East, Latin America and Asia Pacific

Úrsula Oswald Spring, Hans Günter Brauch, Serena Eréndira Serrano Oswald and Juliet Bennett

1.1 On Regions and Regional Development

The processes of globalization and global environmental change have created increasing socioeconomic imbalances among continents, nations and social classes within the countries. Twenty-five years ago, with the end of the Cold War, the bipolar division of the world has been overcome and in several parts of the world regional cooperation among developing countries has intensified. Multiple mechanisms are still subordinating developing countries (*hinterlands*) and social groups to the hegemonic necessities of corporate capitalism, and its dominant countries.

A new regional cooperation between Russia and four key developing countries and strategic zones in South America, Asia and Africa—*Brazil, Russia, India, China and South Africa* (BRICS)—was established in 2006 and expanded in 2010 to include South Africa representing a total of 3 billion people or 42 % of world population and 20 % of global GNP. In July 2014 the BRICS set up a *New*

Prof. Dr. Úrsula Oswald Spring, full-time Professor/Researcher at the *National University of Mexico* (UNAM) in the *Regional Multidisciplinary Research Center* (CRIM); co-convenor, IPRA's Ecology and Commission (2012-2016); Email: uoswald@gmail.com.

PD Dr. Hans Günter Brauch, chairman, Peace Research and European Security Studies (AFES-PRESS), since 1987; co-convenor, IPRA's Ecology and Commission (2012-2016), Mosbach, Germany; Email: brauch@afes-press.de.

Dr. Serena Eréndira Serrano Oswald; researcher, *Regional Multidisciplinary Research Center* (CRIM); president of AMECIDER Mexico; Email: sesohi@hotmail.com.

Juliet Bennett, PhD candidate, University of Sydney; co-convenor, IPRA's Ecology and Commission (2014-2016); Email: juliet.bennett@sydney.edu.au.

Ú.Oswald Spring et al. (eds.), *Regional Ecological Challenges for Peace in Africa, the Middle East, Latin America and Asia Pacific*, The Anthropocene: Politik—Economics—Society—Science 5, DOI 10.1007/978-3-319-30560-8_1

Development Bank (NDB)[1] to partly balance the influence of the World Bank, the *International Monetary Fund* (IMF) and the *World Trade Organization* (WTO).

The BRICS have attempted to counter the economic and political dominance of the United States as the only remaining military superpower and of the OECD world. As an emerging intraregional organization the BRICS link five major countries in South America (Brazil), Europe and Asia (Russia, India, China) and Africa (South Africa), including three nuclear powers and two permanent members of the UN Security Council. On the regional level, international organizations with different levels and intensity of cooperation have developed. In Europe, since 1990 the *European Union* (EU) has both widened (to include 28 countries) and deepened (with a common currency), and as a result the freedom of movement of capital goods and people has increased. In South East Asia, the *Association of Southeast Asian Nations* (ASEAN) has expanded to ten countries uniting the whole region.

In North America, in 1994 the *North American Free Trade Agreement* (NAFTA) was set up to boost trade while preventing the free movement of people (especially from Mexico to the USA and Canada). In South America the Mercosur and the Andean Pact have not yet resulted in a common market. In Africa, the *African Union* (AU) has tried to play a major role on issues of peace and security in the region, while sub-regional organizations have emerged in West Africa [*Economic Community of West African States* (ECOWAS)], in Southern Africa [*South African Development Community* (SADC)], and in Eastern Africa [East African Community (EAC)].

In 2001, in Asia the *Shanghai Cooperation Organization* (SCO) was established as a Eurasian political, economic and military organization in Shanghai by the leaders of China, Kazakhstan, Kyrgyzstan, Russia, Tajikistan, and Uzbekistan. On 10 July 2015, the SCO decided to admit India and Pakistan as full members, and they are expected to join by 2016.

Across the Pacific, already in 1989 with active membership of the United States and Australia several political and economic organizations were launched, such as the *Asian Pacific Economic Cooperation* (APEC) with 21 members in Asia, Australia and South America while the *Pacific Economic Cooperation Council* (PECC) is a private non-governmental tripartite partnership of senior individuals from business and industry, government, academic and other intellectual circles who all take part in their private capacity discussing current, practical policy issues of the Asia Pacific region.

Within the framework of the neoliberal paradigm (or 'Washington Consensus') of the Post Cold War era, the different levels of intensity and efforts of regional

[1]The goal of the NDB is to "mobilize resources for infrastructure and sustainable development projects in BRICS and other emerging economies and developing countries" (Agreement on the New Development Bank, Fortaleza, July 15, 2015), in: *Government of Brazil*. 15 July 2014; *Wall Street Journal*, 16 July 2015. NDB headquarter is in Shanghai, China and each of the five participants holds an equal number of shares with equal voting rights. There is no veto right. The proposal is to pay to the NDB directly and during the next seven years 20 % of half up to one million of shares, with a value of USD 100,000 each of them.

association and cooperation also indicate a growing complexity involved in the free flow of capital and goods and in the deregulation of public affairs in many countries. There is a need to overcome the remnants of existing protectionisms and subsidies that many OECD countries in the North in addition to threshold countries in the South e.g. China, India and South East Asia, have benefitted from, while the poverty in many developing countries has increased, especially in Africa, in parts of Asia and Latin America.

The European Union has emerged as the only supranational organization of 28 European countries of different levels of economic development which has neither the properties of a state (sovereignty, people, system of rule), but its own tripartite governance structure (of the Council as the representative body of the 28 members countries, the European Commission and the directly elected European Parliament) with their own sources of income with an inbuilt solidarity system that has resulted in financial transfers to poorer regions, both in Southern and Eastern Europe and financial support for countries with severe economic and financial and debt problems (e.g. in Ireland, Spain, Portugal, Greece and Italy).

We now live in an era of financial globalization and the "great recession that began in 2008, millions of people in America and all over the world lost their homes and jobs" (Stiglitz 2010: xi). It is a time in which the impacts of global environmental change are increasing in visibility (Brauch et al. 2008, 2009, 2011a, b), and in which there is an increasing complexity in the social, political, financial and cultural developments required from analysts to explore different approaches to regionalism and regional studies, not always referring to neighbouring territories, but also to hegemonic or counterhegemonic interests (e.g. Cuba, Venezuela, Bolivia and Brazil).

From a postcolonial and exploitative approach of people and resources by former colonial powers and the superpower, new factors such as security, cooperation, culture, biodiversity, identity, coherence, governance, sustainability, threats, challenges, vulnerabilities and risks, and related to global environmental change and climate change have widened and deepened the regional analysis. From a strict coercive approach, free cooperation among nations increased as a reflex of a long-term historical process. Hettne et al. (1999, 2000, 2001) proposed to conceptualize regions as processes with different phases of formation, similar to the process of evolution of species proposed by Charles Darwin (1859). Together with Bassols (2002), they started with a *regional space* as a geographical zone, delimited by physical obstacles such as watersheds, mountains etc.; for example, Rio Grande being the border between Mexico and the United States. Without any doubt the roots of a region are related to its territory, and whenever this unity is administrated by communities they are increasingly interrelated (in the pre-Westphalian phase). There exist multiple conflicts related to the expansion of the territory and the appropriation of the natural resources, which during the 19th and 20th century were basically resolved by invasion and occupation or financial and commercial penetration (e.g. the United States open-door policy in China).

Paradoxically, conquest, invasion and coercive processes of regionalisation produced a second phase, the *regional complex* (Telo 2001), where relations among neighbouring communities deepened. These interrelations brought communities to achieve certain consensus and an incipient peaceful conciliation process was able to bring some stability and security to its inhabitants (Oswald Spring 2002). These organizations represent a type of embryonic state, where the initial anarchy has been replaced slowly by an organization of power equilibrium. New conquest brought major cohesion thanks to alliances (e.g. Cantons of Switzerland who allied in 1291 against Habsburg, or as in the triple alliance among the Aztecs in Tenochtitlan in 1565).

In a third phase *regional societies* emerged, when different nations signed formal cultural, social, economic and political agreements. This cooperation was often imposed from top-down (colonial states such as Congo or India and Pakistan) and produced a formal region. Other attempts started by an integration process from bottom-up related to collective interests, which produce regions with stable integration. From a legally constituted nation-state, several states can ally according to common interests (e.g. UN, APEC, SCO, NAFTA). This phase represents a *regional community* (Telo 2001), able to produce a stable and durable association with social communication, and convergence of common values and actions. These regional communities were basically based on common economic interests, and were the building blocks of the African Union (AU). For example, the Arab Maghreb Union (UMA), Common Market for Eastern and Southern Africa (COMESA), Community of Sahel-Saharan State (CEN-SAD), East Africa Community (EAC), Economic Community of Central African States (ECCAS), Economic Community of West African States (ECOWAS), Intergovernmental Authority on Development (IGAD) and South African Development Community (SADC). These types of supranational associations are based on mutual confidence and joint interests. In all these phases plural interests are then involved in the negotiation processes and differences are agreed through dialogue, and not by war or the destruction of the other.

With the growing complexity of interaction, a *regional institutionalized system* is created by interested states, which has a democratic structure of decision-making and binding legal agreements. It includes an institutionalized system of global democracy. Citizens are consulted, a strong civil society lobbies their government, and the citizens approve a common legal framework by personal vote, thus the laws are respected by all their members. Hüller (2012) asks if these global democratic structures encounter the normative standards of democratic accountability and transparency. He starts by studying the European Union as the most advanced cosmopolitan democracy, and finds still structural democratic deficits in the EU, when compared to national democracies. He writes:

> The EU faces a gradual deficit in democratic capacities and the global reality of cosmopolitan democracy … The main findings is: Vertical accountability is either more ineffective or more inegalitarian or both. Neither unitary nor federal systems should be seen

as a plausible solution for the threat of 'Verselbständigung' caused by multilevel politics.[2] And nationally segmented public spheres will not promote a similar type of politicised discourses around 'common' global issues (Hüller 2012: 249).

Breslin/Higgott (2000) mention certain logic of historical evolution in this development process of understanding of regionalism, where greater complexity is progressively integrated. They also indicate that the present nation states and exogenous and endogenous regional policies have created a complex mosaic of globalization, where the diverse processes of regionalization obey different logics. They integrate human actors, often with antagonistic interests, thus the integration to a higher level of regionalism may fail. Furthermore, not all *regional institutionalized systems* are based on consensus and the optimization of wellbeing among the participants. As the recent wars in Iraq, Syria, Palestine, Sudan, etc. indicate, there exist hegemonic interests on strategic resources and geopolitical calculation of regional and global powers. On the other side, the historical evolution of globalization and global interaction indicates that regional autarchy and decoupling is no longer viable and all countries are pushed to take a global integration towards the present globalization.

Experience indicates, as Stiglitz (2010) emphasises, that faith in the invisible hand of free markets and globalization has not brought the promised prosperity. On the contrary, with greater deregulation and financial engineering, risks of global economic crises have increased and promoted selectivity, destruction of human and natural well-being, crisis, and conflicts (Toussaint 2015). To continue with the present model of globalization based on the *Bretton Woods* agreements and the dollar as the basic currency for international interactions, the future of nature and human beings is under risk (Beck 2011).

Nevertheless, there is no obligation to continue with the dominant model of globalization, characterized by an extreme concentration of wealth, power and goods in hands of a small oligarchy. The limited power of most nation states and the threats of global environmental change oblige the world society to explore different sustainable and peaceful ways to deal with the challenges of the 21st century.

This book analyses the outcomes of hegemonic power impositions for different regions and socio-political contexts, where human well-being, health and livelihood have been marginalised. Chapters analyse the cultural capacity for resilience and sustainable care as bases for new ways to deal with conflicts and to improve livelihood and ecosystem services. The book starts with chapters focusing on Africa and the Middle East, then goes to Latin America and Asia and concludes with an outlook by the editors.

[2]'Verselbständigung' means a way back to a paradigm dominated by nation state, requirements. This includes to introduce strong borders controls, limit foreign workers, control on national currency, taxes on imports, high subsidies for local products, etc.; in synthesis a step back from open global economy and policy to a nation state controlled political economy.

1.2 Organization of the Book

In Chap. 2, *Charles Christian and Heather Speight* from the United States analyse "Water, Cooperation, and Peace in the Palestinian West Bank". From a theoretical background of conflict transformation they discuss the potential of environmental peacebuilding when natural resources are scarce for both parties involved in the conflict. Their chapter explores the possibility for engaging parties in the conflict in shared natural resources, e.g. reuse of grey water. Starting from nested conflict theory the authors develop a map for conflict transformation and analyse the interacting levels, such as issues-specific, relational, structural, and cultural. In the case of environmental peacebuilding they did not see progress at the structural level (Levy-Strauss 1958; Mauss 1950; Parsons 2004). They explored further the potential in building trust and fostering cooperation in other areas. Starting with Lederach's notion of transformational platforms (2003) the chapter tests the hypothesis that environmental cooperation can transform relationships, especially through the process of peacebuilding. They found that culturally shared transboundary ecosystems have intrinsic cultural significance, where ecological, historical and symbolic understanding are shared and are further developed. This interchange creates relations between the two countries involved and facilitates sharing experiences based on communities' perceptions of their common identities.

As both countries experience water scarcity, grey water reuse increases the potential for agriculture and industrial activities. Nevertheless, the Israeli-Palestinian conflict is not a strict interstate conflict, but rather recognized as a "nation-state occupying a semi-autonomous, displaced and stateless people". Israel's hydro-hegemony denies Palestine equal access to water and often the water available is insufficient for productive activities. Given this power imbalance, the Arava Institute of Environmental Studies in Israel cooperated with the institutional Center for Transboundary Water Management and the Palestinian Wastewater Engineers Group on capacity building, professional development, and wastewater and solid waste management. Their approach transcended power asymmetries and fostered common goals with a simultaneous approach from both below and top-down and opened space for small-scale wastewater interventions. Prioritizing the professional instead of the national identity facilitated the development of the project, improved the management of scarce water resources, and reduced the danger of pollution. The success enhanced the relational sphere, but was not able to promote a transformation of the conflict dynamics and oppression. The existing asymmetry creates a political situation of conflict intractability and community initiative's efforts get stuck "within a peacebuilding purgatory". The authors consider transboundary environmental cooperation to have a strategic ability for overcoming territory-based identities. They suggest that analysing the structural and cultural layers of conflict together can help to overcome situations of extreme power asymmetry that limits peacebuilding initiatives.

In Chap. 3, *Tania Galaviz* from Mexico examines "The Peace Process Mediation Network between the Colombian Government and the April 19th Movement", better known as M-19. Galaviz specifically reviews the role of mediation networks in this peace process. She applies a conceptual model offered by Lederach (1997) and Paffenholz (2007) to develop a deeper understanding of the negotiation process between two intrastate groups. From a systemic dissipative open system approach, the author analyses the dynamic elements that support or limit peace efforts. Galaviz argues that the presence of citizen and religious movements and the absence of high-level mediation, often used in negotiation processes (e.g. Clinton mediating in the Israeli-Palestinian conflict), provides a stable base for progress, and the possibility to overcome the obstacles during the peace process. *Autopoeises*, understood as the capability that systems must maintain a dynamic stability and equilibrium, is especially useful when the system is confronted with external pressure. With Luhmann's (1998) systemic approach in mind, the author applies three types of system analysis: the *baseline* that "breaks-down the system elements according to their relationships", the *procedural* that explores the temporal evolution of the elements of the conflict, and *systemic* that discovers the effects among interactions and elements on the system and in relation to its surrounding conditions. In a dissipative systemic approach dynamic and adaptive process are in permanent change and adaptation give the mediation process a form, a purpose and a direction, where trust becomes the key factor of selection and legitimization of the mediator(s).

Galaviz shows that three decades of war have left Colombia in high social marginalization. The partisan dialogue of ally and enemies characterized the dominant political discourse. The members of M-19 came from bottom-up social movements and critical church members with support from several universities. Their struggle appealed to national symbols such as the flag and the national anthem. The peace process was complex and with nonlinear, erratic and multidirectional trajectories and got permanent adaptation to the surrounding conditions and its own needs. It started in 1978 and ended in 1990, when the M-19 offered to demobilize, regardless of the conditions and terms of the process. Simultaneously narco-terrorism was in a peak and the Colombian society, peace movements, the Catholic Church, university and trade unions performed marches, rallies, meetings and seminars that forced the government to accept the peace deal. At the same time a National Constituent Assembly generated synergies with the peace process.

The actors of the mediation network coming from the locally affected community (including displaced people) created an arena of peacebuilding at the *meso* level by legal, religious, academic and governmental groups and at *macro* level by international pressure from different governments, especially the USA. The mechanisms of solidarity, trust and reciprocity were strengthened and exercised pressure on the military and the president. Social processes of empowerment and forgiveness, community resilience and personal and collective reconciliation were supported by exogenous organizations. The capacity of the affected communities was fostered by solidarity, where people hoped that the conflict could be resolved nonviolently. Human rights, truth, justice, damage repair, and non-repetition permitted the building of an infrastructure for sustainable peace. The M-19 peace process influenced six other armed groups in Colombia, but the greatest contribution was the integrated and networked participation of civil society, who learned during this long negotiation process new tools as mediator and nonviolence.

In Chap. 4, *Serena Eréndira Serrano Oswald* from Mexico analyses the "Social Resilience and Intangible Cultural Heritage: A Mutually Fertilizing Potential Seen in a Case Study in Mexico". Her paper is a historical, sociological, and anthropological study, where intangible cultural heritage strengthens social resilience through festivities. Social resilience is understood as a dynamic communitarian concept that looks at concrete subjects and collectives and is rooted in a socio-cultural framework. With participant observation, fieldwork notes and in-depth recorded interviews, Serrano Oswald examines the social and psychological capital of resilience that does not need adversity or enemies for existing. She argues that resilience "operates beyond the specific crises. Once the costume [for the *mojiganga*] is ready and the person joins the feast with a mask, some frontiers of the 'self' break, other ways of being and behaving are explored, a ritual catharsis may take place". During this process, participants reencounter with migrants, history, life and death, and thus consolidate transgenerational heritage, which opens the dialogue among civilizations.

In terms of living together peacefully, the feast of festivities reinforces interchange, reciprocity, and *convivencia* in an open, creative and flexible space. The author synthetizes that "resilience is a wide, dynamic, flexible concept that implies tensions, transitions and competences, paving the road for a positive vision of development and boundless potential from the individual level up to the collective level (*to be-to grow*), and not only understanding it as coping with adversity in a state of damage, crisis and disaster (*keeping up*)". Thus immaterial patrimony is an effective tool to overcome local and regional conflict and social resilience and it provides the dynamism to challenge the threats related to global environmental change, risk of disasters and social anomy.

In Chap. 5, *Audil Rashid, Feng Feng and Fakhra Rashid* from Pakistan study the "Community Perceptions of Ecological Disturbances Caused during Terrorists Invasion and Counter-insurgency Operations in Swat in Pakistan". The Swat valley is located in the northwestern part of Pakistan, and represents a strategic region of South Asia, Central Asia and China in military, economic, social, cultural, ecological and political terms. Counter-insurgency operations in the Swat created lasting effects among local communities and people in Pakistan have witnessed the direct violence against defenseless civilians justified by terrorist groups and by religious extremism. The physical violence destroyed also a region with a fragile ecological equilibrium, especially when the government launched in 2009 a counter insurgency to restore the local government. Nevertheless, there are lasting effects among the population, including poverty, demographic changes, travel insecurity, damages to schools and hospitals, health concerns, loss to the landscape and cultural and amenity values. More than 200 schools were destroyed and hundreds more affected; especially threatened where female teachers and girls' school.

With quantitative and qualitative research methods the dual environmental and social vulnerability of the affected people is analysed (Oswald Spring 2013). The results show a decrease in their sense of belonging, combined with an increased desire to migrate. Compared with other social regions, differences on livelihood were found. In the Swat area people protect less their crops, orchid farms and plantations. Most of their children are unable to attend school, due to destruction of infrastructure or fear of child kidnapping. Both earning mechanisms and educational future of their children have failed because of attacks produced by extremists and the outcome of an ineffective counter insurgency policy by the government. Numerous reports pointed to serious social, security and political problems in the Swat region, but they rarely addressed ecological concerns. The authors insist that a stable peace process must integrate both the human and the environmental factors.

People are conscious about the possibility to locally increase their human security. Nevertheless, when the solutions were imposed from outside and without considering ecological and geographical norms, they were detrimental to peace efforts and destroyed those developed locally. Without doubt, militants and religious extremists have brought terror to the whole valley. They have undermined the environment, which is closely linked to the earning and livelihood of the local people. There is also a lack of trust by the local population in peace efforts carried out by the government. Based on past experiences, the incongruity between counter-insurgency actions and community's ideology seems to produce greater failure in peace efforts. Swat inhabitants were all in favour of conflict resolution; however, their demand has been to avoid warfare and militarization. Human, gender and environmental security were central demands of the Swat population; instead, they received both military security and terrorism.

Michiko Yoshii from Japan reviews in Chap. 6 the "Structure of Discrimination in Japan's Nuclear Export—A Case of Ninh Thuan Power Plant in Vietnam". The author is concerned about a deal between the governments of Japan and Vietnam to build nuclear power plants in Vietnam starting in 2015. As Vietnam cannot pay 10 billion USD, Japan will grant credits and Vietnamese staffs are trained by Japan with the support of *Official Development Assistance* (ODA). This chapter focuses on the Vietnamese perspective on this project, where the Japanese researcher finds evidence of discrimination. Yoshii claims that most Vietnamese have limited or no access to information, mostly from webpages developed by enterprises. No scientific papers on these nuclear power plants were published and elaborated in both countries. Thus, Vietnamese specialists cannot evaluate in depth these projects and the risks related to nuclear power plants. The Japanese disaster in the Fukushima Daiichi Nuclear Power Plant in March 2011 is downplayed, and is unknown by fishermen and women from the Thai An Hamlet in Ninh Thuan, Vietnam. In the same region Russia plans another nuclear power plant.

With US aid in 1961, the Dalat Nuclear Research Institute in Vietnam was founded in the former Republic of (South) Vietnam. After the war situation the demand for electric energy increased exponentially. The 7th National Development Plan adopted a policy of mixed energy resources (oil, natural gas, nuclear and renewables), but there are not enough human resources to deal with all requirements for power development. Thus, Vietnam depends on technical support and training from Japan to maintain its nuclear power plants. Yoshii argues that field studies in Vietnam and documentation indicates that Japan is exporting discrimination through these projects "between big cities and rural areas, between large companies and workers, and between present and future generations". In Vietnam, the author also observes discrimination against the indigenous Cham, an ethnic minority group living in the Ninh Thuan Province. The chapter discusses also the role of Japanese researchers in Vietnamese studies and emphasizes their important role in informing the Vietnamese and Japanese civil societies about the real risks. Modernization projects in foreign countries with lower level of development must place the information in a historical context of structures of discrimination between the United States, Japan and Vietnam to avoid discrimination and later conflicts.

Seiichiro Takemine from Japan discussed in Chap. 7 on "Overlooked Invisible Victims of the U.S. Nuclear Testing in the Marshall Islands: Why were the Local People Exposed to Radiation?" Here the author introduces a new concept of 'Global Hibakusha', which analyses the longer term impact of radiation-related effects on victims and survivors and on the environment affected by radiation from nuclear testing. In the Marshall Islands in the Pacific, where the United States detonated nuclear tests, these effects were often overlooked. From the impacts of the two nuclear bombs launched against Hiroshima and Nagasaki, and from the first bomb test in New Mexico, the US Government had already knowledge about the radioactive fallout. Nevertheless, in 1946 the United States started nuclear testing in the Marshall Islands and exposed the land, sea, flora and fauna of native people and Japanese fishermen to radiation.

The concern of the US Government was to find testing sites far away from their mainland, to maintain their lead on nuclear bombs. The US military tested with the Bravo experiment 67 nuclear explosions in the Marshall Islands, despite a world-wide opposition against these tests. "Over 7000 Hiroshima-sized bombs, measured in terms of *trinitrotoluene* (TNT), were dropped on the Marshall Islands alone over a 12-year period." The Health and Safety Laboratory of the US Atomic Energy Commission had established before the first nuclear test a global network to monitor in 122 stations the fallout of its radioactivity. Thus, the so-called accident —"unexpected wind" and "exceeded the estimates"—did not exist, but it was a systematic testing of nuclear bombs and their impacts on people and environment that affected a region far beyond the Marshall Islands.

The Hibakusha approach includes the invisible aspects of nuclear damages, especially on the Marshall Islands where the region today is once again covered with tropical vegetation. With Japanese survivors from the two nuclear bombs, a 'Global Hibakusha' created vertical links among survivors and victims "across time, connecting historical suffering to present and future issues". This research became part of the work of the Peace Studies Association of Japan. The knowledge between both regions was spread by peace studies and worldwide protests against nuclear testing and treated by a global nuclear conflagration. The invisible impact on native people in the Marshall Islands indicates a hegemonic behaviour of the superpower disrespecting human rights and the basic right to life and health, but also the right to a safe environment. The "United States' double standards of security, justice and human rights in the framework of nuclear development" is clearly exposed in this chapter.

Margaret Ifeoma Abazie-Humphrey from Nigeria analyses in Chap. 8 "The Nigeria Home-Grown DDR Programme—Its Impacts on Empowering the Niger Delta Ex-Militants", a federal government programme of Nigeria, called the Niger Delta Amnesty Programme. Its mandate was to initiate, plan and develop a *Disarmament, Demobilization and Reintegration* (DRR) programme. The aim has been to integrate 30,000 former agitators into civil life, to transfer their weapons to the government and to get in exchange a monthly stipend with vocational and academic training within the country and abroad. This *Presidential Amnesty Programme* (PAP) has strengthened livelihoods through training as a strategy for economic empowerment, job creation by supporting academic, vocational and entrepreneurial training, and engaging in business setups. Her chapter discusses—from an inside perspective—the impact of the DDR programme on the economy and on peace in Nigeria's Niger Delta region. It reviews how academic training could improve individual performance and have a positive influence on economic development.

The Nigerian authorities compared their programme with other DRR efforts from donors and UN piloted DDR programmes in other parts of Africa. The author asks whether the Nigerian DRR programme has added anything beyond other programmes? A key question is whether this DDR programme in Nigerian Delta has created capacities of relevance for other national DRR programmes. A crucial point is whether the improvement in the economic development in the Niger Delta has become a transformative mechanism for a long-term structural change. Nigeria as all African countries and developing regions suffer from inequality, where historical social exclusion has triggered several conflicts and where the colonial heritage has increased religious and ethnic conflicts. The analysis also discusses the expectations of the leaders of the militants, who often sabotaged the DRR programme and as the peace efforts threatened their privileges. As a home-grown programme, local cultural elements were integrated and training programmes for ex-combatants had a long-term impact on these people, offering them peaceful ways for a nonviolent livelihood. The amnesty policy intervention impacted on artisanal fishing and agribusiness. The DRR programme trained over 14,000 'delegates' in different human capitals of whom 2000 were supported to set up small-scale businesses. Both training and economic support improved the livelihood in different rural riverine communities in the Niger Delta and may support a peaceful outcome of the Niger Delta conflict.

In the concluding chapter, Juliet Bennett reflects on "Moving Toward Ecological Civilization and Positive Peace." Bennett points to the alignment of positive peace with emerging ideas about 'ecological civilization', both which entail the aim of bringing about a more socially just and ecologically harmonious global society. Bennett surveys initiatives that are working to bring about change on structural, cultural and direct levels, corresponding with Galtung's (1996) notions of structural peace, cultural peace and direct peace. Under these headings, Bennett presents a small selection of initiatives that she personally finds hope for humanity. For example, she considers the research and action being done in the interdisciplinary fields of process philosophy and ecofeminism, to bring about deep cultural change toward a more peaceful and ecological civilization. On a structural level, Bennett considers changes in technology, business, laws and economic systems. She links these changes to direct changes that individuals can make within their realms of influence to encourage the broader structural and cultural change, for example, choosing to invest in renewal technologies and divest from fossil fuels, and building the political will to support governments to do the same. Within this framework one can consider how issues discussed in the other chapters of the two volumes fit into the matrix of structural, cultural and direct violence, and what kind of changes and actions at each of these levels can help contribute to positive peace. Overall this essay will leave readers with a sense of hope, that humanity can together work to change their habits and structural constrains and move toward a more peaceful and ecological civilization.

1.3 Conclusions

These case studies analyse across three continents the conflictive potential, possible peacebuilding, and resilience processes, and their impacts on the environment. The case of Mexico is an example of a *regional institutionalized system*. In 1994 NAFTA integrated Mexico with Canada and the United States in terms of financial flow and commerce (but not for freedom of transit). Nevertheless, the resilience through immaterial heritage reinforces interchange, reciprocity, and conflict resolution from the bottom-up. In the case of Japan, there is a transition in process between *regional society* and *regional community*. Both authors link traumatic experiences in their country (atomic bombs, nuclear accident) with other existing or possible disasters in poorer countries that lack the technological and institutional know-how to deal with these threats. In the case of Colombia's three decades of war, and in the case of the Swat valley of Pakistan where terrorist and religious fanatics have pushed their countries to a second stage of regional organization, we can see examples of *regional complex* (Telo 2001). In the case of the Israeli-Palestinian conflict, coercive relationships maintain the occupation of Palestinian territory, which correspond also to the second stage of regional organization (in the sense of Telo 2001).[3]

In synthesis, southern countries are still in a lower level of regional development and complexity, due to the colonial and postcolonial processes of domination, exploitation of natural resources, terrorist attacks and power inequalities. Whenever

[3]Not understood in the sense of Buzan/Wæver (2003), who used the same concept, but did not review the former conceptualizations.

there are intents in South America to find independent ways and different alliances among themselves and with China, the pressure of the United States and Bretton Woods organizations, covered interventions and proxy wars, protest marches (Brazil, Venezuela, Argentina, Ecuador, Bolivia) and cues (Paraguay, Honduras, Brazil) put limits to a country's goals of independence from the superpower. Also high internal inequality is limiting a genuine development process. In the case of Mexico, the border control with United States and the lack of some articles agreed within NAFTA (e.g. transport system, corn import, etc.) have limited its development. Out of all the Latin American countries, Mexico has experienced the lowest reduction in poverty alleviation rate during the last three decades and in absolute terms, an increase of the number of poor people (CEPAL 2015). Therefore social resilience is crucial for poor people to strengthen through immaterial patrimony networks and human relations.

In Palestine a territorial and resource control imposed by Israel and supported by the superpower have imposed a model of domination and exploitation, taken away from the people the most basic need, clean water and sanitation. Conditions of unequal relations are also found between Japan and Vietnam, where the cascading effects of earthquake, tsunami, affectation of three nuclear power reactors, and radioactive pollution of air, soil and sea have limited the development of new nuclear power plant in their own country. In order to avoid losing market and profit, Japanese corporations are now constructing nuclear power plants in Vietnam and abroad, transferring new risk to this country. Finally the Global Hibakusha approach explored physical and invisible aspects of nuclear damages. Among Japanese and Marshall Islands survivors from nuclear bombs and tests created vertical links among survivors and victims, who shared their historical suffering by nuclear pollution? The knowledge and exchanges of suffering between both regions got reinforcement by peace studies. Protests worldwide against nuclear testing helped also to prevent a global nuclear conflagration with serious destruction of the environment. The lack of consultation with native groups of Marshall Islands is another proves of hegemonic behaviour of the superpower disrespecting human rights.

The regional analysis among different conflict areas in three continents indicates various processes of regional consolidation. The reflection may open new ways for peacebuilding and environmental restoration, where the southern countries are not only suffering from hegemonic power of corporate multinational enterprises supported by industrialized countries, but may find through mediation process, self-reliance and social resilience paths to sustainable peace. All the developing and emerging countries analysed in this book (Vietnam, Marshall Islands, Pakistan, Palestine, Nigeria, Colombia and Mexico) have high biodiversity, long-term historical suffering from colonization, exploitation, and military occupation. They have developed strong cultural immaterial resistance to the struggle with adverse conditions imposed by an unjust globalization, where often their weak governments are unable to deal with and to prevent economic, social and environmental crises, letting the people to find ways to peaceful conflict resolution.

References

Bassols Batalla, Ángel, 2002: "Son inevitables los desequilibrios regionales en México", in: Delgadillo, Javier and Irracheta, Alfonso (eds.), *Actualidad de la investigación regional en México* (México: CRIM-UNAM, Colegio Mexiquense, Colegio de Tlaxcala and Plaza y Valdés): 15-26.

Beck, Ulrich, 2011: "Living in and Coping with World Risk Society", in: Brauch, Hans Günter; Oswald Spring, Úrsula; Mesjasz, Czeslaw; Grin, John; Kameri-Mbote, Patricia, Chourou, Béchir; Dunay, Pal; Birkmann, Jörn (Eds.): *Coping with Global Environmental Change, Disasters and Security—Threats, Challenges, Vulnerabilities and Risks* (Berlin—Heidelberg—New York: Springer-Verlag): 11–16.

Brauch, Hans Günter; Dalby, Simon; Oswald Spring, Úrsula, 2011: "Political Geoecology for the Anthropocene", in Brauch, Hans Günter; Oswald Spring, Úrsula; Mesjasz, Czeslaw; Grin, John; Kameri-Mbote, Patricia, Chourou, Béchir; Dunay, Pal; Birkmann, Jörn (Eds.), 2011: *Coping with Global Environmental Change, Disasters and Security—Threats, Challenges, Vulnerabilities and Risks* (Berlin—Heidelberg—New York: Springer): 1453-1485.

Brauch, Hans Günter; Oswald Spring, Úrsula; Grin, John; Mesjasz, Czeslaw; Kameri-Mbote, Patricia; Behera, Navnita Chadha; Chourou, Béchir; Krummenacher, Heinz (Eds.), 2009: *Facing Global Environmental Change: Environmental, Human, Energy, Food, Health and Water Security Concepts* (Berlin—Heidelberg—New York: Springer).

Brauch, Hans Günter; Oswald Spring, Úrsula; Mesjasz, Czeslaw; Grin, John; Kameri-Mbote, Patricia, Chourou, Béchir; Dunay, Pal; Birkmann, Jörn (Eds.), 2011: *Coping with Global Environmental Change, Disasters and Security—Threats, Challenges, Vulnerabilities and Risks* (Berlin—Heidelberg—New York: Springer).

Brauch, Hans Günter; Oswald Spring, Úrsula; Mesjasz, Czeslaw; Grin, John; Dunay, Pal; Behera, Navnita Chadha; Chourou, Béchir; Kameri-Mbote, Patricia; Liotta, P. H. (Eds.), 2008: *Globalization and Environmental Challenges: Reconceptualizing Security in the 21st Century.* Hexagon Series on Human and Environmental Security and Peace, vol. 3 (Berlin—Heidelberg —New York: Springer).

Breslin, Shaun and Higgott, Richard, 2000: "Studying regions. Learning from the Old Constructing the New", in: *New Political Economy*, 5,3: 333-352.

Buzan, Barry; Wæver, Ole, 2003: *Regions and Powers: The Structure of International Security* (Cambridge: Cambridge University Press).

Darwin, Charles R., 1859: *On the Origin of Species.*

Galtung, Johan, 1996: *Peace by Peaceful Means: Peace and Conflict, Development and Civilization* (London: Sage Publications Ltd).

Hettne, Björn; Inotai, András; Sunkel, Osvaldo (Eds.), 1999: *Globalism and the New Regio-nalism* (Basingstoke – London: Macmillan; New York: St. Martin's Press).

Hettne, Björn; Inotai, Andras; Sunkel, Osvaldo (Eds.), 2000: *The New Regionalism and the Future of Security and Development* (Basingstoke – London: Macmillan, New York: St. Martin's Press).

Hettne, Björn; Inotai, Andras; Sunkel, Osvaldo (Eds.), 2001: *Comparing Regionalisms. Implications for Global Development* (Basingstoke: Palgrave).

Hüller, Thorsten, 2012: "On Infeasibilities of Cosmopolitan Democracy – Lessons from the European Union", in: *Swiss Political Science Review*, Special Issue: *The (Democratic) Legitimacy of Global Governance: New Theoretical and Empirical Perspectives*, 18,2 (June): 249–271.

Lederach, John P., 1997: *Building Peace: Sustainable Reconciliation in Divided Societies.* (Washington, D.C.: United States Institute of Peace).

Lederach, J. P., 2003: *The Little Book of Conflict Transformation* (Intercourse, Pa: Good Books).

Levy-Strauss, Claude, 1958: *Anthropologie Structurale* (Paris: Plon).

Luhmann, Nicolas, 1998: *Sistemas Sociales. Lineamientos para una Teoria General* (Barcelona: Anthropos, Universidad Iberoamericana, Pontificia Universidad Javeriana).

Mauss, Marcel, 1950: *Sociologie et Anthropologie* (Paris: PUF).
Oswald Spring, Úrsula, 2002: "Presentación", *Regiones y Desarrollo Sustentable* 2(3): 5-10.
Oswald Spring, Úrsula, 2013: "Dual Vulnerability among Female Household Heads", in: *Acta Colombiano de Psicología*, 16,2: 19-30.
Paffenholz, Thania, 2007: *Civil Society and Peacebuilding Potential, Limitations and Critical Factors*. Report No. 36445-GLB; at: http://www-wds.worldbank.org/external/default/WDSContentServer/WDSP/IB/2008/03/27/000333038_20080327071355/Rendered/PDF/364450SR0REPLA1nd1Peacebuilding1web.pdf.
Parsons, Charles, 2004: "Structuralism and Metaphysics", in: *The Philosophical Quarterly*, 54,214 (January): 56-77.
Stiglitz, Joseph E., 2010: *Freefall. America, Free Markets, and the Sinking of the World Economy* (New York-London: W.W. Northon)
Telo, Mario, 2001: *European Union and the New Regionalims* (Alderhot: Ashgate).
Toussaint, Éric, 2015: *Bancocratie* (Brussels: CADTM - Ed. Aden).

Chapter 2
Water, Cooperation, and Peace in the Palestinian West Bank

Charles Christian and Heather Speight

Abstract This chapter tests the conflict transformation potential of environmental peacebuilding, exploring the possibility for engagement between conflicting parties over shared natural resources in building trust and fostering cooperation in other areas, positively influencing wider conflict dynamics. *Nested conflict theory* (NCT) serves as a conflictual roadmap for judging transformative potential as it conceptualizes a single conflict at four discrete yet interacting levels: issues-specific, relational, structural, and cultural. A critical examination of a joint Israeli-Palestinian greywater reuse system is employed as a case study to run the model. Our examination finds the environmental peacebuilding case study fails to show progress at the structural level. The initiative's efforts are stuck within a "peacebuilding purgatory." The authors believe this indicates a need for environmental peacebuilding initiatives to consciously develop mechanisms that can leverage gains at the issue-specific and relational levels into counter-normative institutions and behaviours.

Keywords Water and conflict · Wastewater · Greywater reuse · Israeli-Palestinian cooperation · Environmental peacebuilding · Nested conflict theory · Conflict transformation · Epistemic communities

---

Charles Christian, Program Associate, Middle East and North Africa, Search for Common Ground, USA; Email: charlesdavidchristian@gmail.com.

Heather Speight, Research Scientist, United States Army Corps of Engineers, Engineer Research and Development Center, USA; Email: heather.a.speight@gmail.com.

This chapter is the result of work carried out through a graduate practicum organized by the American University School of International Service (USA) and, therefore, would not have been possible without the contributions of additional team members: Joanna Fisher, Moses Jackson, Christina Kehoe, Courtney Owen, Valerie Puleo, and Erin Rosner.

Ú.Oswald Spring et al. (eds.), *Regional Ecological Challenges for Peace in Africa, the Middle East, Latin America and Asia Pacific*, The Anthropocene: Politik—Economics—Society—Science 5, DOI 10.1007/978-3-319-30560-8_2

2.1 Introduction

This chapter explores the extent to which cooperation over natural resources can catalyze movement from violent conflict to positive peace. Using nested conflict theory as a conceptual roadmap for gauging environmental peacebuilding's potential, we assess the ability of a particular environmental peacebuilding initiative to make a positive impact at different levels of the Israeli-Palestinian conflict.

We begin with a review of key literature on conflict transformation and environmental peacebuilding theory. Mapping the theoretical landscape is key as we seek to highlight the links and lacks between theory and practice. We will examine at length (1) the meaning and mechanisms of conflict transformation, (2) environmental peacebuilding's claims to transformative power and, (3) how conflict theory frames the Israeli-Palestinian issue.

Following the theoretical discussion, a brief summary of why the Israeli-Palestinian conflict, and our case study initiative in particular, will be provided. Lastly, the initiative's relative successes and failures are analysed. The hope is that the level analysis will not only highlight the idiosyncratic successes and failures of the case study, but that they can provide guidance and direction in conceiving of environmental peacebuilding elsewhere.

2.2 Literature Review

2.2.1 Conflict Transformation

Curle (1971: 1–23) describes conflict as 'unpeacefulness' stemming from a relational imbalance where one party in a relationship is able to dominate another—with or without the knowledge of the parties involved. Galtung (1996: 72, 79–80) also refers to conflict in terms of domination, however, he refers more broadly to the domination of disharmonious aspects of a formation with both harmonious and disharmonious elements. In Galtung's view, conflict in its latent and manifest forms can be thought of as a formation of attitudes or assumptions, behaviour and contradictions, the interactions of which form a conflict triangle. Burton (1996: 7) understands conflict as, "struggles between opposing forces." For Francis (2002: 3), conflict is, "the friction caused by difference, proximity, and movement … [ultimately] a sign of life." Rupesinghe (1995: 73) notes that conflict can be viewed as a situation where different actors pursue incompatible—or seemingly incompatible—goals. Lederach (1995: 15–6, 2003: 23) suggests that conflict is a transformative phenomenon lodged naturally in human relationships—with personal, relational, structural, and cultural implications. Lederach (2003: 3–4, 13–4, 18) further emphasizes the normality of conflict calling it a gift, an opportunity, a necessity, and a motor of change. As Ramsbotham et al. (2005: 164) share, "[i]n many cultures conflicts are explained as 'tangles' of contradictory claims that must be unravelled … at the root of conflict is a knot of problematic relationships, conflicting interests and differing world-views." For Wallensteen (1991: 151), conflict can be thought of as, "... processes, where 'resolutions' are often only part of continuous development."

When expressed violently, conflict may serve as a mechanism for taking or preserving power, maintaining internal cohesion, or pursuing external expansion (Väyrynen 1991: 1). Violent conflict can become "... an ideology, a form of life without any clear-cut objectives ... an instrument intended to produce desired political effects ... a means of communication ... [or] ... a method of destruction ..." (Väyrynen 1991: 2). Importantly, Deutsch (2014: 27–38) adds that conflicts can be interpersonal, intergroup, organizational, or international in scope and character. Whether conflict is viewed by theorists and practitioners as a process, discrete incident, facet of human relationship or other such formation, its acknowledged presence becomes a meaningful starting point for change and a foundation for the study of conflict transformation.

Väyrynen (1991: 4–6) acknowledges the continuously transforming nature of conflict and proposes that intractable conflicts may require a process of transformation in order to find solutions. To this end, he offers a taxonomy of transformation distinguishing between actor, issue, rule, and structural transformation. Actor transformation may be characterized by the emergence or recognition of new actors but can also result from internal changes within major parties. Issue transformation makes, "dissonant issues less weighty and salient, while making consonant ones more clearly perceived and stronger" (Deutsch 1978: 195–7). It promotes an opening of the agenda and a focus on issues of commonality. Rule transformation focuses on changing the rules of the game by redefining the norms that typically guide the actors in their relationships. Structural transformation is more comprehensive as power between actors is substantially redistributed or mutual relations undergo qualitative change.

According to Francis (2002: 26), conflict transformation, "... embraces the different processes and approaches that are needed to address conflict constructively in different contexts and at different levels, in the short term and the long term, including engagement in conflict as well as its management and resolution." Emphasizing conflict transformation's social justice demands, Francis outlines a series of dynamic stages and processes needed "if a situation of oppression, with an extreme imbalance of power, is to be transformed into one of genuine peace." She begins with situations of latent conflict where there is an unequal distribution of power but oppressed parties are not aware of their oppression. She then moves through shifting power relations, conflict resolution, long-term cooperation, and continuous peace maintenance and violence prevention. Francis suggests that conflict resolution processes and nonviolent methods work together to realize conflict transformation—like two sides of the same coin.

Ramsbotham et al. (2005: 29), however, suggest that conflict transformation is conflict resolution at its deepest level; engaging in the underlying tasks of structural and cultural peacebuilding by transforming the parties in conflict, the relationships between those conflicting parties, and the institutions and discourses that perpetuate violence. For Galtung (1996: 90), transforming conflict becomes identifying the parts that make up the conflict triangle and then engaging in processes of (dis) articulation, (de)conscientization, complexification and simplification, (de)polarization, and (de-)escalation across time, recognizing that conflict transformation is a never-ending process responsive to old and new contradictions as they arise.

According to Galtung (1996: 73–8, 90–1), articulation refers to a fully realized conflict with all elements (attitudes, behaviors, contradictions) clearly articulated; disarticulation considers the dissipation of conflict with, "attitudes dying out, behavioral patterns receding into oblivion and contradictions dissolving." The concept of conscientization is borrowed from the work of Freire (1993: 35–40) and refers to the process of making conflict attitudes and contradictions visible. As Galtung asks, "… how can a conflict be consciously transformed unless the parties to the conflict are conscious subjects, true actors?" The opposite process is thought of as deconscientization. Complexification considers the balance between understanding conflict elements at a high enough level of complexity to identify opportunities for transformation while not overcomplicating the elements thereby making them too complex for the human mind to handle. When reducing complexity—or engaging in the process of simplification—Galtung warns against reductionist tendencies favoring a healthy balance between complexity and simplicity. The process of simplification may produce polarization as conflicts are pared down to their more basic, elemental parts—"assigning all parties … to one or the other of *two* camps, wrapping all … conflict themes together in one supra-theme." Escalation and de-escalation refers to the increase or decrease of violent behaviors in a conflict.

Expanding on the concepts of simplification and complexification, Galtung (1996: 93, 103) suggests that, to transform structural conflicts, other structural arrangements that reinforce verticality, repression and exploitation must be transformed—namely those preventing conscientization and those preventing mobilization. Arrangements that prevent conscientization, tend to manifest as either the oppressed being conditioned by the oppressor (penetration) or exhibiting a limited view of reality (segmentation). The prevention of mobilization occurs when the oppressed are either split away from each other (fragmentation) or isolated from others (marginalization). Galtung suggests a number of strategies for overcoming these structural arrangements but adds that transformations do not happen on their own; rather, they must be willed. Conflict transformation can occur at any time and in any location between a range of actors including, but not limited to, state, civil society, corporations, or individuals, by engaging in a communication process with other actors in the conflict.

Although not directly using the term conflict transformation—but building on the work of Galtung (Miall 2004: 4)—Curle (1971: 15) notes that, in order to transition from unpeaceful to peaceful relationships, the relationship itself must undergo radical change focused on mutuality—mutual understanding, assistance, and concern—rather than domination or imposition. He argues that peacemaking is born of the changes—both incremental and large-scale—that bring relationships to the point that full development can occur.

Rooted in the work of Galtung and Curle, Lederach (2003: 22) describes conflict transformation as a capacity "to envision and respond to the ebb and flow of social conflict as life-giving opportunities for creating constructive change processes that reduce violence, increase justice in direct interaction and social structures, and respond to real-life problems in human relationships." Influenced by Dugan's (1996: 9–19, 2001: 365–9) nested conflict theory, Lederach offers a taxonomy of change goals in conflict transformation suggesting that constructive processes in the personal, relational, structural, and cultural domains of social conflict can promote transformation. Goals focused on personal change seek to minimize the destructive aspects of social conflict while maximizing the potential for physical, emotional, intellectual, and spiritual growth. Relational change goals minimize poor communication and maximize understanding of hopes and fears as connected to emotions and interdependence in a relationship. Structurally oriented change goals focus on understanding and addressing the root causes of conflict while promoting nonviolent methods and substantive and procedural justice. Culturally oriented change goals focus on uncovering and understanding the underlying cultural patterns that can lead to the violent expression of conflict.

As noted by Lederach, when transitioning from conflict transformation theory to practice, a key challenge emerges, "… how to develop and sustain a platform or strategic plan that has the capacity to adapt and generate ongoing desired change, while at the same responding creatively to immediate needs" (Lederach 2003: 33–4). Lederach asserts that change is simultaneously circular and linear; the circular nature of change recognizes that things are connected in relationship with growth emerging from its own multi-directional process. The linear nature of change demands thoughtful consideration of the overall flow of change—both its direction and purpose. Creative balance of the circular and linear aspects of change is key to creating transformational platforms that are both responsive in the short term and strategic in the long term. Transformational platforms provide, "a base to stand on and jump from." (Lederach 2003: 45) They include, "an understanding of … the 'big picture'…, processes for addressing immediate problems and conflicts, a vision for the future, and a plan for change processes which will move in that direction." (Lederach 2003: 45). Lederach (2005: 48–9) elaborates on this concept further sharing that platforms for ongoing change should be,

1. Built by supporting the constructive engagement of people who have been historically divided and who are or may remain in significant levels of conflict,
2. Permanent and continuously adaptive; platforms to produce change are more important than the individual solutions they create,
3. Capable of producing solutions that meet particular demands in temporary discrete timeframes providing answers to pressing problems, but ephemeral rather than permanent.

To consider the applicability of environmental peacebuilding as a viable means of conflict transformation, the concepts highlighted by these key theorists in aggregate provide a useful framework for analysis.

2.2.2 *Environmental Peacebuilding*

In understanding the concept of environmental peacebuilding, it is critical to first understand peacebuilding in a broader sense and then consider what possibilities for conflict transformation emerge when linking peacebuilding directly to environmental cooperation.

2.2.2.1 Peacebuilding

Despite its ubiquitous use in peace and conflict studies, there is no one agreed upon definition of peacebuilding (Call/Cooke 2003: 235; Jenkins 2013: 35). Galtung is often credited with first using the term in reference to structures that encourage sustainable peace by addressing the underlying causes of conflict and supporting indigenous capacity-building for conflict management and resolution.[1] For Bertram (1995: 388–9), peacebuilding is also thought of as tackling the roots of conflict but by fostering the political conditions necessary for a sustainable, democratic peace including—but not limited to—remaking a state's political, security, and economic institution or arrangements.

The UN Agenda for Peace (UN 1992: 822–5), makes distinctions between preventative diplomacy, peacemaking, peacekeeping, and peacebuilding. Preventative diplomacy refers to actions intended to either prevent disputes or their escalation. Peacemaking describes processes that bring parties to an agreement while peacekeeping involves deploying forces for a region to keep the peace. Peacebuilding activities are critical in post-conflict settings as they are meant to deter a return to violence. Further illuminating these concepts, the Brahimi Report (UN 2000: 2–3) notes that peacemaking attempts to end conflicts that are in progress by employing the tools of diplomacy and mediation while peacekeeping involves both military and civilian forces engaging in the work of building peace in the, "dangerous aftermath of civil wars." Peacebuilding, however, "defines activities undertaken on the far side of conflict to reassemble the foundations of peace and provide the tools for building on those foundations something that is more than just the absence of war." The UN (2010: 5) visited the concept of peacebuilding again in 2007 determining:

> Peacebuilding involves a range of measures targeted to reduce the risk of lapsing or relapsing into conflict by strengthening national capacities at all levels for conflict management, and to lay the foundations for sustainable peace and development. Peacebuilding strategies must be coherent and tailored to specific needs of the country concerned, based on national ownership, and should comprise a carefully prioritized, sequenced, and therefore relatively narrow set of activities aimed at achieving the above objectives.

[1]UN (United Nations); at http://www.un.org/en/peacebuilding/pbso/pbun.shtml (1 June 2015).

Call/Cooke (2003: 235), note an additional body of literature in the peacebuilding arena that make no clear distinctions between peacemaking, peacekeeping, and conflict prevention. Rather, these scholars assert that peacebuilding can be thought of as an umbrella term that captures peacemaking, peacekeeping, conflict prevention, and related concepts (Jarstad 2008). It is this broad concept of peacebuilding that is employed herein.

2.2.2.2 Peacebuilding and Environmental Cooperation

In their seminal work, *Environmental Peacemaking*, Conca/Dabelko (2002: 8–12, 220–32) consider the extent to which environmental cooperation can bring about, "movement along a peace continuum, rendering violent conflict less likely or less imaginable." They outline two pathways for exploiting environmental challenges to promote synergies for peace—by reframing these challenges as opportunities or by emphasizing the transboundary nature of environmental issues to promote shared identities. They suggest that environmental peacemaking can help to "create cooperative knowledge … [,] establish a tradition of cooperation … [and] push actors to broaden the time horizons that frame bargaining processes." Furthermore, they assert that "a strategy of environmental peacemaking would emphasize creating and exploiting positive forms of trans-societal interdependence, building transnational civil-society linkages, fostering new norms of environmental responsibility and peaceful dispute resolution, and transforming opaque, security-minded institutions of the state."

By viewing the environment with a peacemaking—or peacebuilding—lens, an opportunity emerges to examine the extent to which environmental cooperation can serve as a platform for conflict transformation. In the following subsections, claims that the environment can be leveraged to promote peacebuilding through its emphasis on long time horizons, potential to create shared identities, and ability to encourage mutual cooperation will be subjected to an analysis rooted in the tenets of conflict transformation.

Emphasis on Long Time Horizons. According to Conca and Dabelko, negotiations and discussions about the environment are unique because they demonstrate the need for reciprocity and cooperation by emphasizing long time horizons (Conca/Dabelko 2002: 10–11; Conca 2000: 225–250; Axelrod 2006: 3–24). The long time horizons afforded to environmental planning and management are especially important given that, as Saunders and Slim found, sustained dialogue is needed to change conflictual relationships (Saunders/Slim 1994: 43–56). For environmental peacebuilding to effectively leverage its potential to "push actors to lengthen 'the shadow of the future" (Conca/Dabelko 2002: 10) and promote conflict transformation, it must allow actors to create solutions that are both circular and linear. That is, it must be responsive to the needs of the present moment and the anticipated future.

For examples of how peacebuilding practitioners hold the dual concepts of present and future in constructive tension, consider the works of Boulding and

Dugan. Inspired by Polak's *Image of the Future* (1973), Boulding (2001: 373) and her contemporaries developed a workshop format in the late 1970s designed to empower peace activism. In the workshop, participants were invited to imagine a peaceful world thirty years into the future and then work backwards in time to identify the steps needed to secure that future. Since then, others have borrowed from that workshop format to actively engage in the work of conflict transformation. For example, in explaining her nested conflict theory—which emphasizes the interconnectedness of issue-specific, relational, and structural layers of conflict—Dugan (2001: 365–72) notes the importance of acknowledging the shortcomings of existing social arrangements in spaces of intractable conflict, and then in conceptualizing new arrangements that could be implemented in the future. For conflicts expressed in the relational and structural arenas, Dugan outlines a six stage process for parties to envision transformation: goal statement, clarification, future present moment, futures history, policy team creation, and action planning in the present. By working through this process, parties to a conflict identify goals they would like to work toward achieving, clarify the meanings associated with those goals in an effort to build a shared vocabulary, share a vision of what their imaged future looks like, imagine the steps it took to get to that future, self-identify others present who they could work with to achieve their imagined future, and then develop a plan to make that imagined future a reality.

As Dugan (2001: 371) reflects, engaging in this type of envisioning provides, "an enhanced possibility of fashioning a way out of … existing turmoil …". Notably, however, Dugan suggests that conflicts expressed primarily as issues may not lend themselves to envisioning processes because they are resolved primarily by analytical means and do not necessarily challenge existing relational or structural patterns. This point becomes especially important when considering the extent to which environmental cooperation can promote transformation as environmental efforts can easily remain in the issues-specific domain focusing on, "urban air and water quality, sanitation and toxic contamination" (Conca/Dabelko 2002: 3). To capitalize on the peacebuilding potential associated with long time horizons, structures must be in place that allow actors to actively connect the issue of the moment to the long term goals of an imaged future. Otherwise, the transformative potential of long time horizons remains latent, at best.

Potential to Create Shared Identities. A similarly vital tenet in environmental peacebuilding theory is the relevance of shared identities around the natural environment. Environmental peacebuilding implies that there is an emotional and spiritual sentiment that is tied to the natural world and influences how people perceive and value their communities (Cheng et al. 2003, 87–104). According to Carius (2006: 12), transboundary environmental cooperation has the strategic ability to substitute mutually-exclusive, territory-based identities with ones envisaged by a shared environmental community. More than just a physical space, such transboundary ecosystems have intrinsic cultural significance resulting in ecological, historical and symbolic ramifications on communities' perceptions of their shared identities (Greider/Garkovich 1994: 1–24). Through the creation of shared environmental identities, environmental peacebuilding is distinct from territorial boundaries and can transcend national identities that have been developed by political borders. By catalyzing a shared identity around natural resources, environmental peacebuilding can provide a basis for opposing groups to act collectively.

Critics to the environmental peacebuilding field argue that there are deep-seated political and cultural barriers to the creation of a shared identity over natural resources. National identity is a highly critical factor, especially in regards to normalization campaigns between such parties. Given asymmetrical power relations, the creation of a shared and unifying identity might not be possible if inequality and injustice are rampant within the regional community. Critics contend that the creation of a shared identity may actually contribute to the normalization of such oppression. In anti-normalization efforts, the conflicting groups perceive their identities and their understanding of their "own humanity in contrast to the demonized other" (Abu-Nimer/Lazarus 2007: 23). A Middle Eastern human rights activist organization surmised such perspectives by explaining that "[i]t is helpful to think of normalization as a 'colonization of the mind' whereby the oppressed subject comes to believe that the oppressor's reality is the only 'normal' reality … and a fact of life that must be coped with."[2] From this understanding, transboundary environmental cooperation might not be meaningful since beliefs on normalization and hegemonic oppression are tied to the identity of the oppressor in conflict situations, thereby negating the key functions of environmental peacebuilding.[3]

To counteract these claims, environmental peacebuilding theory suggests that conflict actors can be brought together by a shared common identity by emphasizing collective problem solving and understanding about their transboundary environment in addition to shifting conflict-driven interests (Clayton/Opotow 2003: 1–24). Environmental cooperation can debunk normalization concerns in the effort to promote the development of shared values, norms and practices that result in building such a shared identity (Harari/Roseman 2008: 12). Transboundary environmental cooperation can create awareness of the transboundary nature of ecosystems and of commonality between communities. Scholars Akçali/Antonsich (2009: 944) suggest that this environmental perspective is "seen to generate a 'we' feeling inclusive of the whole population, beyond ethnic or religious divides, thus confirming the discursive strategy of using the environment to foster a common identity." With changes in identity, "individuals may come to see commonalities in their experience. They may come to consider themselves members of a community and view themselves in collective terms" (Miller 1992: 32).

Ability to Encourage Mutual Cooperation. Conca/Dabelko (2002: 11) consider the potential positive side effects associated with environmental cooperation including "trust-building … the identification of mutual gains, or a growing habit of

---

[2]Palestinian Campaign for the Academic and Cultural Boycott of Israel (PACBI); at: http://www.pacbi.org/etemplate.php?id=1749 (1 June 2015).

[3]PACBI; at: http://www.pacbi.org/etemplate.php?id=1749 (1 June 2015).

cooperation …" Carius (2006–2007: 62) suggests that environmental cooperation can be utilized as a platform for dialogue, particularly when diplomatic or political approaches have not produced significant gains. As Carius (2006–2007: 62) shares, "[i]n many instances, hostile—if not openly warring—countries have found that environmental issues are one of the few topics on which they can sustain an ongoing dialogue." He further asserts, "… common environmental challenges can also be used to replace distrust, suspicion, and divergent interests with a shared knowledge base and common goals, and thus could transform relationships marred by conflict."

To test the hypothesis that environmental cooperation can transform relationships, it is valuable to keep in mind Lederach's notion of a transformational platforms and, in particular, the way that these platforms are built. According to Lederach, transformational platforms are built by supporting the constructive engagement of people who have been historically divided and who are or may remain in significant levels of conflict. To better understand what is meant by supporting constructive engagement, a brief primer on contact theory and its limitations is essential.

Efforts rooted in contact theory are, "based on the assumption that working together toward a common, superordinate goal reduces intergroup hostilities, increases liking and cooperation, and fosters a common identity transcending the separate identity of each group" (Moaz 2011: 115–25). As Allport (1954: 206–220) notes: positive interpersonal contact between members of different groups reduces prejudice, in turn leading to cooperation. Contact theory's assertion that limited, interpersonal contact can broaden into intergroup amicability is based on the notion of generalization, or the transferring of a positive view of an individual to an entire group (Pettigrew 1998: 65–85).

The aspirations of initiatives rooted in the ideals of contact theory can fall short if prevailing power relations and social discourses retard the process of generalization. As contact theory asserts, institutional or authority support for changing attitudes is considered part of the 'optimal' conditions under which contact theory operates. A second optimal condition is that representatives must share equal status in order for positive intergroup contact to occur (Allport 1954: 261–84). More recent meta-data research has found that "although authority support appears to play an important role, this condition should not be conceived of or implemented in isolation. Institutional support for contact under conditions of competition or unequal status can often enhance animosity between groups, thereby diminishing the potential for achieving positive outcomes from contact" (Pettigrew/Tropp 2006: 751–83). Indeed, studies have shown that certain contact theory methods replicate the macro power asymmetry within the group microcosm (Moaz 2000: 259–77). Contact exercises thus may inadvertently reinforce normative, culturally violence attitudes and perceptions. Moreover, even when positive personal interaction does occur, personal affinity and understanding are not enough to reduce structural inequality. In fact, it is possible that positive intergroup contact "may nurture bonds of affection yet leave intact political commitments that sustain institutional discrimination" (Dixon et al. 2005: 697–711). These findings suggest that, while environmental cooperation may promote engagement, it may not be of a constructive nature and, as a result, may not be sufficient for building transformational platforms capable of promoting sustained and adaptive peacebuilding.

2.2.3 *Conflict Theory*

This final theoretical review concerns the typological classifications of the Israeli-Palestinian issue. Having reviewed the means of and claims to conflict transformation above, it is necessary that we indicate what is in exact need of transformation. This section will frame the Israeli-Palestinian conflict as asymmetric, hegemonic, and protracted. In each instance, the classification necessitates a transformative approach at the expense of traditional tools of mediation and dialogue.

2.2.3.1 Asymmetric Conflict, Hegemonic Power, and Protracted Conflict

The Israeli-Palestinian conflict is neither a strict inter- or intrastate conflict but rather a case of a recognized nation-state occupying a semi-autonomous, displaced and stateless people. By nature, the conflict is characterized by extreme power asymmetries. These institutionalized power asymmetries contribute to the conflict's intractability (Azar et al. 1978: 41–60; Azar/Farah 1981: 317–35, Azar 1985: 59–70). Thus it is necessary to describe and develop the concepts of asymmetry and protraction which will lead into a discussion of hegemonic power. Throughout this exploration, we will refer back to the Israeli-Palestinian conflict as an illustrative tool that both gives shape and form to the theoretical literature as well as contextualizes our case study examination.

At its most basic definition, asymmetric conflicts "are those in which conflict parties are unequal in power, either quantitatively (e.g. strong vs. weak states) or qualitatively (e.g. state vs. non-state actors) or both" (Ramsbotham et al. 2011: 59). Respectively, these are inequalities in power of *force* and power of *status* (Miall 2004: 3). Suleiman further disaggregates asymmetry by naming five key areas by which conflicting parties can be compared: political status, access to resources, institutional development, external support (e.g. moral, financial, political), and the privilege to discriminate (i.e. agency to determine one's own future) (Suleiman 2000: 40, cited by Abitbol 2013: 6). As an example, consider the notion of external support. In the form of arms, external support bolsters a party's power of force. In the form of political recognition of a party's statehood or independence, however, external support augments the party's power of status. These two notions of power while distinctive are also interactive in nature: recognition of one's statehood can help legitimize marital support. In either case, Cascão/Zeitoun (2010: 28) state that "power asymmetries determine to a significant (not total) extent the fundamentally political distributional issue of 'who gets what, when, where and why' (Lasswell 1936)."

In the case of the Israeli-Palestinian conflict, relative strength is extremely asymmetric (Zeitoun/Allan 2008: 10). In both force and status power, Israel is a clear heavyweight: it is an officially recognized state with full United Nations privileges, possesses the most quantitatively and qualitatively superior armed forces in the region—let alone in comparison to Palestine[4] and continues to grow and modernize its economy (OECD 2013: 1–37). The extent of Israel's asymmetry may be said to be hegemonic.

The denotation of hegemony is important as it explicitly incorporates ideational power:

> … the concept of hegemony provides a means of analysing and communicating about asymmetric international power relations. The hegemon has a disproportionate capacity to coerce a weaker [party]. As the greatest form of power lies in the realm of ideas, hegemons have the option to write the agenda. They have the ability to determine the knowledge that is included, regardless of how analysts judge the merit or legitimacy of the outcomes (Zeitoun/Allan 2008: 9).

The power of ideas is the power of discourse. Fröhlich (2012: 126) notes that discourse differentiates "between 'right' and 'wrong' knowledge, between different constructions of reality, between that which is 'sayable' and that which is 'unsayable.'" By all accounts, Israel has "the option to write the agenda for … contestation"—that is, what is sayable—within the hydrological conflict. As an example, the Israeli-Palestinian Joint Water Committee (JWC) which is responsible for writing the agenda for hydrological contestation/cooperation has been criticized on a number of grounds, most notably for "dressing up domination as cooperation," and effectively reproducing Israeli hydro-hegemony (Selby 2003: 121–138). As a result of this domination, the JWC is able to leverage bureaucratic and discursive arrangements to effectively hinder Palestinian water sector development which is well acknowledged to be sorely lacking (World Bank 2009: 9–25, 33–42, 47–53).

In addition to being asymmetric and hegemonic, the Israeli-Palestinian conflict can further be understood as a protracted social conflict. Protracted social conflicts, or intractable conflicts, are conflicts where antagonistic relations between different communal groups persist over a long period of time (Azar et al. 1978: 41–60; Azar/Farah 1981: 317–35; Azar 1985: 59–70). Mitchell (1991: 245–26) notes that such conflicts are commonly waged between competing ethnonationalist groups within discrete jurio-territorial borders—essentially, a competition between competing identity groups over the mechanisms of political power. The stakes of this conflict are existentially high as it is a contest to either preserve or invalidate a political system that innately favours a single and exclusive ethnocentric definition of citizenship and personhood.

As a result of the difficulties associated with maintaining high levels of violent intensity over extended periods of time, protracted asymmetric conflicts thus tend to

[4]Haaretz; at: http://www.haaretz.com/news/diplomacy-defense/1.623249 (28 October 2014).

wax and wane in their expressions of direct, physical violence with structurally and culturally violent frames and relationships remaining intact. Given the length of the conflict, violent expressions may alter their forms of expression in accordance to changing historical circumstances (Azar et al. 1978: 41–60; Mitchell 1991: 28). Miall (2004: 3) observes that protracted conflict cross "repeatedly into and out of violence and thus [defy] cyclical or bell-shaped models of conflict phases. By virtue of this undulation, it is highly unlikely that parties will reach a mutually hurting stalemate, a qualification that a significant portion of the conflict resolution literature holds as a necessary precondition for a negotiated settlement (Mitchell 1991: 35–37). As contests for ethnonational supremacy, protracted conflicts present little to no space for altering the basic grievance. Rather (Azar et al. 1978: 51),

> They tend to generate, reinforce, or intensify mutual images of deception. They tend too to increase the likelihood of confusion in the direct and indirect communications between the parties and their allies. They increase the anxieties of the parties to the conflict, and they foster tension and conflict-maintenance strategies. In the protracted conflict situation, the conflict becomes an arena for redefining issues rather than a means for adjudicating them; it is therefore futile to look for any ultimate resolution. The conflict process becomes the source rather than the outcome of policy.

Resolving protracted social conflicts requires addressing the undergirding notions of group incompatibility and the associated notions of belonging, citizenship, and personhood.

The preceding designations—asymmetry, hegemonic power, protracted social conflict—all have meaningful repercussions vis-à-vis conflict resolution: "In these circumstances critics have seen traditional negotiation/mediation, dialogue and problem-solving approaches as inadequate, if not counterproductive, insofar as the assume equivalence between the conflict parties" (Ramsbotham et al. 2011: 59). It is clear that a conflict transformation approach, one that fundamentally alters relationships on the immediate interpersonal level, structural and cultural level, and all points in between must be initiated.

2.3 Case Study

2.3.1 Israeli-Palestinian Context

The Israeli-Palestinian conflict is characterized by extreme power asymmetries with Israeli hegemony expressed through many capillaries of power. It is not our purpose here, however, to critique them all. This exploration will focus squarely on Israeli's *hydro*hegemony. We acknowledge this is an incomplete picture of the conflict but one that, nevertheless, carries great weight and great potential for transformation.

In the water sector, conflict asymmetry results in an Israeli hydrohegemony whereby Israel denies Palestinians equal access to water—a shared and necessary resource. Strict water access regulations imposed by the 1967 occupation of the

Palestinian West Bank remain in place today with Israel disproportionately controlling shared surface and—most importantly—groundwater. Roughly 90 % of Israel-Palestine's groundwater comes from the Mountain Aquifer, which lies underneath both Israel and the Palestinian West Bank land. The Mountain Aquifer serves as a major source of freshwater for key Israeli population centers and is the only water source for most Palestinians in the Palestinian West Bank. Israel abstracts approximately 80 % of the aquifer's estimated potential and the Palestinian West Bank extracts the remainder.

The Oslo Interim Agreement of 1995 sought to facilitate cooperative water management by establishing the Israeli-Palestinian Joint Water Committee (JWC). Like many initiatives implemented throughout the peace process, however, the JWC has not lived up to expectations. A brief consideration of the permitting process does much to illustrate the asymmetric patterns that are reproduced, rather than interrupted, by the JWC. Any infrastructure project in Area C of the West Bank—approximately 60 % of the territory designated for the future Palestinian state—requires JWC and Israeli Civil Authority permitting. Anecdotal complaints about the JWC's near systematic refusal to grant permits for Palestinian water projects (e.g. Christian et al. 2013: 16–17) have been supported by academic inquiry (Selby 2007: 203–212; World Bank 2009; Zeitoun 2008: 149). Reasonable technical or regulatory concerns no doubt account for some number of JWC permitting decisions. Still, numerous technical experts believe the Israeli government blocks or delays large-scale water infrastructure projects in the Palestinian West Bank "even when no permitting objections or Israeli conditionalities are raised." Thus there remains a perception that the Israeli government's blocking of infrastructure projects is "a means of limiting Palestinian populations and strengthening Israeli control" (Christian et al. 2013: 18).

Curtailing Palestinian capacity building contributes to the discourse of water securitization that supports Israeli hydrohegemony. Water securitization frames national survival as predicated upon access to a sustainable and unpolluted water supply. One of the perceived central threats to water security is the Palestinian other (Sherman 2001: 188–191; Fröhlich 2012: 129–130). Within this narrative Palestinians are perceived as unable and/or unwilling to be environmental stewards, thereby compromising the quality and quantity of water available for Israeli consumption (Abitbol 2013 28–33; Christian et al. 2013: 61). This is an example of Mitchell's ethnonationalist competition over jurio-territorial control in action through the use of ideational power. The discourse is self-reinforcing (Foucault 1980: 40–46) as Israeli hydrohegemony and the occupation severely handicap Palestinian development, thus preserving Israel's metropole-like control (Cairo 2006: 305). Water access, rights, and governance are not only reflective of the ongoing conflict but also potentially affective (Zeitoun et al. 2013: 86–106). Water is one of the "final status" issues in Israeli-Palestinian negotiations, as well, meaning that any future peace agreement must address the cooperative management of shared water resources.

2.3.2 *The Arava Institute of Environmental Studies and the Palestinian Wastewater Engineers Group*

The Arava Institute of Environmental Studies (AIES) is an Israeli-based institution that focuses on environmental education and research programs, including The Center for Transboundary Water Management (CTWM) which provides an institutional basis for developing projects that ensure equitable access to ground and surface water in the Middle East. The Palestinian Wastewater Engineers Group (PWEG) is a Palestinian nonprofit NGO dedicated to capacity building and professional development within the wastewater and solid waste sectors. The two organizations have partnered to provide a cooperative model for providing sustainable wastewater infrastructure in the Palestinian West Bank.[5]

The initiative is designed to address environmental, technical, and social components of wastewater infrastructure[6] on a small scale. The initiative's key feature is a low-cost domestic greywater treatment and reuse system that protects groundwater degradation by diverting wastewater from household cesspits and making it available for agricultural use. System installation and monitoring is a cooperative process meant to encourage transboundary communication between Israelis and Palestinians.

The CTWM-PWEG initiative is comprised of unique characteristics that make it a viable testing ground for our framework. Firstly, CTWM and PWEG have a close and long-lasting partnership. In analyzing their relationship in the conflict context, we see that they are prime examples of the "power with" that transcends asymmetries. Both CTWM and PWEG "seem to understand the potential generated through pooling resources and are leveraging their individual and collective skills and influence to effect change in the region. In this way, they are highlighting the importance of building 'power with' rather than 'power over' partnerships" (Christian et al. 2013: 49–50).

Secondly, the CTWM-PWEG partnership is centered around shared goals and agreement on the intended benefits from the initiative which include increased water availability; increased income from reduced water costs—e.g. "cash savings on cesspits emptying and on drinking water cost," and greater agricultural productivity; and a reduction in hygienic and environmental risks meant to protect and to save the scarce water resources (Christian et al. 2013: 32).

Finally, the two organizations are positioned as mid-level actors whose ability to engage actors both 'above' and 'below' allows for a bridging of the divide between civil society/grassroots and elite actors. To be sure, the organizations, and most

[5]"4.2 The Implementing partner organizations", in *Decentralized Wastewater Treatment and Reuse: A transboundary approach to environmental, social and technical issues of wastewater infrastructure development, A Pilot Project in Al 'Oja Village, Palestine*: 5.

[6]"4. Problem Statement", in: *Decentralized Wastewater Treatment and Reuse: A transboundary approach to environmental, social and technical issues of wastewater infrastructure development, A Pilot Project in Al 'Oja Village, Palestine*: 3–4.

particularly their program staff, do not share the same degree of agency. As an organization registered in Palestine and staffed almost exclusively by Palestinians, PWEG's ability to efficiently and effectively develop international partnerships is severely truncated. For instance, despite being approved by the Joint Water Committee and the Israeli Ministry of Finance, an EU funded water treatment plant to service the Palestinian villages of Taybeh and Ramoun has been delayed for over two months due to the Israeli government, citing security concern, withholding crucial technology provided by a German manufacturer (Christian et al. 2013: 18). While this plant is not a wholly PWEG project, the example is illustrative of the general issue of curtailed privilege to discriminate, i.e. agency to determine one's own future, experienced by Palestinians. In this instance, the ability to enter into equal partnerships designed to improve one's quality of life.

2.4 Results and Discussion

The following analysis borrows from nested conflict theory as first developed by Dugan (1996: 9–19, 2001: 365–9) and then further elaborated upon by Lederach (2003: 27) to organize the research findings. Before engaging in our analysis, however, it is important to note that, while we have chosen to organize our findings in such a way so as to illuminate potential strengths and challenges associated with environmental peacebuilding as a tool for conflict transformation, neither CTWM nor PWEG have explicitly identified their joint partnership and the potential fruits of their work as 'peacebuilding' in nature. Rather, they have focused their attention on achieving environmental and development goals and fostering capacity building. However, the influential Brundtland Report (UN 1987: 240–3), which emphasized the centrality of environmental concerns for development and the importance of sustainability for societal stability, provides a strong foundation and implicit justification for our analysis as we consider the rich nexus between the environment, development, and peacebuilding. Additionally, it is relevant to note that the CTWM-PWEG initiative represents one of many similar transboundary-based projects in the region. This analysis is a modest attempt to consider ways that projects like the CTWM-PWEG initiative could deepen the impact of their efforts and potentially produce change-oriented ripple effects throughout the conflict strata. In the following subsections, we have grouped research findings into issue-specific, relational, structural, and cultural levels in an attempt to better understand the extent to which the CTWM-PWEG initiative—which has been successfully executed and fully realized on an issue-specific level—could also produce relational and societal gains.

2.4.1 Issues-Specific Level

From an issues-specific standpoint, the CTWM-PWEG initiative is primarily concerned with improving wastewater treatment capacity in underserved Palestinian communities. Wastewater infrastructure is sorely lacking in the Palestinian West Bank; 10 % of wastewater is treated and very little is reused (Christian et al. 2013: x). Only 31 % of Palestinians in the Palestinian West Bank were connected to sewerage networks in 2009 and only four major towns had wastewater treatment plants (World Bank 2009: v). Existing sewerage networks are over 50 years old and poorly managed. The World Bank estimates that 25 MCM of raw sewage is discharged from 350 locations annually, and Israeli sources estimate annual discharge rates at up to 64 MCM.

The wastewater problem stems from and is exacerbated by the broader political conflict, which hinders the development of large-scale, centralized wastewater treatment plants in the Palestinian West Bank. Though centralized treatment plants are the preferred solution, small-scale "off-the-grid" wastewater interventions are more politically feasible. Recognizing this, the CTWM-PWEG initiative is designed to skirt intractable political arenas by adopting a decentralized and collaborative approach. The project focuses on installing low-cost greywater recycling technology in individual Palestinian households. This can, in theory, augment household water availability; protect shared water supplies from contamination; and provide more agricultural water to improve livelihoods, food security, and income generation.

Treating and reusing greywater increases water availability and decreases the volume of wastewater entering household cesspits, creating additional economic and environmental benefits. Recycled water can be used to irrigate crops for production and consumption, in some cases enabling agricultural diversification. Water is five to six times more expensive in rural areas without piped water (Assaf et al. 2004: 185–228). Greywater recycling can help lower water costs by 30 % after overhead,[7] in part by reducing cesspit pumping expenses (Christian et al. 2013: 5). Household cesspits are often unlined, allowing wastewater seepage to contaminate transboundary water supplies. Because there are few cesspit pumping companies and few centralized treatment facilities, wastewater is often collected at the household level only to be discharged into shared water supplies elsewhere. The CTWM-PWEG thus has a positive impact at the issues-specific level of conflict by effectively addressing wastewater concerns shared by both Israelis and Palestinians.

[7]"Cost Effectiveness", in: *Environment Agency, Greywater for domestic users: an information guide* (May 2011): 18–20.

2.4.2 Relational Level

The Israeli-Palestinian conflict encompasses much more than a particular set of issues. Shared water supplies are central to the conflict, for example, but it is unlikely that focusing on water alone will achieve enduring peace; relationships between Israelis and Palestinians are critical. The notions of contact theory and generalization are an assumed mechanism at the relational level in the CTWM-PWEG initiative's theory of change. Indeed, the initiative progress report states:[8]

> Collaboration is envisaged by combining Israeli and Palestinian expertise in wastewater treatment and reuse. The cross fertilization of ideas will allow for both Israelis and Palestinians to resolve the wastewater treatment problem in the West Bank to the benefit of both parties… Relationships yield partnerships, regional environmental projects and inter-municipal agreements and thereby reduce conflict.

In practice, relationship building is primarily evidenced between CTWM and PWEG project staff, but also, to a much lesser extent, relationships between CTWM staff and Palestinian project beneficiaries and stakeholders. In conversation, a number of technical actors associated with this project—and similar projects in the region—focused on the importance of placing their identity as 'professionals' above 'Israeli' or 'Palestinian' identities in order to help projects move forward. The initiative has helped develop a cadre of technical experts from both sides of the conflict that work together toward shared goals around wastewater treatment. As AIES notes, it provides "a platform whereby … real and long-lasting relationships built on trust and integrity are created among those who are responsible for the sustainable management of the region's fragile water resources."[9] Likewise, PWEG's brochure speaks to its ambitions to build technical and organizational capacity by connecting like-minded professionals.[10] Professional cooperation in regional wastewater management may be a particularly advantageous mechanism for forging relationships, since "focusing on common environmental harms (or aversions) is psychologically more successful at producing cooperative outcomes than focusing on common interests" (Ali 2007: 6). By establishing and strengthening new relationships, the CTWM-PWEG initiative is realizing gains at the relational level.

[8]"2. Project Goal", in: *Decentralized Wastewater Treatment and Reuse: A transboundary approach to environmental, social and technical issues of wastewater infrastructure development, A Pilot Project in Al 'Oja Village, Palestine*: 3.

[9]"4.2 The Implementing partner organizations", in: *Decentralized Wastewater Treatment and Reuse: A transboundary approach to environmental, social and technical issues of wastewater infrastructure development, A Pilot Project in Al 'Oja Village, Palestine*: 5.

[10]'Mission', in: *Palestinian Wastewater Engineers Group (PWEG) Information brochure* (2013): 2.

2.4.3 *Structural and Cultural Levels*

Reducing conflict at the structural level involves addressing institutions and behaviors that reproduce structural violence. Tackling cultural violence, requires shining a light on the, "symbolic sphere of our existence—exemplified by religion and ideology, language and art, empirical science and formal science" (Galtung 1990: 291) in hopes of better understanding how these aspects of culture are used to, "justify or legitimize direct [or physical] or structural violence." (Galtung 1990: 291)

Research findings suggest that the issue-specific and relational gains associated with the CTWM-PWEG initiative are not translating into structural or cultural change. To cite an example, when a respondent interrupted a conversation about regional infrastructure and water management to give an impassioned soliloquy about the injustices and affronts to human dignity that he encounters daily, other respondents became silent and failed to comment directly on the issues he raised. Instead, after a brief pause, individuals returned to their conversations. In this way, the moment—and its potential—went largely unacknowledged by the group. This example suggests that, while the CTWM-PWEG initiative has successfully created a space for facilitating dialogue and venting frustrations, the dialogue produced is not being used to extend action beyond the relational sphere. This can be problematic given that dialogue without action can, in the long run, reinforce rather than transform conflict dynamics and existing oppression (Abu-Nimer 2004: 405–422).

Building peace requires purposeful contact between conflict actors (Lederach 1997: 23–35): relational contact is unlikely to be effectual beyond the relational level unless it translates into sustained social action. Evidence suggests that the CTWM-PWEG initiative is not currently promoting these actions which, we believe, explains why peacebuilding does not occur beyond the relational level.

2.5 Conclusion

This chapter has explored the potential of a cooperative wastewater development initiative in the Palestinian West Bank to be a lever for transformative change within the greater asymmetric conflict in which it is situated. The initiative has made positive impacts at both issues-specific and relational levels but was unable to leverage those gains to realize structural and cultural change. Conflict theory makes clear that the necessary targets of transformation are deeply rooted, namely the asymmetric (not one-sided, non-collaborative) ideational power and the ethnonationalist discourse sustaining Israeli hegemony and incompatible notions of belonging and personhood, respectively. Christian et al. (2013: 29–35, 46–54, 57–64) posit potential rectifying mechanisms in epistemic community capacity building, institutionalizing benefit sharing, and curating peace constituencies. These hold potential promise to directly address the structural, and subsequent cultural, levels of conflict left untransformed. While grounded in the specifics of the Israeli-Palestinian conflict, this examination makes clear the need for conscious and coordinated targeting of the structural and cultural layer of conflict on the part of able actors to build in multiplying and leveraging measures into peacebuilding initiatives widely.

References

Abitbol, Eric, 2013: "Hydropolitical Peacebuilding: Israeli-Palestinian Water Relations and Transformation of Asymmetric Conflict in the Middle East" (Ph.D., University of Bradford).

Abu-Nimer, Mohammed, 2004: "Education for Coexistence and Arab-Jewish Encounters in Israel: Potential and Challenges", in: *Journal of Social Issues*, 60,2: 405–422.

Abu-Nimer, Mohammed; Lazarus, Ned, 2007: "The Peacebuilders Paradox and the Dynamics of Dialogue: Psychosocial Approaches to Israeli/Palestinian Peacebuilding" in: Kuriansky, J (Ed.): *Beyond Bullets and Bombs: Grassroots Peacebuilding between Palestinians and Israelis* (Santa Barbara: Greenwood Press): 19–32.

Akçali, Emel; Antonsich, Marco 2009: "'Nature Knows No Boundaries': A Critical Reading of UNDP Environmental Peacemaking in Cyprus" in: *Annals of the Association of American Geographers*, 99,5: 940–947.

Ali, Saleem H., 2007: *Peace Parks: Conservation and Conflict Resolution* (Cambridge: MIT Press).

Allport, Gordon W., 1954: *The Nature of Prejudice* (Reading: Addison-Wesley).

Assaf, Karen; Attian, Bayoumi; Darwish, Ali; Wardam, Batit; Klawitter, Simone, 2004: *Water as a Human Right: The Understanding of Water in the Arab Countries of the Middle East—a Four Country Analysis* (Ramallah: Heinrich Böll Foundation, Arab Middle East Office).

Axelrod, Robert, 2006: *The Evolution of Cooperation* (New York: Basic Books).

Azar, Edward E., 1985: "Protracted International Conflicts: Ten Propositions" in: *International Interactions*, 12, 1: 59–70.

Azar, Edward E.; Farah, Nadia, 1981: "The Structure of Inequalities and Protracted Social Conflict: A Theoretical Framework" in: *International Interactions*, 7,4: 317–335.

Azar, Edward E.; Jureidini, Paul, McLaurin, Ronald, 1978: "Protracted Social Conflict; Theory and Practice in the Middle East" in: *Journal of Palestine Studies*, 8,1: 41–60.

Bertram, Eva, 1995: "Reinventing Governments: The Promise and Perils of United Nations Peace Building" in: *The Journal of Conflict Resolution*, 39,3: 387–418

Boulding, Elise, 2001: "Designing Future Workshops as a Tool for Peacebuilding", in: Reychler, Luc; Paffenholz, Thania (Eds.): *Peacebuilding, A Field Guide* (Boulder: Lynne Rienner Publishers): 373–375.

Burton, John W., 1996: *Conflict Resolution: Its Language and Processes* (Lanham: Scarecrow Press Inc.).

Cairo, Heriberto, 2006: "The Duty of the Benevolent Master: From Sovereignty to Suzerainty and the Biopolitics of Intervention", in: *Alternatives: Global, Local, Political*, 31,3: 285–311.

Call, Charles T.; Cooke, Susan E., 2003: "On Democratization and Peacebuilding" in: *Global Governance*, 9,2: 233–246

Carius, Alexander, 2006: "Environmental Cooperation as an Instrument for Crisis Prevention and Peacebuilding: Conditions for Success" (unpublished).

Carius, Alexander, 2006-2007: "Environmental Peacemaking: Conditions for Success" in: Dabelko, Geoffrey (Ed.): *Environmental Change and Security Report 12* (Washington, D.C.: Woodrow Wilson Center): 59–75.

Cascão, Ana Elisa; Zeitoun, Mark, 2010: "Power, hegemony and critical hydropolitics", in: Earle, Anton; Jägerskog, Anders; Ojendal, Joakin (Eds.): *Transboundary Water Management: Principles and Practice* (London: Earthscan): 27–42.

Cheng, Anthony S.; Kruger, Linda E.; Daniels, Steven E., 2003: "'Place' as an Integrating Concept in Natural Resource Politics: Propositions for a Social Science Research Agenda" in: *Society & Natural Resources*, 16,2: 87–104.

Christian, C.; Fisher, J.; Jackson, M.; Kehoe, C.; Owen, C.; Puleo, V.; Rosner, E.; Speight, H., 2013: "Water, Cooperation, and Peace" (Graduate Practicum Report, American University).

Clayton, Susan D.; Opotow, Susan (Eds.) 2003: *Identity and the Natural Environment: The Psychological Significance of Nature* (Cambridge: The MIT Press).

Conca, Ken, 2000: "Chapter 11: Environmental Cooperation and International Peace." in: Diehl, Paul F.; Gleditsch, Nile Petter (Eds.): *Environmental Conflict: An Anthology* (Boulder: Westview Press): 225–250.

Conca, Ken, 2002: "Chapter 1: The Case for Environmental Peacemaking." in: Conca, Ken; Dabelko, Geoffrey (Eds.): *Environmental Peacemaking* (Washington, D.C.: Woodrow Wilson Press): 1–22.

Conca, Ken; Dabelko, 2002: "Chapter 8: The Problems of Possibilities of Environmental Peacemaking." in: Conca, Ken; Dabelko, Geoffrey (Eds.): *Environmental Peacemaking* (Washington, D.C.: Woodrow Wilson Press): 220–234.

Curle, Adam, 1971: *Making Peace* (London: Tavistock Publications Limited).

Deutsch, Karl W., 1978: *The Analysis of International Relations, Second Edition* (Englewood Cliffs: Prentice-Hall).

Deutsch, Morton, 2014: "Introduction", in Coleman, Peter T; Deutsch, Morton; Marcus, Eric, C, (Eds): *The Handbook of Conflict Resolution, Theory and Practice, 3rd Edition* (San Francisco: Jossey-Bass): 27–50.

Dixon, John; Durrheim, Kevin; Tredoux, Colin, 2005: "Beyond the Optimal Contact Strategy: A Reality Check for the Contact Hypothesis" in: *American Psychologist* 60, 7: 197–711.

Dugan, Máire A., 1996: "A Nested Theory of Conflict" in: *A Leadership Journal: Women in Leadership*, 1: 9–19.

Dugan, Máire A., 2001: "Imagining the Future: A Tool for Conflict Resolution", in Reychler, Luc; Paffenholz, Thania (Eds.): *Peacebuilding, A Field Guide* (Boulder: Lynne Rienner Publishers): 365–372.

Foucault, Michel, 1980: "Prison Talk" in: Gordon, Colin (Ed.): Power/Knowledge: Selected Interviews and Other Writings, 1972-1977 (New York: Pantheon): 37–54.

Francis, Diana, 2002: *People, Peace and Power: Conflict Transformation in Action* (Sterling: Pluto Press).

Freire, Paulo, 1993: *Pedagogy of the Oppressed* (New York: Continuum International Publishing Group).

Fröhlich, Christiane J., 2012: "Security and Discourse: The Israeli–Palestinian Water Conflict" in: *Conflict, Security & Development*, 12,2: 123–148.

Galtung, Johan, 1990: "Cultural Violence", in: *Journal of Peace Research* 27,3: 291–305.

Galtung, Johan, 1996: *Peace by Peaceful Means: Peace and Conflict, Development and Civilization* (London: SAGE Publications).

Greider, Thomas; Garkovich, Lorraine, 1994: "Landscapes: The Social Construction of Nature and the Environment" in: *Rural Sociology*, 59,1: 1–24.

Harari, Nicole; Roseman, Jesse, 2008: *Environmental Theory and Practice: A Case Study of the Good Water Neighbours Project and In Depth Analysis of the Wadi Fukin / Tzur Hadassah Communities* (Amman, Bethlehem, and Tel Aviv: Friends of the Earth Middle East).

Jarstad, Anna K., 2008: "Dilemmas of war-to-democracy transitions: theories and concepts", in: Jarstad, Anna K; Sisk, Timothy D. (Eds.): *From War to Democracy, Dilemmas of Peacebuilding* (Cambridge: Cambridge University Press): 1–20.

Jenkins, Robert, 2013: *Peacebuilding, From Concept to Commission* (New York: Routledge).

Lasswell, H. D., 1936: *Politics: Who Gets What, When, How* (New York: McGraw-Hill).

Lederach, John Paul, 1995: *Preparing for Peace, Conflict Transformation Across Cultures* (Syracuse: Syracuse University Press).

Lederach, John Paul, 1997: *Building Peace: Sustainable Reconciliation in Divided Societies* (Washington, D.C.: United States Institute of Peace).

Lederach, John Paul, 2003: *The Little Book of Conflict Transformation* (Intercourse: Good Books).
Lederach, John Paul, 2005: *The Moral Imagination: The Art and Soul of Building Peace* (New York: Oxford University Press, Inc.).
Miall, Hugh, 2004: "Conflict Transformation: A Multi-Dimensional Task" in: Austin, Alex; Fischer, Martina; Ropers, Norbert (Eds.): *Transforming Ethnopolitical Conflict, The Berghof Handbook* (Berlin: Springer): 67–89.
Miller, Byron, 1992: "Collective Action and Rational Choice: Place, Community, and the Limits to Individual Self-Interest" in: *Economic Geography*, 68,1: 22–42.
Mitchell, Christopher R., 1991: "Classifying Conflicts: Asymmetry and Resolution", in: *The Annals of the American Academy of Political and Social Science* 518,1: 23–38.
Moaz, Ifat, 2011: "Does Contact Work in Protracted Asymmetrical Conflict? Appraising 20 Years of Reconciliation-Aimed Encounters between Israeli Jews and Palestinians" in: *Journal of Peace Research*, 48,1: 115–125.
Moaz, Ifat, 2000: "Power Relations in Intergroup Encounters: A Case Study of Jewish–Arab Encounters in Israel" in *International Journal of Intercultural Relations*, 24,2: 266–275.
OECD, 2013: *OECD Economic Surveys: Israel* (Paris: OECD).
Pettigrew, T.F.; Tropp, L.R., 2006: "A Meta-Analytic Test of Intergroup Contact Theory" in: *Journal of Personality and Social Psychology* 90, 5: 751–783.
Pettigrew, Thomas, 1998: "Intergroup Contact Theory", in: *Annual Review of Psychology*, 49: 65–85.
Polak, Fred, 1973: *Image of the Future* (Amsterdam: Elsevier Scientific Publishing Company).
Ramsbotham, Oliver; Woodhouse, Tom; Miall, Hugh, 2005: *Contemporary Conflict Resolution, Second Edition* (Cambridge: Polity Press).
Ramsbotham, Oliver; Woodhouse, Tom; Miall, Hugh, 2011: *Contemporary Conflict Resolution, Third Edition* (Cambridge: Polity Press).
Rupesinghe, Kumar, 1995: "Conflict Transformation", in: Rupesinghe, Kumar (Ed.): *Conflict Transformation* (London: Macmillan Press Ltd): 65–92.
Saunders, Hal; Slim, Rwanda, 1994: "Dialogue to Change Conflictual Relationships", in: *Higher Education Exchange*: 43–56.
Selby, Jan, 2003: "Dressing up Domination as 'Cooperation': The Case of Israeli-Palestinian Water Relations", in: *Review of International Studies*, 1: 121–138.
Selby, Jan, 2007: "Joint Mismanagement: Reappraising the Oslo Water Regime", in: *Water Resources in the Middle East* 2: 203–2012.
Sherman, Martin, 2001: "The Hydro-Political Implications of the Oslo Agreements: An Israeli Perspective" in: Stav, Arieh (Ed.): *Israel and a Palestinian State: Zero Sum Game?* (Shaarei Tikva: Zmora-Bitan Publishers and Ariel Center for Policy Research Publishers): 182–202.
Suleiman, Ramzi, 2000: "Jewish-Palestinian Relations in Israel" in: Halabi, Rabah (Ed.): *Israeli and Palestinian Identities in Dialogue* (New Brunswick, NY: Rutgers University Press): 31–46.
UN (United Nations), 1987: *Report of the World Commission on Environment and Development: Our Common Future*, annex to document A/42/427.
UN (United Nations), 1992: *Report of the Secretary-General, An Agenda for Peace,* A/47/277 (New York; UN).
UN (United Nations), 2000: *Report of the Panel on United Nations Peace Operations*, A/55/305, S/2000/809 (New York; UN).
UN (United Nations), 2010: "Section 1: The Scope of Peacebuilding", in: *UN Peacebuilding: An Orientation* (United Nations Peacebuilding Support Office).
Väyrynen, Raimo, 1991: "To Settle or to Transform? Perspectives on the Resolution of National and International Conflicts", in: Väyrynen, Raimo (Ed.): *New Directions in Conflict Theory, Conflict Resolution and Conflict Transformation* (London: Sage Publications Ltd): 1–25.
Wallensteen, Peter, 1991: "To Settle or to Transform? Perspectives on the Resolution of National and International Conflicts", in: Väyrynen, Raimo (Ed.): *New Directions in Conflict Theory, Conflict Resolution and Conflict Transformation* (London: Sage Publications Ltd): 129–152.

World Bank, 2009: *West Bank and Gaza: Assessment of Restriction on Palestinian Water Sector Development* (Washington, D.C.: World Bank).
Zeitoun, Mark; Eid-Sabbagh, Karim; Talhami, Michael; Dajani, Muna, 2013: "Hydro-Hegemony in the Upper Jordan Waterscape: Control and Use of the Flows" in: *Water Alternatives*, 6,1: 86–106.
Zeitoun, Mark, 2008: *Power and Water in the Middle East: The Hidden Politics of the Palestinian-Israeli Water Conflict* (New York: I.B. Tauris).
Zeitoun, Mark; Allan, J.A., 2008: "Applying Hegemony and Power Theory to Transboundary Water Analysis" in: *Water Policy* 10, Supplement 2:10.

Other Literature

Globetrotter Berkeley; at: http://globetrotter.berkeley.edu/people/Haas/haas-con0.html (2 June 2015).
United Nations; at: http://www.un.org/en/peacebuilding/pbso/pbun.shtml (1 June 2015).
PACBI; at: http://www.pacbi.org/etemplate.php?id=1749 (1 June 2015).

Chapter 3
The Peace Process Mediation Network Between the Colombian Government and the April 19th Movement

Tania Galaviz

Abstract This chapter explores the role of mediation networks in the peace process. It considers the case of negotiations between the Colombian government and the April 19th Movement (also referred to as M-19), and the effectiveness of mediation networks in creating a successful environment to demobilize the movement. Systems Theory is used to study the peace processes, along with conceptual models for analysing mediated conflict management by John Paul Lederach and Thania Paffenholz. Mediations are considered as dynamic elements that help and support efforts to consolidate peace in societies incurring conflict. This perspective allows the chapter to transform the traditional concept of mediators to one of mediations, which is more dynamic and inclusive. This concept provides a basis for exploring the presence of citizen movements during M-19, and the absence of traditional high-level mediation during this particular peace process.

Keywords Mediation network · Systems theory · Peace process · April 19th movement

3.1 Introduction

This study focuses on the involvement of civil society in the peace process between the Columbian government and the "19 de abril" movement (M-19). Based on Luhmann's (1998) systemic approach, the related components appearing throughout its development were considered as influential to a larger and more complex structure. This allowed to considerer the peace processes as non-linear, erratic and

Dr. Tania Galaviz, professor, Humanities Faculty, Autonomous University of Morelos (UAEM); Edif.19 Av. Universidad 1001, Col. Chamilpa, Cuernavaca, Morelos, México, C.P. 62209; Email: tgalaviz@gmail.com.

This work is the result of a review of some sections of the doctoral thesis "Mediations in the peace process between the Colombian government and the M-19, 1980–1990" defended in October, 2014 at the Political and Social Science Graduate Program of the National Autonomous University of Mexico.

Ú.Oswald Spring et al. (eds.), *Regional Ecological Challenges for Peace in Africa, the Middle East, Latin America and Asia Pacific*, The Anthropocene: Politik—Economics—Society—Science 5, DOI 10.1007/978-3-319-30560-8_3

multidirectional that responds to its environment and needs. Traditionally conflicts develop through four phases: pre-conflict, conflict, mitigation and post-conflict; is an idea that can be contested (Paffenholz/Spurk 2006: 15). For example, post-conflict is difficult to understand without mitigation. This would make peace processes more similar to a system that responds to its own variability, pressures and *autopoiesis*, which rarely follow a linear trajectory (Galaviz Armenta 2014: 14).

Autopoeises is the capability that systems have to maintain stability, especially useful when confronting external pressure (Galaviz Armenta 2014: 30). In the specific peace process in question between the M-19 and the Columbian government, this implied generating and reproducing the necessary conditions for the disarmament, demobilization and reintegration of M-19's members. Civilian participation through network mediation—as its *autopoietic* expression—allowed a favourable environment for the peace process. It also aimed at creating a strong social foundation for sustainable peace characterized by smart flexibility[1] to contextual variations and ability to build cooperative links at different levels.

To further the analysis of these developments this chapter is structured in four sections. The first will discuss social system theory applied to social conflict. Following are John Paul Lederach's and Thania Paffenholz' models for mediation methodology. The third section studies the Colombian armed conflict and the peace process in the light of social system theory. Finally, the network mediation model applied to the case study is presented.

3.1.1 Social Systems Theory

In the theory of social systems by Luhmann (1998), the system is defined with binding to its environment, that is, the system sets its scrutiny and boundaries of interaction regarding this precept: "systems are established and maintained through the creation and preservation of difference to the environment, and use their boundaries to regulate such difference" (Luhmann 1998: 40). Thus, the system will exist due to the environment and the environment—as environment—will require the system for its own distinction. Therefore, according to Luhmann, "the systems … are established and maintained through the production and maintenance of a difference to the environment and use their boundaries to regulate this difference" (Luhmann 1990: 50).

One of the key features of the systems is their consistency and independence from other systems. In other words, a system behaves not only as a simple compound of independent elements, but as an inseparable whole and coherent. This is because even though a system is part of another system, the component parts

[1]Smart flexibility is how network mediation attends to communication requirement and to resolve conflicts produced by inter-systemic pressures. It includes a growing complexity based on the collectives and the individuals involved, as the nature of the necessities (Poggiese et al. 1999: 11).

interact in a complex way that to make a change in one of these, a modification occurs in the other.

This capacity is referred to as 'recursivity', and is what allows a system to hold and contain, in turn, to other subsystems. The latter can be defined as the elements whose properties are reflected throughout the entire system. This total system can also influence the properties of subsystems, to the degree of their interrelationship.

Subsystems are created by the differentiation between the system and its environment: "Thus the overall system acquires the function of 'internal environment' for the subsystems, which, however, is specific to each" (Luhmann 1990: 42). This distinction is based on the different yet complementary functions of each system regarding its environment.

Identifying the internal processes of a system needs a second-order of observation it is considered of second-order because the observation is performed externally. It requires two types of references: hetero-reference and self-reference. That is, the properties that the observer attributes to the system and to itself—for instance the concepts by which the facts are analysed. The objective of the second-order observation is to identify causal relationships between the inside and outside to ascribe their purposes (Corsi 1996: 119).

3.1.2 *Analysis of Social Conflicts*

The second-order observation involves an analysis that differentiates between the events[2] and processes[3] they present and that transform the present into the past; that modify the entire system. Luhmann proposes three types of system analysis: baseline, procedural and systemic. Baseline analysis breaks-down the system elements according to their relationships. Procedural analysis relates to the temporal evolution of the element's internal relations and their association with the environment. Both of these approaches could be considered as part of the theory of systemic complexity. Systemic analysis studies the effects that the interactions and the elements have on the system with respect to its environment distinction (Luhmann 1998). In this case study the author is applying a systemic form of analysis.

This chapter examines the peace process involved in the M-19 movement in Colombia between 1981 and 1990. Here the M-19 movement is treated as complex system with capacity to generate its own structures and components. The analysis focuses on participation mechanisms for mediations as well as the grade of incidence that was involved in creating a favourable environment.

---

[2]Events are phenomena promptly fixed in time and only occur once.

[3]Processes are constituted by a sequence of events based on a double selection of possibilities. The first limits the succession of events that may arise. The second selection occurs when determining which event can be updated consecutively.

3.2 Approaches to Mediation

Traditionally, the mediator has been defined as a third person unconnected to the conflict who seeks to approach both parties with objective neutrality—with the capacity to generate empathy and look for solutions without pronouncing in favour of any involved parties.

However, in conflicts with multiple actors and a high level of complex interactions, the mediator is limited during negotiations and eventually isolated from the peacebuilding process. Accordingly, Lederach/Wehr (1991) proposed that mediators to become a part of society affected by conflict. This will allow them to understand its causes, the underlying variables, the needs and attitudes of the population, which can facilitate building links or networks for reconciliation and transformation of societies (Lederach/Wehr 1991).

3.2.1 Transform Approach

The proposal of John Paul Lederach was nurtured by his experience in mediation and training in peacebuilding as well as his academic work at the universities of Notre Dame and Eastern Mennonite. From this reasoning Lederach makes his conflict transformation proposal that considers peace as "centered and rooted in the quality of relationships. These relationships have two dimensions: our face-to-face interactions and the ways we structure our social, political, economic, and cultural relationships" (Lederach 2003b: 20). So, peace becomes a dynamic, adaptive, changing process, which holds simultaneously a form, a purpose and a direction.

To address the conflict, Lederach proposes to analyse the immediate problem, the underlying patterns and context. With this a web of actions can be created that allows building changes in the processes involved in a conflict. Thus the temporal and spatial dimensions acquire centrality in the conflict transformation approach. As mentioned earlier, Lederach proposes that the mediation is performed by actors of society that come from the conflict and having some connection with any of the parties to the conflict. This model of mediation is called a trust-based model.

In this model, trust becomes the principal criteria to select and legitimate the mediator. It is the result of a good knowledgeable relationship between the parts. Key words for understanding the trust-based model are: legitimacy, tradition and positive connection (Lederach/Wehr 1991: 88).

Lederach stresses the importance of relationships between the different actors. Hence the trust-based model of conflict transformation establishes three levels in which the organizations and actors are grouped with different characteristics and leaderships.

The first level of the trust-based model is denominated top-level leadership. At this level the actors' profiles are public and their activities are concentrated on retaining position and influence (Lederach 2001: 146–147). The second level locates mid-level leadership characterized that allows communication with other levels serving as a liaison. The actors participating in this level are not subject to political and electoral calculation, which allows them greater diversity and dynamism. Generally, they are members of academia circles, intellectuals and civil society organizations. This level involves training in resolving conflicts, which lays the basis for sustainable peacebuilding (Lederach 2001: 152–153). The third and the last level is base leadership. It consists of organizations and individuals that aim to meet the immediate needs of the population such as food, shelter, clothing, safety and education (Lederach 1997: 51–52).

The mid-level leaderships are capable of vertical mobility by linking base leaderships with high-level negotiations. It also has horizontal mobility, through its capacity to reunite organizations with ethnic, religious or linguistic differences, for instance (Lederach 2005: 79–80). According to Lederach, this mobility and interaction of middle level leaderships allows them to perform networking. The advantage of this type of relationships is their smart flexibility. In the face of environmental changes they are able to generate processes that address these flows (Lederach 2005: 85), and maintain the entire system as a dynamic totality characterized by self-organization, favouring the establishment of a new order in both time and space (Oswald Spring 2005).

3.2.2 *Aid for Peace Approach*

Returning to the Conflict Transformation model, Thania Paffenholz develops a model of peacebuilding based on the involvement of civil society, where 'civil society' is defined as an:

> (…) arena of un-coerced collective action around shared interests, purposes and values. As a public sphere where citizens and voluntary organizations freely engage, it is distinct from the state, the family and the market, although since civil society is closely linked with these spheres, strict boundaries may be difficult to establish (Foster/Mattner 2007: 3).[4]

The approach Aid for Peace aims to ensure the relevance of the intervention in a society in conflict; enable the improvement of its effects and avoid risks and unwanted results. The interventions considered comprise a wide range of activities taking place in areas affected by violent conflict or aftermath of a war. For Paffenholz and Spurk, the importance that civil society organizations have in building peace lies in their ability to reveal changes that armed conflict has on society both at the individual—attitudes, behaviour, confidence and security—and at the community level with respect to the change in power relations, as well as the political, legal and economic impacts from armed conflict (Paffenholz/Spurk 2006: 11).

Thus, civil society can be recognized as a mediator with features and activities that allow them to contribute to building a sustainable peace that enables

[4]This is the definition for civil society used from here on in this study.

reconciliation in society. The proposals by Lederach and Paffenholz are relevant to the transition from the traditional concept of mediator to the figure of mediations, which are much more dynamic, inclusive and with capacities to influence the creation of an environment conducive to the peace process.

3.3 Colombian Armed Conflict

In this section the Colombian armed conflict will be considered with reference to Lederach's theory, using temporal and spatial dimensions as reference parameters. It also carries out a baseline and procedural methodology of the conflict considering it as a system. In other words, it will analyse the elements comprising the system, the relationships between them and their environment.

The armed conflict in Colombia has origins in the deep economic marginalization derived from the unfair distribution of land, the isolated location of the population, and the unequal distributions of wealth. The Colombian territory is fragmented by three ridges that create six bio-cultural regions: Andean, Northern coast, Orinoco, Amazon, Pacific coast and Insular. Most of population and political power is concentrated in the Andean region, which also generates most of the country's wealth. Property value is determined by rich agricultural soil, hydraulic resources, as well as communication infrastructure. Gradually, the best lands were occupied by big owners, who constantly expanded their properties through forced purchase or dispossession. Faced with such impunity, Colombia's rural population transited from relative economic stability to misery.

According to World Bank figures, between 1950 and 1980 the annual *gross domestic product* (GDP) growth stood at 5 % annually (see Arboleda/Garfield 2003: 46). The industry growth rate remained 9.2 % per annum, which was linked to the diversification of the penetration of the United States (Medina 1989: 22). However, this economic development was not experienced by the majority of the population. According to the World Bank, in 1980 the Gini index was 59.9, indicating that social development was not homogeneous nor equitable (see Table 1. Poverty and Inequality Indicators, Colombia 1978–99, Vélez et al. 2003: 91).

From the second half of the 1980s, land use and the distribution of the population abruptly changed not only due to the entry of illegal practices such as drug traffickers and paramilitaries, but also by the rise of oil exploitation and open pit mining.

These elements helped to define the Colombian system as exclusionary with a high level of social marginalization. The exclusion which the political system operated contributed to increase instability of the system. The process to assimilate —or reject—the entry of a new flow or element implied an increase in the complexity of its operation, characterized by entropic trends to respond to these pressures.

According to Mauricio García Villegas, "Political parties monopolize most of the state, so that everything is subject to the ally/enemy conflicts, typical of partisan debate" (García Villegas/Rebolledo 2009: 32). Belonging to one of the political parties, for the Colombian population, meant participating in traditions of mutual exclusion. Paradoxically, elite party leadership was narrow due to family ties through marriage and cronyism that ensured inclusion and permanence in the political system.

For the rest of Colombians belonging or identifying with one of the political parties did not mean a real chance to participate in the governing bodies. Therefore, the design of policies did not reflect the demands of the population, especially those of marginal urban settlements.

An example of this situation of political exclusion—deriving in economic marginalization—was the National Front, a political pact between the Liberal and Conservative parties that sought to guarantee parity in the exercise of power. From 1957 to 1974 party alternation was agreed; to equally share in the legislature and in the presidential cabinet.

During the National Front a formal exclusion of emerging political parties was established (Bushnell 1994: 306), however, the presidential elections of 1970—the last presidency of the National Front—included a coalition between members of the Liberal and Conservative parties to nominate General Rojas Pinilla as candidate (López de la Roche 1994: 68).[5] Official results showed that Rojas Pinilla captured 39.0 % of the vote, against 40.6 % of the official candidate Misael Pastrana Borrero (Bushnell 1994: 313). In the absence of a second round, these figures were enough for the Electoral Court to proclaim Pastrana winner.

The legality of the triumph of Pastrana was not linked to the legitimacy of it, as there is a very high possibility that a fraud was committed. This possibility caused discontent among the population; therefore, various political groups were integrated into an armed political movement called M-19 (Lara Salive 1987: 34–35).

The M-19 was founded by two organizations, 'comuneros' that included Jaime Bateman, Iván Marino Ospina, Álvaro Fayad, Carlos Pizarro, Augusto Lara, Rosemberg Pavón, María Eugenia Vázquez and Vera Grabe Loewenherz (Díaz 2008: 26); (Lelièvre et al. 2004: 75–76).[6] Most of them were active in the *Revolutionary Armed Forces of Colombia* (FARC) but left or were expelled due to ideological and strategy differences.

The second group that founded the M-19 was the Golconda movement. It was initially a group of priests that lobbied for socioeconomic change (Ramírez Orozco 2007: 268). Gradually the group expanded to incorporate university and professional sectors highly connected with grassroots organizations (Fajardo/Roldán 1980: 69).

---

[5]Colombian general, who after a coup, occupied the presidency between 1953 and 1957. His government ended the period of *La Violencia* in negotiating the demobilization of the Liberal guerrillas. He was deposed by a military coup that was ushered in by the National Front.

[6]Part of the M-19 was assassinated. Several survivors later joined leftist organizations such as *Polo Democrático Alternativo* or formed the opposition party *Opción Centro* (now *Alianza Verde*.) Other members like Camilo González Posso and Vera Grabe Loewenherz have since dedicated themselves to research and peacebuilding. Another survivor, Maria Eugenia Vázquez, now works in social work.

The M-19 was founded on the idea of uniting the Colombian people, so they did not use external references to legitimize their struggle; instead, it appealed to the national symbols like the flag and national anthem. Also, the M-19 defined itself as a 'democracy in arms,' considering it a tool to express the people's interests. Therefore, one of its main objectives was the creation of a National Democratic Convention that allowed for the discussion of new economic and social policies for Colombia.

With this proposal as a parameter of action, the M-19 proposed that the government begin a peace process that would allow the participation of civil society organizations in the construction of a new national pact. This involvement implies that the M-19 is not a conventional guerrilla force, besides the fact that it was capable to manipulate public images and representations to legitimate its actions and to "achieve important levels of public communication and sympathy" (García Durán et al. 2009: 52). Simultaneously, the Colombian government issued a peace proposal that would start a peace process that ended with the demobilization of the M-19 in 1990.

3.3.1 Peace Process Between Colombian Government and April 19th Movement

By analytically linking systems theory and the proposed of conflict analysis by Lederach, the peace process was conceptualized as a system with nonlinear trajectories that are erratic and multi-directional and that respond to their environment and its own needs.

To frame the analysis of the peace process between the Colombian government and M-19, a series of time periods were identified based on the presidential terms of Julio César Turbay Ayala (1978–1982), Belisario Betancur Cuartas (1982–1986) and Virgilio Barco Vargas (1986–1990); the various actions which together form the peace process with the M-19 were subsequently analysed according to this periodization.

A baseline and procedural analysis of these time periods was conducted by examining the component elements and the relationships that are maintained between them and their environment, as well as the temporal and spatial dimensions of their operation.

3.3.1.1 The Beginning of the Peace Process, Presidency of Julio Cesar Turbay Ayala (1978–1982)

On 27 February 1980, the M-19 took the headquarters of the Embassy of Dominican Republic to denounce human rights violations in the country and the release of its imprisoned members. After 61 days of negotiations to free the hostages, the seizing of the embassy concluded with positive results for both the Colombian government and the M-19. In particular, the intention of both parties to begin the search for a peaceful solution to the armed conflict was announced.

However, neither the operation of the integrated Peace Commission to mediate between the parties, nor the Amnesty Law sent to the Colombian Congress for approval, was made concrete. This was largely due to the confusing messages from the Colombian government and the declaring of M-19 as a non-political criminal group. As such, negotiations between with the Colombian government and M-19 had to focus on the delivery of weapons and not on the discussion of a political agenda.

In contrast, the public discussion of a political agenda was the central point of the M-19 peace proposal. The movement considered democratic openness as one of the principles that would allow for the building of processes to eliminate economic differences in the population (Jiménez Ricardez 1986: 6). During this period, the participation of civil society was restricted to denouncing the violation of human rights. So it could not affect or accompany the scant initial stage of the peace process.

3.3.1.2 Peace Process as a War Strategy, Presidency of Belisario Betancur Cuartas (1982–1986)

From the start of the administration of Belisario Betancur Cuartas, the pressure exerted by both the public and the economic and political groups made the option to revive the proposal of the peace process with the M-19 an unavoidable task for the government. The Peace Initiative from Betancur answered to his analysis of the causes of the emergence—and prolongation—of armed conflict. For him, violence was the product of two factors that were both objective and subjective; the former were gaps in service provision and access to goods; the latter were the consequences of the actions of individuals, who analysed reality from a particular ideological perspective and made efforts to change it (Betancur 1990: 48).

The government proposal consisted of two phases. The first focused on promoting economic and social development that could eliminate the objective causes; the second phase was the negotiation with the armed movements.[7] To do this, the government designed a strategy of four elements: the reactivation of the Peace Commission, the appointment of High Commissioners of Peace, performing a Multiparty Policy Summit and the adoption of a wide amnesty law.

The Commission was composed of 40 members, who represented various aspects of political, social and cultural life of Colombia. President Betancur conducted the integration personally, so participation and even consultation, was impossible with the legislature, the judiciary, the armed forces or political parties. The Commission had no power of decision (Arias 2008: 13), and their interaction

[7]President Belisario Betancur's peace policy was aimed mainly at M-19. Nonetheless, it was the *Revolutionary Armed Forces of Colombia* (FARC) who responded with most interest, and the *Popular Liberation Army* (EPL) also later involving itself in Betancur's peace process.

was directly with the President, who kept it isolated from the rest of the cabinet and the other powers.

During the four years of government, the Commission gradually lost its capacity to influence the peace process besides his constant flirtation with informality, for instance they operated on the basis of the willingness of its members, without access to a specific budget.

The High Commissioners for Peace—a second element of the negotiation strategy—were responsible for the operation of building development plans, as well as the budgetary exercise of the Peace Commission. These figures generated confusion among the public because they were unclear as to the limits of its operation or aims of its creation (Morales Benitez 1991).

As for the realization of a Multiparty Policy Summit, it was intended to discuss the scope and limitations of the peace process and the political reforms needed to achieve it (Jaramillo 2003: 46). Despite the diversity of the participants in this, their work could not be successful because they did not explicitly commit themselves to get results. Thus, in the first quarter of 1983 the meetings of the summit concluded with only two bills submitted to Congress, both of which were rejected.

Finally, the Amnesty Law was approved on 18 November 1982, benefiting 339 political prisoners—among them members of the High Command of the M-19. The release of these prisoners generated discontent in various sectors of the population, especially in the Armed Forces, who operated as spoilers of this stage of the peace process (Ramírez/Restrepo 1989: 115).

During this stage, mediations driven by intellectuals and artists, such as Gabriel García Márquez, and social organizations, ecclesial base communities,[8] and others formed a favorable environment for the peace process. However, there was little they could do when both the Colombian government and the M-19 operated as spoilers of the peace process. For example, President Betancur on several occasions blocked the work of the Negotiating Committee to delay hearings to review the progress of the process, which hampered the continuity itself. He also made misleading statements to influence the international public opinion, which was received by the M-19 as an attempt to sabotage the process. As for the M-19, its internal division was reflected in the divergent actions and statements regarding the peace process.

The failure of the second stage of the peace process was framed by the takeover of the Palace of Justice by the M-19 and the bloody military recovery operation. This event, and the resulting increase in drug violence, determined the electoral commitments in presidential campaigns, which agreed to reject the continuation of the peace process.

---

[8]In 1985 the Jesuits sold a gold and jeweled religious relic to the Colombian Bank of the Republic and used the sale to startup its Peace Programme. From 1987 to 1997 the program financed close to one thousand projects focused on strengthening civil society in conflict and marginal areas (Romero 2001: 411). Also important to mention is that the Mennonites advanced their relationship with civil society through their Christian Center For Justice, Peace and Non-Violence Action (García Durán 2006: 234).

3.3.1.3 Peace Process as a School of Organized Civil Society, and the Presidency of Virgilio Barco Vargas (1986–1990)

During the first two years of the administration of Virgilio Barco there was a refusal to resume the peace process with the M-19. However, on 29 May 1988, the M-19 abducted Alvaro Gomez Hurtado, the leader of the Conservative Party. The objective of this action was to announce his new peace proposal, which consisted of a National Dialogue to build the foundations for a democratic transition.

Due to pressure from politicians and the public, the government considered the proposal of the M-19 and resumed the peace process. Because the environment of the process was characterized in a peak moment of narco-terrorism, the same stability was based on the commitment of the M-19 to demobilize, regardless of the conditions and terms of the process.

This generated great expectations among different sectors of Colombian society, and unlike the previous phase of the peace process, in this, the participation of civil society was to create a favourable environment for the process. In particular, peace movements and the Catholic Church began to perform activities such as marches, rallies, meetings and seminars in favour of peace; these were all broadcast for national public opinion.

In addition, the implementation of the Working Tables—and the Analysis Tables and agreements derived from it—allowed various sectors of society to discuss the proposals, focusing on three points: the drafting of a new constitution, the design of an economic and social development plan, and the redefinition of the social democratic framework (Bejarano 1990: 108–109). This favoured the integration of civil society organizations into the peace process and allowed for the strengthening of both the network of mediations that they had begun to build and the enabling environment for the development of the peace process.

The development of the peace process coincided with the mobilization for the convening of a *National Constituent Assembly* (NCA). Both events generated a synergy that would create an enabling environment for the realization of its objectives.

Thus, in the context of armed violence produced by narco-terrorism, as well as guerrilla and paramilitary activities, social mobilization generated environments favourable to the articulation of consensus for building mechanisms to reduce gun violence. In 1990, following the signing of peace agreements between the M-19 and the Colombian government, and the installation of the NCA, mobilization for peace decreased. This did not see the disappearance of such movements, which remained stable, however, and grew steadily in the following decades.

3.4 Mediation Network for Sustainable Peace

Lederach's proposal for mediation focuses on the involvement of mediators in peacebuilding activities. It builds interactions that synergistically moderate the intensity of the conflict and create a favourable environment for negotiation and processes for building peace. Thus, mediations acquire the ability to become a dissipative structure. That is, mediations must allow for the stability of a system by absorbing instabilities, by creating multiple channels of feedback flows. In this way mediations can respond to the complexity of interactions between the system and its environment, and increasing its complexity. Also, mediations meet the needs generated at the levels where armed conflict is present, for instance, local, regional, national and international.

This type of mobility, allows the mediations to create a mediation network that is characterized by its ability to maintain smart flexibility. For instance, it is able to face changes in the environment, to generate processes that address these flows (Lederach 2005: 85) and to articulate mediation processes into a network; it is a peace-building dynamic that is responsive to its cycles of conflict (Lederach 2003a: 37). It is precisely this flexibility that allows mediation networks to establish effective cooperative links with peace processes since these are characterized by erratic and multidirectional trajectories. The network flexibility gives it the ability to meet communication needs and resolve conflicts arising from intersystem pressures, making it an emerging dynamic element that generates favorable environments for peace processes.

Mediation networks are dynamic social processes with the ability to create activities and actions that address the changing needs of building sustainable peace. Mediation networks are characterized by the actors' ability to transform, translate and modify the information they receive. For example, in the case of Colombian negotiations, a mediation network modified the initial objective of M-19 to convene a constituent opening of the political system for the integration of that movement, allowing the integration of unarmed, social organizations. Thus, interactions with the social movements could be woven into mediations with the NCA to provide feedback and strengthen the peace process.

Furthermore, mediation networks tend to lead to co-managed projects as a mechanism to reduce opportunistic behaviour. These projects see each of the network actors involved in the management of resources at meso and macro levels by partnering with another—or other—actors, either by sharing methodologies for planning or by implementing shared management mechanisms which are based on solidarity, trust and reciprocity.

Mediation networks work within a spatial approach to peacebuilding. That is, they transform the concept of peacebuilding as an international effort to address the structural causes of conflict into a more collaborative approach between international actors and the territories and regions affected by violence. At the individual level, mediation networks promote a process of transition, where the victims become actors in the development of peace. This reflects notions of peace from a gender perspective, allowing for the development of more comprehensive proposals in order to foster more equitable and fair relations (Serrano Oswald 2009: 1156).

Those activities are accompanied by social processes of empowerment and forgiveness, which allow for the development of processes of social healing through community resilience. That is an intermediary element between individual health and the development of collective reconciliation, which requires communities to develop resilience, either by themselves or with the accompaniment of exogenous organizations. It involves strengthening the capacity of a community to foster solidarity based on hope and purpose so as to handle conflicts creatively and nonviolently.

In this manner, mediation networks promote the four pillars of human rights: truth, justice, damage repair, and non-repetition, which, in turn, permit the building of an infrastructure for sustainable peace.

3.4.1 The Colombian Mediation Network for Sustainable Peace

As a final note, the mediation network for sustainable peace in Colombia is based on the work of the Christian-based communities, and the Catholic Church itself. These have laid the foundation for the creation of social movements and peace. Although these social movements have not been directly involved in the negotiation process itself, they have helped to create a network fabric that has kept the peace process from being seriously affected by environmental pressures. Moreover, the pressure exerted on the Colombian government began to attract small-but-constant changes in the political system so that the military option began to be questioned as the only way for social change.

This process has over passed M-19 developments by achieving greater potential for social impact. The activities of social movements and ecclesial bases aimed at solving social and environmental problems helped decrease the pressure that these elements may have on the peace process. Simultaneously, these projects became social impulses that strengthened citizen activism.

3.5 Conclusions

Lederach's and Paffenholz' perspectives allowed identifying civil society as a dynamic element assisting the peace process between the Colombian government and the M-19. They allowed us to transit from the traditional concept of mediator to one of mediations, which are more dynamic and inclusive. They also facilitated an analytical juncture with systems theory that beyond considering dynamism distant from stability, propose it as a descriptive element of the studied case *autopoietic* qualities.

The peace process was affected by meso and macro interactions around it. Yet, despite the lack of civil society participation in negotiations, it was able to create a favorable environment that blocked outside interference. The activities carried out by social movements and ecclesial base communities to address social and environmental problems allowed for a reduction in the pressure that these elements could have had on the peace process. Their activities also created information channels that operated together with the media to counteract the manipulation of the political class.

The peace process between the Colombian government and the M-19 had several results. The first was the demobilization of the movement. This later on influenced peace processes with other six armed groups[9] in the country. However, it must be said that one of the greatest contributions was the networked participation of civil society as mediators.

Considering these achievements, it was suggested here the most important result of the mediation network during the peace process was the experience. It allowed citizens to be peace-builders in the following decades and, while creating peace from conflict.

References

Arboleda, Jairo; Garfield, Elsie, 2003: "Violence, Sustainable Peace and Development", in: Giugale, Marcelo; Lafourcade, Oliver; Luff, Connie. (Eds.): *Colombia, The Economic Fundation of Peace* (Washington, D.C.: The World Bank): 35–58.

Arias O., Gerson Iván, 2008: *Una mirada atrás: procesos de paz y dispositivos de negociación del gobierno colombiano.* (Bogotá: Fundación Ideas para la Paz).

Bejarano, Ana María, 1990: "Estrategias de paz y apertura democrática: un balance de las administraciones Betancur y Barco", in Leal Buitrago, Francisco. (Ed.), *Al filo de caos. Crisis política en la Colombia de los años 80.* (Bogotá: Instituto de Estudios Políticos y Relaciones Internacionales-IEPRI): 52–124.

Betancur, Belisario, 1990: *El homo sapiens se extravió en América Latina. Teoría de la subversión y de la paz.* (Bogotá: El Navegante Editores, Tercer Mundo Editores).

Bushnell, David, 1994: *Colombia, Una Nación a pesar de sí misma. De los tiempos precolombinos hasta nuestros días*, (Bogotá: Planeta)

Corsi, Giancarlo, 1996: *GLU: Glosario de la teoría social de Niklas Luhmann*, (México: Universidad Iberoamericana, Instituto Tecnológico y de Estudios Superiores de Occidente (ITESO), Anthropos).

Díaz, Lina Paola, 2008: *La Paz y la Guerra en Femenino: Historias de Mujeres ex combatientes del M-19 y las AUC.* (Bogotá, Pontificia Universidad Javeriana).

Fajardo, José, Roldán, Miguel Ángel, 1980: *Soy el Comandante 1.* (Bogotá: La Oveja Negra).

Foster, Reiner, Mattner, Mark, 2007: *Report No. 36445-GLB Civil Society and Peacebuilding Potential, Limitations and Critical Factors;* at: http://www-wds.worldbank.org/external/default/WDSContentServer/WDSP/IB/2008/03/27/000333038_20080327071355/Rendered/PDF/364450SR0REPLA1nd1Peacebuilding1web.pdf (11 April 2011).

[9]EPL (founded 1967 as the armed branch for the Colombian Marxist-Leninist Communist Party); Quintín Lame armed movement (MAQL; mainly indigenous from the South West of the Cauca Department); the Workers Revolutionary Party (PRT; a Marxist-Leninist-Maoist armed movement); the Popular Militias of the People and for the People along with the Metropolitan Militias (urban armed groups based in marginal areas of Medellín) and the Independent Militias from Aburrá Valley (another urban armed group, but based in marginal areas in Central Antioquía Department).

Galaviz Armenta, Tania, 2014: *Las mediaciones en el proceso de paz entre el Gobierno colombiano y el Movimiento-19 de abril, 1980–1990*. (Tesis de Grado, Universidad Nacional Autónoma de México, Ciudad de México).

García Durán, Mauricio, 2006: *Movimiento por la paz en Colombia 1978–2003*. (Bogotá: Centro de Investigación y Educación Popular, Colciencias, Programa para el Desarrollo Humano de las Naciones Unidas).

García Durán, Mauricio; Grabe Loewenherz, Vera; Patiño Hormanza, Otty, 2009: "El camino del M-19 de la lucha armada a la Democracia: una búsqueda de cómo hacer política en sintonía con el país", in García Durán, Mauricio. (Ed.), *De la Insurgencia a la Democracia*, Vol. 1 (Bogotá: Centro de Investigación y Educación Popular, CINEP, Berghof Research Center for Constructive Conflict Management): 43–106.

García Villegas, Mauricio; Rebolledo, Javier, 2009: *Mayorías sin democracia. Desequilibrio de poderes y Estado de Derecho en Colombia, 2002-2009*. (Bogotá: Centro de Estudios de Derecho, Justicia y Sociedad).

Jaramillo, Daniel, 2003: "El viejo congreso y la paz. Una breve historia del papel de la rama legislativa en los procesos de paz de Betancur y Barco", in *Historia Crítica*, 7, (Enero- Junio): 45–49, at: http://historiacritica.uniandes.edu.co/view.php/119/index.php?id=119, (23 May 2011.)

Jiménez Ricardez, Rubén, 1986: "M-19: Paz y Guerra en Colombia", in Cuadernos Políticos, 45, (enero-marzo): 82–104.

Lara Salive, Patricia, 1987: *Siembra Vientos y recogerás tempestades* (Bogotá: Planeta).

Lederach, John Paul; Wehr, Paul, 1991: "Mediating Conflict in Central America", *Journal of Peace Research*, 28:1, 85–98. at: http://www.jstor.org/stable/424196 (26 September 2011.)

Lederach, John Paul, 1997: *Building Peace: Sustainable Reconciliation in Divided Societies* (Washington, D.C.: United States Institute of Peace).

Lederach, John Paul, 2001: "Levels of Leadership", in Paffenholz, Thania. (Ed.), *Peacebuilding A Field Guide* (Colorado: Lynne Rienner Publishers, Inc): 145–156.

Lederach, John Paul, 2003a: "Cultivating Peace: a Practitioner's View of Deadly Conflict and Negotiation", in Darby, John; Mac Ginty, Roger (Ed.), *Contemporary Peacemaking. Conflict, Violence and Peace Processes* (New York: Palgrave MacMillan): 30–37.

Lederach, John Paul, 2003b: *The Little Book of Conflict Transformation* (Intercourse Pennsylvania: Good Books).

Lederach, John Paul, 2005: *The Moral Imagination: The Art and Soul of Building Peace* (New York: Oxford University Press).

Lelièvre, Christiane, Moreno Echavarría, Graciliana; Ortiz Pérez, Isabel, 2004: *Haciendo memoria y dejando rastros. Encuentros con mujeres ex combatientes del Nororiente de Colombia* (Bogotá: Fundación Mujer y Futuro, Fondo de Desarrollo de las Naciones Unidas para la Mujer UNIFEM).

López de la Roche, Fabio, 1994: *Izquierdas y cultura política, ¿oposición alternativa?* (Bogotá: Cinep).

Luhmann, Niklas, 1990: *Sociedad y Sistema: La ambición de la teoría* (Barcelona: Paidós).

Luhmann, Niklas, 1998: *Sistemas Sociales. Lineamientos para una Teoría General* (Barcelona: Anthropos, Universidad Iberoamericana, Pontificia Universidad Javeriana).

Medina, Medófilo, 1989: "Bases urbanas de la violencia en Colombia", in: *Historia Crítica*, (Enero-Junio): 20–32. at: http://historiacritica.uniandes.edu.co/view.php/11/index.php?id=11 (08 November 2011)

Morales Benitez, Otto, 1991: *Papeles para la paz*.

Oswald Spring, Úrsula, 2005: *El valor del agua: una visión socioeconómica de un conflicto ambiental*. (Tlaxcala, México: El Colegio de Tlaxcala, A.C. FOMIX, Gobierno del Estado de Tlaxcala, SEFOA, Coordinación General de Ecología).

Paffenholz, Thania; Spurk, Chris, 2006: "Civil Society, Civic Engagement, and Peacebuilding", in: *Conflict prevention & reconstruction*, Paper 36, (October), at: http://siteresources.worldbank.org/INTCPR/Resources/WP36_web.pdf (09 April 2011).

Poggiese, Héctor.; Redín, María. Elena; Alí, Patricia, 1999: *El papel de las redes en el desarrollo local como prácticas asociadas entre Estado y Sociedad.* (Buenos Aires, Facultad Latinoamericana de Ciencias Sociales).

Ramírez Orozco, Mario, 2007: *Estrategias para una Paz Estructural. Caso Colombia.* (México, D.F.: Universidad Nacional Autónoma de México).

Ramírez, Socorro y Restrepo, Luis A. (1989). *Actores en Conflicto por la paz. El proceso de paz durante el gobierno de Belisario Betancur (1982–1986).* (Bogotá: CINEP siglo XXI).

Romero, Mauricio, 2001 "Movilizaciones por la paz, cooperación y sociedad civil en Colombia", in Archila Mauricio; Pardo, Mauricio. (Eds.), *Movimientos sociales, Estado y democracia* (Bogotá: Centro de Estudios Sociales, Facultad de Ciencias Humanas, Universidad Nacional de Colombia, Instituto Colombiano de Antropología e Historia): 405–440.

Serrano Oswald, Serena Eréndira, 2009: "The imposibility of Securitizing Gender vis á vis Engendering Security", in Brauch Hans Günter, Oswald Spring, Úrsula; Grin, John; Czeslaw, Mesjasz (Eds.), *Facing Global Environmental Change, Environmental, Human, Energy, Food, Health and Water Security Concepts.* (Berlin-Heidelberg: Springer): 1143–1156.

Vélez, Carlos Eduardo; Rawlings, Laura; Paqueo, Vic; Riaño, Juanita, 2003: "Shared Growth, Poverty, and Inequality", in Giugale, Marcelo; Lafourcade, Olivier; Luff, Connie (Eds.), *Colombia. The Economic Fundation of Peace* (Washington, USA: The World Bank): 89–129.

Chapter 4
Social Resilience and Intangible Cultural Heritage: A Mutually Fertilizing Potential Seen in a Case Study in Mexico

Serena Eréndira Serrano Oswald

Abstract This chapter looks at the relationship between social resilience and *Intangible Cultural Heritage* (ICH) in a local setting, positing that each nurtures the other and that they constitute important pillars for sustainable, long-term, and context-coherent peace. Specifically, the chapter seeks to explore the way in which cultural heritage renews itself through the centrality of social resilience, which is conceptualized systemically as a process and explored in a case study of the Mojiganga festival in the state of Morelos in Mexico. A significant ICH practice becomes a social resilience pillar of the social system, as it enables the system to reconfigure its internal coherence and sense of identity (to *be*), mediate change (to *continue*), and develop (to *grow*) with endless potential. At the same time, however, this process of social resilience provides feedback and reconfigures ICH.

Keywords Intangible cultural heritage (ICH) · Social resilience · Mexico · Morelos · Mojiganga · Zacualpan de amilpas

4.1 Introduction

This chapter looks at the relationship between social resilience and *Intangible Cultural Heritage* (ICH) in the municipality of Zacualpan de Amilpas, Morelos, Mexico. Looking at the most important festival in Zacualpan, the 'Mojiganga', it seeks to explore the ways in which intangible cultural heritage renews itself through the centrality of social resilience. Social resilience is conceptualized systemically as a process, part of the dynamism and fluidity of cultural life. Social resilience enables a collective subject or system to reconfigure its identity in the face of change (to *be*), solving the problems, contradictions and crises inherent in change (to *continue*) in order to re-equilibrate and have continuity. So on the one hand it effectively protects itself, and on the other hand it may also integrate novelty,

Dr. Serena Eréndira Serrano Oswald, researcher, Regional Multidisciplinary Research Center, National Autonomous University of Mexico (CRIM–UNAM); Email: sesohi@hotmail.com.

Ú.Oswald Spring et al. (eds.), *Regional Ecological Challenges for Peace in Africa, the Middle East, Latin America and Asia Pacific*, The Anthropocene: Politik—Economics—Society—Science 5, DOI 10.1007/978-3-319-30560-8_4

actualize its potential, and develop (to *grow*) across time. The case study provides important insights into the importance of ICH in the generation of social resilience across time in order to avoid negative outcomes from conflict and crises, creatively yet coherently mitigating negative externalities, equilibrating conflicts, integrating stressors, renewing identity and avoiding a collapse of the system. In turn, social resilience provides feedback that dialectically actualizes and reconstitutes intangible cultural heritage. This work thus highlights the potential of *Intangible Cultural Heritage* (ICH) and social resilience as important pillars for sustainable, long-term, and context-coherent peace.

The methodology is qualitative, situated in the framework of critical ethnography, and it is based on participant observation, fieldwork notes, recorded interviews with key people and the transcription of the interviews, conversations, free association, and also fieldwork undertaken in order to prepare an ICH documentary in which local people describe and analyse the way in which they create, transform and document their cultural heritage.[1] Citations throughout the text are taken directly from interviewees; age and name are included in parentheses following each quote. Photographs and complementary internet sources such as videos, websites and social networks are included to illustrate the text.

Following this brief introduction (Sect. 4.1), a conceptual framework is discussed linking resilience and social action through culture via intangible cultural heritage (Sect. 4.2), which paves the way for the general characterization of the festival (Sect. 4.3) and the history of the particular Mojiganga in the locality in order to understand its importance and singularity (Sect. 4.4). The ensuing section presents the findings, namely the axes of resilience present in the Mojiganga in Zacualpan, Morelos (Sect. 4.5). Finally, concluding remarks (Sect. 4.6) are offered.

Readers who want a detailed ethnographic and historical account should read all sections; those who are interested in the analysis of resilience should focus on the conceptual framework (Sect. 4.2) and the empirical findings (Sects. 4.5 and 4.6).

4.2 Conceptual Framework: Resilience and Social Action Through Cultural Heritage

The concept of 'resilience' derives from the Latin term *resiliens—resilire* (*re-salire*), and refers to a property or characteristic of a material which enables it to return to its original state or position, to rebound, recover, recoil and sometimes even to regenerate, reanimate itself or be reborn. Since 1824 it has meant 'elasticity'.[2] In engineering, resilience denotes the capacity of an elastic material to recover its

[1]See "INTANGIBLE. Reencuentro: La Mojiganga en Zacualpan de Amilpas"; at: https://www.youtube.com/watch?v=obP5UPAdto4 (5 May 2015).

[2]See the "Online Etymology Dictionary"; at: http://www.etymonline.com/index.php?term=resilience&allowed_in_frame=0 (5 May 2015).

shape, despite being manipulated, as it bounces back energy without absorbing it. In environmental studies, the concept of resilience takes a more historical perspective as it refers to the ability of an ecosystem to adapt itself in order to tolerate perturbations such as risk and disasters, adapting to change and maintaining its function (Holling 1973). In psychology, the concept of resilience has become very important; it is also understood to result from a live process, although it typically addresses the individual level (a person or human being as part of a family, community or social system). It is understood as the long-term human aptitude for facing and overcoming environmental or structural (constitutive) adversity, stress, change, illness and severe trauma, leading to adaptation, growth and development (Rutter 1987; Dyer/McGuiness 1996; Luthar et al. 2000).

'Social resilience', understood as a dynamic concept, may be a part of, and the result of, a historical process in a particular social context. However, being 'social' implies that it has a relational component, it is systemic, and it must include the collective-communal-communitarian dimension. Researching 'social resilience' systemically implies looking at the history of concrete subjects and collectives, seen as agents of change and equilibrium, rooted in a sociocultural framework that propitiates specific interactions, exchanges, and meanings (Walsh 2005; Villalba 2004; Berkes/Folke 1998; Berkes et al. 2003; Walker/Salt 2006; Uriarte 2013). Thus, resilience is not only an individual trait or competence, nor a fixed characteristic of an inert element. Societies are characterized by permanent change. It is misleading to evoke a totalitarian, abstract or indefinitely over-general concept of resilience. Socially, it makes no sense to conceive of a rigid notion of resilience such as an idealized fixed departure or end point, nor to think of it as a rigid equilibrium, or look at it as a sense of invulnerability. Social resilience is a dynamic process, the capacity of a social system to transform itself thanks to its cultural capital, mediating its singularity and plurality within its internal cohesion, coherence and identity (to *be*), solving the problems, crises and contradictions inherent in change (to *continue*) in order to effectively protect itself and at the same time develop and realize its many potentials (to *grow*).

Although in this vision it is still conceived of using an evolutionary outlook, and even though the concept does not refer to a linear growth process, the concept in the global era implies potential access to a significant and productive life in a multilevel framework. Within this framework the individual, micro and meso group dynamics are understood systemically as interrelated with the macro and global sociocultural dimensions. The subject-agent protects its integrity at the same time as a process of actualization, transformation, growth, and development takes place which enables qualitative leaps and a projection leading to plenitude (the axes to *be*—to *continue*—to *grow*). Resilience speaks of a reconfiguration of identity, of innovations in the nucleus of a 'self', who can be an individual or a collective subject, even both at the same time, always considering its social nature. Resilience is relative (not absolute) and it is not fixed (it is dynamic and varies). Seen in the context of discussions about intangible cultural heritage (Arizpe 2011, 2015; Arizpe/Amescua 2013;

Lacarrieu 2004; Guanche 2008), it must be defined as collaborative and convivial[3] (Arizpe 2014) since it comprises the individual, intra- and inter-group and collective levels understood in a relational, temporal and interactional sociocultural frame that is both singular and plural. That is, we reconfigure our 'self' and its constituting elements as we encounter others, and that meeting also provides feedback and transforms others. The temporary facet of resilience establishes a dialectic dialogue between past and present; we are a product of history yet history is always re-signified at present, the past is redefined and the future framed here and now.

Since this work draws on the importance of the Mojiganga festival as the core practice of intangible cultural heritage in Zacualpan de Amilpas, Morelos, Mexico, the following two sections provide a brief ethnographic and historical account of this heritage. Section 4.3 introduces the Mojiganga performance, and Sect. 4.4 describes the history of Mojiganga in Zacualpan. This provides a basis for the analysis that follows in Sect. 4.5, which examines the way intangible cultural heritage translates into social resilience in the example of Mojiganga.

4.3 The Mojiganga

'Mojiganga', a Spanish term that has no English equivalent, refers according to the *Diccionario de la Lengua Española* (Dictionary of the Royal Spanish Academy, DRAE)[4] to one of three things: "(1) short dramatic play, designed for laughter, with ridiculous and extravagant characters; (2) mocking or playful action; and (3) public festival featuring odd costumes, especially representing animals". It evokes the term 'Bojiganga' "from *voxiga*, variant of *vejiga* (bladder)" which in turn according to DRAE means "a small company of travelling players who performed comedies and plays in small towns in the past". Elaborating from this historical definition, alluding to theatre and its picaresque nature during the Spanish Golden Age, we find the following elements that might prove helpful in order to understand the Mojiganga in the locality of Zacualpan: a brief and comic play and/or an event of mockery and/or a public festival with costumes presented by a company of actors in small towns. What calls for special attention is that the Mojiganga in Zacualpan developed from religious motives, in order to announce the feast of the Virgin of Rosario, and today it still incorporates religious displays in its allegorical floats. Perhaps this may be explained by the fact that, unlike in Spain, in New Spain Mojigangas were used as evangelizing theatre, and they also featured as street dances in carnivals; both these elements are reflected in the locality. In present-day popular festivals in Mexico, Mojigangas are popular in the states of Oaxaca,

[3]'Convivial' following from *convivencia* as defined by Arizpe (2014: 3, footnote) in the work on Intangible Cultural Heritage as: "*Convivencia* in Spanish means not only the conviviality of sharing an agreeable feast as in English or in French. Vivencia in Spanish means a life experience so that *convivencia* means not only sharing together but actually living the experience together.".

[4]See the "Royal Spanish Dictionary"; at: http://www.rae.es (5 May 2015).

Veracruz, Morelos, and Jalisco, with a diversity of displays such as disguise, pantomimes, animal displays and giant puppets. Although popular festivals in Mexico are quite popular, and Mojigangas are very much alive in some areas of the country whereas in other areas they are extinct, there are some displays of the Mojiganga which stand out in relation to other more common forms of it. In the state of Morelos, the Mojiganga in Zacualpan de Amilpas is unrivalled, making it one of the most important festivals in the area. Furthermore, given its characteristics, its history, its regional impact on the border between states, and the small size of the municipality where it takes place make it also unique in the country and deserving of closer research attention (Figs. 4.1 and 4.2).

In Zacualpan de Amilpas, in the state of Morelos in Mexico, there is an annual traditional festival known as Mojiganga that has been celebrated during many generations on the last Sunday of September in order to announce the arrival of the Festival of the Virgin of Rosario. Unlike other Mojigangas, the festival in Zacualpan does not include giant puppets, it goes further than the mockery by indigenous peasants of the creoles and the landowners (the 'chinelo' tradition in Morelos), and it does not only mean a festival in which people wear animal or cross-sex costumes. It is not a carnival or a procession, although it includes elements of both religious and pagan festivals (Fig. 4.3).

Fig. 4.1 Comparsa Cacomixtles. *Source* Mijoganga 2013, Zacualpan de Amilpas. The photo was taken by the author who holds the copyright

Fig. 4.2 Comparsa Falfan. *Source* Mijoganga 2013, Zacualpan de Amilpas. The photo was taken by the author who holds the copyright

Fig. 4.3 The study area: Zacualpan de Amilpas, state of Morelos in Mexico. *Source* Ursula Oswald Spring (2014: 89). The graphic design is taken from: http://www.inafed.gob.mx/work/enciclopedia/EMM17morelos/municipios/17032a.html

In the Mojiganga of Zacualpan there is a public parade through the main streets of the town with wind bands and dancing, in which families, neighbourhoods and groups of friends and acquaintances take part on foot or on allegorical floats as troupes (*comparsa* in Spanish) presenting a theme with artistic, historical or cultural and religious topics. It is open to the townspeople, to migrants, to neighbouring towns, and to people of the region, as well as to national and international guests. Driven by themes of re-encounter, *convivencia*, fun, creativity, cult and happiness, the Mojiganga in Zacualpan stands out as an example of the dynamism and

Fig. 4.4 Saint Juan Diego cart. *Source* Mijoganga 2013, Zacualpan de Amilpas. The photo was taken by the author who holds the copyright

diversity of the living heritage of the state of Morelos, a living ethnographical treasure and seal of Zacualpan's identity and resilience (Fig. 4.4).[5]

4.4 The History of the Mojiganga in Zacualpan

In order to contextualize the importance of the festival, it is useful to provide a brief paragraph in order to characterize the locality. Zacualpan de Amilpas—'on top of something covered' stemming from *tzacualli* 'covered thing' and *pan* 'on top'—is one of the thirty-three municipalities in the state of Morelos. It was created in 1826 and has a population of 9087 people (8579 urban and 508 rural; 96.1 females for every 100 males) and an area of 63.6 km^2 made up of private and *ejido* lands, with economic activities such as agriculture, commerce and services (INEGI 2010). It is located on the border with the state of Puebla, in the vicinity of the volcano Popocatépetl, approximately two hours by car from Mexico City in the oriental region of the state of Morelos. The people's religion in Zacualpan is 90.3 % Catholic and 5.2 % Pentecostal, Evangelical and Christian of other denominations.

According to local interviewees, the Virgin of Rosario is central to this Mojiganga. Despite not being the patron saint of Zacualpan, the Virgin of Rosario has an extended cult which dates back to the eighteenth century. The exact origins of the celebration are unknown, although looking back two centuries one understands that the forms of communication at the time were different and it makes sense to think that the Mojiganga originated as the public announcement of the beginning of the festivities for the Virgin of Rosario one week before the first Sunday of October. These announcements were cried at every main corner of the streets of the town. A group of people from the church and the town, disguised or not, sought to attract the attention of others and gather crowds in order to spread the word using music, games, and costumes such as the '*torito*'—a person disguised as a little bull who used to chase children in the streets.

As time passed, this announcement grew and was nurtured by circus influences from the small entertainment companies that have typically accompanied most religious festivals throughout the country, together with the arrival of temporary markets and funfairs, causing visitors from the region to congregate. Since

[5]For the UNESCO-UniTwin ICH Chair/CRIM/IMRyT documentary in which local people describe and analyse the Mojiganga in Zacualpan, see "INTANGIBLE. Reencuentro: La Mojiganga en Zacualpan de Amilpas"; at: https://www.youtube.com/watch?v=obP5UPAdto4. For other public videos portraying the Mojiganga in Zacualpan, see: https://www.youtube.com/watch?v=UqCoCTvTYkg, https://www.youtube.com/watch?v=eyn_MeJqo5Y, https://www.youtube.com/watch?v=OsbueXsXaik, https://www.youtube.com/watch?v=aaV9PpT1t1g, https://www.youtube.com/watch?v=7qyfmuQjDqI, and https://www.youtube.com/watch?v=cyqvYZDaccA. If you wish to see more pictures by local people displayed on social networks, see: https://www.facebook.com/AyuntamientoZacualpan, https://www.facebook.com/comitefiestaspatronales.zacualpan?fref=ts, https://www.facebook.com/comparsa.falfan?fref=ts, and https://www.facebook.com/pages/COMPARSA-ZACUALPAN-M%C3%81GICO/164,215,380,341,111?fref=ts (5 May 2015).

indigenous times, the region has been known as a trade centre, where commercial exchanges such as '*truque*' (barter) and *tianquiztli* (street markets) are still practised (see Pérez Flores in press). Formerly, it was the Virgin of Rosario's festival in October that played the central role. The Mojiganga was just a procession for announcing the main festival in which agricultural products were offered as presents and '*chirimía*' music was played (a primitive oboe introduced by the Spanish clergy that was popular among indigenous people). Later on, wind bands and the '*chinelo*' dance replaced the '*chirimía*' and agricultural products have generally been replace by sweets. It is very likely that since Zacualpan had three distilleries for '*aguardiente*' or raw rum (La Perla, El Diamante and La Concepción), the so-called 'Zacualpita' liquor was a constitutive element of the Mojiganga from early times. As the Mojiganga grew, town inhabitants and peasants disguised themselves with old clothing or with the clothing of the opposite sex. The people who shouted out were called '*nahuales*'[6] and don Vicente Mancilla, Manuel González, Moises Pinzón and don Eleuterio are specifically mentioned:

> A long time ago, when I was a little girl, I knew them and they were already old. It was like two or three people who used masks that they made themselves with hair, rope and such materials; their costumes were dirty and they were then called '*nahuales*'. It was them we heard shouting in the streets; they stopped at each corner to cry out the announcements of the feast of the virgin: "There will be this and that". They also used a wind band. Back then nobody else would wear a costume, only those three. There were others who accompanied them and shouted 'hurrah', making a scandal with the music (Imelda Ríos Franco, 73 years).

The people of Zacualpan say that according what their grandparents and great-grandparents told them, the Mojiganga was the announcement of the festival as well as a procession in which the banner of the Virgin of Rosario was taken around the main streets of the town in the hands of three small girls riding horses and known as '*Romanitas*'. One carried the banner and the other two held ribbons that hung down, decorating the banner. Today, it is still these three girls called '*Romanitas*' and the peasants representing the Ejido Commissariat who lead the procession so that the festival still seeks the Virgin's protection to favour the agricultural cycle. Also, since the Virgin of Rosario was the virgin of the peasants and of the poorest social groups, she has a much more extended cult than the patron saint. This is a region that had big haciendas and very fertile lands. Although there is no clear consensus, some people say that General Emiliano Zapata[7]—a leading figure of the Mexican Revolution (see Knight 1986; Womack Jr. 1968)—was a faithful devotee

[6]'*Nahual*' from Nahualt '*nahualli*' meaning 'disguised or hidden' is the historical and socially shared belief in Meso-American territories in shamans and people of power turning into animals, mostly their animal spirit guides, for the purposes of magic and ritual.

[7]Emiliano Zapata Salazar (8 August 1870–10 April 1919), peasant leader during the Mexican Revolution, leader of the Liberation Army of the South. One of the most famous and influential figures in Mexican history. For basic information online, see: http://www.biography.com/people/emiliano-zapata-9540356 or http://latinamericanhistory.about.com/od/themexicanrevolution/p/08zapatabio.htm (5 May 2015).

of the Virgin of Rosario. According to some accounts that are part of oral tradition, Zapata asked the Virgin of Rosario for a miracle, since he was losing important battles. When he was favoured by the virgin and he won, he decided to allocate some parcels of land to her. These lands still exist and are cultivated by the peasants, using the returns in order to cover some of the expenses of the Virgin's festival.

Although for some Zapata had personally nothing to do with the Mojiganga, some people also say that from that moment onwards, Zacualpan always had a squad of Zapatistas present at the Mojiganga who participated in the festivities. Although the annual participation of Zapatistas in the Mojiganga at the time is hard to prove, the importance of Zapatismo in symbolic displays remains and is recreated, especially as the Mojiganga grew and became the most important annual event, devoted to the Virgin of Rosario. Currently, the Ejido Commissariat, together with the Committee for the Virgin's Festivities, ensures that the '*Romanitas*' and peasants dressed as *charros* and Zapatistas lead the Mojiganga. Zapata has an important place in the Mojiganga and in the identity of Zacualpan. This is reinforced by the fact that some families such as the Falfán family have researched the federal archives and claim that their ancestors were part of Zapata's army.

The Mojiganga has changed over time. Over the past century, besides the impact of the Mexican Revolution and Zapatismo, there have been two turning points that are especially important: (i) the influence of the Ríos Franco family, and (ii) the impact of the Falfán family. Although the exact dates vary, the first turning point corresponds to the mid-or late 1960s, when besides horses and people walking, motor vehicles were incorporated in the Mojiganga. This is also when people started presenting specific displays of scenes ('*cuadros*'). The first scene was a representation of emperors Charlotte and Maximilian. It was organized by Marino Ríos Franco, Wenceslao Ríos Barreto and the parish priest Victorino Aranda, some claim also Jaime García Alcázar. Marino Ríos earned the nickname "the great Marino". The then somewhat 'invisible' of making the costumes and preparing the accessories was done by Imelda Ríos Franco:

> we cannot take the merit from the creators of the Mojiganga, whom I had the honour of knowing. Señor Marino Ríos and Jaime García Alcázar, they were the fundamental pillars, if not the icons of our Mojiganga with their creations, their taste, their culture. It was they who completely changed the concept of the Mojiganga (José Baeza Alonso, 37 years).

The community as social regulator of change liked the innovations and even reproduced them the ensuing year. Señor Rafael Ramírez began representing circus animals on a float. If he could not hunt or find real animals, he would get people to dress up as animals. Another group emerged called 'Tecuanes' (tigers). They dressed up as animals, women or dead people. Gradually, a spiral of creativity unfolded. People from nearby communities were invited to the Mojiganga, such as the people from San Bartolo who had giant puppets and in the community of San Antón in the capital city of the state of Morelos are known as 'Mojigangas' or in the state of Oaxaca as part of '*calenda*' festivals. At this point, generosity and reciprocity took centre stage. People participated out of joy and shared food and drink with guests, without any kind of support. To this, some local merchants responded by offering to donate products. The Ríos Franco family continued to present new displays every year. Since they owned a sewing workshop and their work meant that they dealt with clients outside Zacualpan, they had novel ideas for their displays and also began to invite distinguished guests to the Mojiganga celebration. In turn, this encouraged more people to experiment informally and develop different artistic forms for the festival based on intuition; different groups organized themselves into troupes. Although most displays at this time had religious themes, other displays included topics such as literature, drama, history and culture. With time Imelda's children put a travel agency. Imelda travelled to many countries, such as Egypt and Italy, bringing ideas and materials to renovate the festivity. Since then it has been the new generations who have innovated most often. Although they were representing religious themes, youngsters started dancing. Since then, everyone dances or does the 'chinelo jump' (Figs. 4.5 and 4.6).

The second turning point is linked to the impact of the Falfán family, the importance of cardboard work, migration and the culmination of the historical process in which the Mojiganga has grown from hundreds to thousands of participants. The particular thing about the Falfán family was that they temporarily left Zacualpan for purposes of work and education, migrating to Mexico City. So when they returned to Zacualpan, they brought new ideas and transformed the festival with the tools and visions acquired during their time away. They also gave a different value to their town

Fig. 4.5 Comparsa Fam. Aroche. *Source* Mijoganga 2013, Zacualpan de Amilpas. The photo was taken by the author who holds the copyright

Fig. 4.6 Comparsa Fam. Hernández Ramírez. *Source* Mijoganga 2013, Zacualpan de Amilpas. The photo was taken by the author who holds the copyright

of origin and its relational exchanges and festivals. With time, the Falfán family has become a professional troupe, inspiring many people in Zacualpan. At what exact moment and in what exact form the Falfán family started participating in the Mojiganga is unclear; accounts vary, although it dates back about forty years. In the beginning, Señor Prócoro Falfán worked under the influence of Marino Ríos, although over time the Falfán family became independent and their leadership at the Mojiganga was recognized by the community by the mid- to late 1980s.

According to Esteban Falfán (24 years), the idea of participating in the Mojiganga and bringing displays from Mexico City came to Prócoro when he worked as a merchant, bringing and taking fruits to one of Mexico City's main markets ('la Merced'). The family says that in order to fulfil a vow to the Virgin of Rosario, he decided to hire a group of '*concheros*'[8] and took them to Zacualpan to the Mojiganga procession. From then onwards, there have been four generations of the Falfán family —many with university degrees and in artistic professions, including figures such as Prócoro, Roberto, Tar, Esteban and Claudio—who have participated and perfected their yearly displays, incorporating the new generations of the family and building an

[8]'*Concheros*', also called Azteca, Mexica or Huehuenche dance, refers to a syncretic ritual dance and dance ceremony, performed by a dance group with music, mixing indigenous and colonial elements. It is a widespread practice of intangible cultural heritage in Mexico.

important network of support which includes cultural institutions, master craftsmen, artists, sponsors, and businesses. As they innovated, perfected, and professionalized their work, the Falfán family stands out because they give a *qualitative turn* to the Mojiganga, preparing and developing their displays throughout the whole year and not only on the eve of the celebration (Figs. 4.7 and 4.8):

> My point is that many people went out to study. Some went to study and some to work. People say that when one travels the world one learns a lot provided one wants to and understands. Well, they went and saw other things, other ideas. Besides that, they studied and got into culture, so when they came back they brought new ideas to all of us who had never been out of here. That is how the Mojiganga got bigger, they did things well and I think that was good (Imelda Ríos Franco, 73).

Besides, this is the second key moment in which the Mojiganga opened themselves up to social action through culture. Street theatre and popular art replaced the predominantly religious displays, which also became more creative. Currently, the Falfán family works in their workshop in Zacualpan and at the same time they have a subsidiary in Mexico City where part of the family lives. From 2008 onwards they have collaborated with the Popular Art Museum of Mexico City. Another significant characteristic is that although they are best known for their cardboard art, they have innovated using various techniques and materials, and this has inspired other groups and generations in Zacualpan. Youngsters have learnt some techniques as

Fig. 4.7 Comparsa Matzongo. *Source* Mijoganga 2013, Zacualpan de Amilpas. The photo was taken by the author who holds the copyright

Fig. 4.8 Comparsa Zacualán Mágico. *Source* Mijoganga 2013, Zacualpan de Amilpas. The photo was taken by the author who holds the copyright

part of the Falfán group and later they have established their own independent troupes; this is the case with the group originally called 'Zacualpan Vive' (Zacualpan lives), which is now called 'Zacualpan Mágico' (Magic Zacualpan).

Through healthy competition in which each person, family and group competes with themselves and each other in order to grow, the qualitative turn has also led to a *quantitative turn*, with a greater number of troupes with innovating vision (for example 'Zacualpan Mágico', 'Juvemor', 'Cacomixtles', 'Nahuales') who present very attractive displays; over time this has attracted a greater number of outside visitors to the Mojiganga. In the year 2013 the government of the state of Morelos officially declared the Mojiganga as Morelos' cultural heritage.

Today the Mojiganga is part of the official programme of the Virgin of Rosario Patronal Festival which is made up of many activities, although the Mojiganga has become the most famous. I shall outline them in order to provide an idea of the local festivities and of the place that the Mojiganga has won in it over time. On the Saturday one week before the first Sunday of October, the festival begins with a cavalcade parade and a *charro* demonstration called '*escaramuza charra*' (3 p.m.) followed by a big horse show and dance (8 or 9 p.m.). On the next day, the last Sunday of September, the morning starts with the ringing of bells and fireworks (6 a.m.) and an opening mass petitioning for marriages and the community's migrants (11 a.m.), followed by the Mojiganga parade (4 p.m.) closing with a dance at the main plaza (8 or 9 p.m.). Throughout the week from Monday to Friday, the morning starts with the ringing of bells and fireworks (6 a.m., repeated at noon) and every day the different barrios (town neighbourhoods) make a pilgrimage departing from the spot known as 'El Arbolito' (the little tree) at 5 p.m. (Barrio de San Pedro; Barrio de San Andrés; Barrio de San Nicolás, Barrio de San Juan, Col. Guadalupe Victoria), together with the neighbouring communities (Tecajec, Popotlan, Temoac, Tlacotepec, Huazulco, and Amilcingo) and with the different associations of cab drivers. Mass is celebrated every day at six in the afternoon.

On the first Saturday of October the morning starts with fireworks and the bells are rung (6 a.m.), and baptisms and first communions take place at the Church of the Immaculate Conception,[9] where the chapel of the Virgin of Rosario is located. There is a performance by the Voladores de Papantla[10] (Dance of the Flyers or Pole Flyers) at 5 or 6 p.m. at the atrium, and a solemn mass (6 or 7 p.m.) followed by a 'Mexican Night' including artists and musical performances. At midnight the Virgin of Rosario gets a mariachi serenade and at 1 a.m. there is a '*callejoneada*' (a 'walking serenade') in the streets of the main neighbourhoods of the town. At 3 a. m. it is the youngsters and adolescents who offer the Virgin of Rosario a new serenade. The traditional Mexican birthday song '*las mañanitas*' is sung to the Virgin, the bells are rung and there are fireworks at 5 or 6 a.m. A circus performance takes place (10 a.m.), followed by a performance by the Voladores de Papantla (11 a.m.) and a solemn mass (noon). At 2 p.m. there is an important raffle and another performance by the Voladores de Papantla, and from 3 p.m. onwards people use flowers and flower petals, grains and sawdust in order to make colourful tapestries covering the main streets of the town (Juárez, Allende, Cuautepec, 5 de Mayo and Hidalgo) so that straight after the rosary (4 p.m.), the Virgin's Procession may take place at 5 p.m. At night there are fireworks and musical shows. The festival closes on the universal day of the Virgin of Rosario on October 7th, sometimes it coincides with the first Sunday of October. The closing includes fireworks and the ringing of the bells in the morning (6 a.m.), a solemn mass offered by the Ejido Commissariat, and a closing procession (4 or 5 p.m.); there may also be a horse show, depending on the resources available. It is important to note that the authorities have tried to make the dates of the "Barter Fair of Zacualpan" coincide with the dates of the Feasts of the Virgin of Rosario, especially with the Mojiganga, which is the day that attracts most visitors and is a Sunday, the day which is typically called 'day of exchange' (used for barter), when street markets (*tianquiztlis*) also take place (Figs. 4.9 and 4.10).

---

[9]The Convent of the Immaculate Conception of the Virgin in Zacualpan is one of the sixteenth-century monasteries in the Popocatépetl volcano hillside area. Since December 1994 it has been on the UNESCO List of World Heritage Sites. Being inscribed on this list consecrates the exceptional and universal value of a natural or cultural good in order for it to be protected for the benefit of humanity.

[10]A pre-Hispanic ritual involving a team of men who ascend a thirty-metre pole, they dance as they fly, and one of them plays music at the top of the pole. Since 2009, it has been catalogued by UNESCO as a Practice of Mexican and Guatemalan Intangible Cultural Heritage (register 00175).

Fig. 4.9 Youth Council representatives. *Source* Mijoganga 2013, Zacualpan de Amilpas. The photo was taken by the author who holds the copyright

Fig. 4.10 *Charro* child horse riding. *Source* Mijoganga 2013, Zacualpan de Amilpas. The photo was taken by the author who holds the copyright

Linked to the present historical moment one could envisage a third turning point that is taking place now, at a time when the Mojiganga is being consolidated as one of the most important traditional festivals in the state of Morelos. Without any doubt, the Mojiganga is today the most important annual event in Zacualpan. Besides this, although there are mixed opinions and divisions among the population, there is a project to turn Zacualpan into the third 'Magical Village'[11] of Morelos, in the hope of attracting government funds and consolidating Zacualpan as a major tourist hub. Important procedures have already been carried out as part of the preparation for this bid, in which the guiding elements are tradition and cultural heritage. As well as this, the establishment of the Cultural Centre of the Falfán Troupe in 2010 is an opening for developing cultural services, popular art, sustainability, information technology, '*convivencia*', exchanges and social organization that will have an important effect in the Mojiganga.

After this brief historical review of the Mojiganga and the range of activities it involves today, I shall turn to more analytical reflection regarding the axes of social resilience surrounding the Mojiganga in Zacualpan, which are crucial in the effort to unravel the importance of intangible culture for developing social resilience and vice versa.

4.5 Axes of Social Resilience in the Mojiganga

Resilience is seen as a process in which a system placed in a specific and multilevel sociocultural context alters and generates resources to re-equilibrate and reconfigure its 'self'; this gives it coherence and continuity over time (to *be*). This process of resilience generates resources that accumulate (experience, knowledge, heritage), and thus are part of the social and psychological capital of the system (they integrate that self and enable it to *be*). The system can be an individual or a collective with an identity that constantly receives feedback in a temporal framework characterized by interactions, exchanges and relations. Cultural heritage can thus become part of the resilience of a system, and at the same time the process of resilience provides feedback and reconfigures heritage. Understanding resilience in a positive way is to understand resilience as a process of experience and knowledge (to *be* and to *grow*) that does not need adversity as precondition in order to exist (to *keep up*). Resilience in this sense operates beyond specific crises (*being* goes beyond a moment of keeping-up—*to continue*). The dynamic and historical process of social resilience involves generating social capital and cultural heritage that is

[11]The government programme of 'Magical Villages' ('*Pueblos Mágicos*') is an initiative developed by the federal Ministry of Tourism, linked to state and local governments, in order to promote tourism in a few selected localities across the country which must fulfil certain criteria: preserve symbolic heritage and architectural beauty, be protagonists of historical feats and legends, be ancient in historical and cultural terms, and maintain a day-to-day lifestyle in which its inhabitants live by their customs and traditions.

always at hand and reconfigures itself constantly. However, if the social system is put under too much stress, it is at risk of collapse. Such a scenario can lead to the disintegration of the system, or to a change of order, leading to a reconfiguration of the system into another system. This is to say that the identity and coherence of the

Fig. 4.11 Temoac's cart present in the Mojiganga. *Source* Mijoganga 2013, Zacualpan de Amilpas. The photo was taken by the author who holds the copyright

system transform themselves, leading to a new system. This breaking point is important in relation to the chronic stress and multiple instances of stress. Although stress also generates resilience and the ability to respond in the short, medium or long term, chronic stress to the system also implies costs that impact the functioning of the system and may lead to the end of the system (Fig. 4.11).

Examining the relationship between social resilience and cultural heritage in the case study sheds light on some of the axes of resilience that have been generated by the Mojiganga or are expressed in Zacualpan. Over time these axes become a key to local identities, in one of the most important public festivals in Morelos. The axes that will be considered are: re-encounter, identity, reciprocity, reconciliation, equality, inclusion, recognition and a creativity spiral. The section will close by considering the areas for opportunity and danger. It is important to clarify that the fact that they are separated for analytical purposes does not mean that these axes are not interrelated or do not provide feedback to each other and the system as a whole in a dynamic way.

4.5.1 Re-encounter

Among the axes of resilience, re-encounter was the most commonly expressed during fieldwork and in the local narratives. The term 're-encounter' refers to a process of getting to know alterity or 'the other' at the deepest levels of identity, and establishing exchanges that are enriching. Re-encounters provide feedback and it is their nurturing capacity that enhances resilience. Since it started, the Mojiganga has caused multilevel, multi-systemic and polysemic re-encounters: of a person with his or her 'self', as an individual (self-reflexivity in the process of self-actualization). It has brought about re-encounters of people with other people to whom they are in a close relationship (couples, families), of people with their in-groups and out-groups at meso-levels (families, extended families, neighbourhoods, committees, troupes, municipalities, the nearby region, the state) and at macro-levels (the country, the historical epoch, the globe, the universe); of shared meanings that people express differently in their displays at the Mojiganga (e.g. 'the dance for the good harvest in Temascalcingo' from the state of Mexico or 'Ali Baba and the Forty Thieves'[12]). Mojiganga has caused encounters and re-encounters with different meanings (e.g. representing Japanese 'samurai'); with other realities (e.g. the themes 'cannibals' or 'Minions'); with other historical times (e.g. portraying 'ancient Egypt'); and even with other worlds (e.g. the theme 'the Martians have landed'). Thus the Mojiganga as an important part of cultural heritage is a meeting point, but also a point of re-encounter, expressed in the public domain and constituting a meta-system (a system of/about other systems) of resilience with a

[12]For example, "Ali Baba and the Forty Thieves" in Spanish rhymes and sounds almost like "Here comes the VAT with its Forty Thieves" ('El IVA va con sus 40 ladrones').

historical trajectory in which the various subsystems periodically provide feedback to each other. This enables the systems to *be* (i.e. it is coherent in identity terms), to *continue* (to face change and adjust, re-equilibrate, compensate for adversity), and to *grow* (to develop towards other potentials of being, as a dynamic and coherent process, unfolding across time although not necessarily heading towards a fixed *telos* since possibilities and goals actualize as the system changes).

This encounter at the intra-individual level implies the capacity of reflexivity, of self-actualization, of introspection. The process to prepare for the Mojiganga is stimulating and questioning at the individual level. This happens on at least three levels: during preparation, at the Mojiganga, and once the Mojiganga has taken place, in preparation for the ensuing year. The person transforms throughout the year in order to come out and participate: "you lose fear and start learning to develop for the best. You learn and go deeper inside yourself" (Juan I. Vargas, 41). However, once the costume is ready and the person joins the festival with a mask, some frontiers of the 'self' break down, other ways of being and behaving are explored, a ritual catharsis may take place: "once I am dressed up, I am transformed" (Edgar Iván García, 29). Taking part in a display at the Mojiganga implies the potential for transforming oneself into the alterity of that which is being represented. It can range from superficial to deeper transformations: "you are alone in the middle of everyone else, it is a very personal and very important moment, deeply spiritual" (Esteban Falfán, 24).

Relationally, the re-encounter inside the group enables '*convivencia*', living a shared experience together, which goes beyond a mere tolerant coexistence. In a troupe or on a committee people must interact, relate to each other, get organized, use personal talents for the common good, differentiate one from the other and at the same time make a team. They collaborate with patience, discipline, perseverance and organization for a year: "teamwork, that is the most important and that is the reason one belongs to a troupe" (Belem Bonilla, 25); "here the most important is that one learns to relate to the others as individual people… despite our differences and misunderstandings… that takes place during an entire year" (Natalia Hernández, 23); "A troupe is useful in order to temper yourself and serve as example to others" (Omar Delgado, 27).

As the groups get together in the public meetings hosted by the Committee for the Virgin's Festivities in the church, before the Mojiganga there is also a re-encounter, a process of solidarity and collaboration that guarantees the continuity of this particular practice of cultural heritage, favouring social cohesion, confronting prejudice, inducing organization and making social relations more dynamic. "It's meeting after meeting. First with the people in charge, with the family, we all organize what is to be done. Then, once we prepare a display we get together to see what each group wants to present. If themes are repeated, we adapt and change in order not to compete. We find points of agreement and we negotiate because we don't do this as competition, we do this out of joy, in order to support each other" (Imelda Ríos, 73).

The day of the festival is the main day of re-encounter, of *convivencia* and of getting together as a much larger collective including the entire town and embracing others at the Mojiganga, seal of Zacualpan's identity. In the voice of its protagonists: "the Mojiganga congregates, reunites family, all those that are not here—no matter how far away they are—follow the celebration and come. They get here on Friday or Saturday, so there is an incredible family gathering that I have not experienced elsewhere. Our Mojiganga is the best excuse to gather, believe me, families gather together more than at Christmas. It is about getting together, supporting each other and enjoying an event that is a hundred per cent from Zacualpan" (José Baeza, 37); "it started as a hobby, it was the way in which the family got together, chatted, worked together. It was an excuse to gather and reunite" (Esteban Falfán, 24); "that is the main intention of this Mojiganga: to be together, united and merry" (Imelda Ríos, 73). With regard to the symbolic family and the extension of self, the friendship bonds consolidate and draw closer once this collective rite is shared: "they come every year and they are part of the family at this moment" (Claudio Falfán, 21); "they danced together with you and they are a part of you now" (Esteban Falfán, 24).

There are other re-encounters that as a flexible process of social resilience the Mojiganga makes possible. The first such re-encounter relates to the community's migrants, whether these are temporary, permanent or itinerant. It is quite probable that the Mojiganga would not have reconfigured in any of its two turning points without the feedback resulting from the itinerant migration of Marino Ríos or the temporary migration of the Falfán family (permanent in the case of some of its members). The same applies to the rest of the people who have migrated due to work or education inside the country or abroad, who keep their vision of returning to take part in the Mojiganga or who have participated by supporting it from a distance for decades: "my brother got himself into this commitment and often our family members in the USA would send us money and cooperate; they would provide the raw material and we would do the work" (Imelda Ríos, 73); "the Mojiganga has the support of many people who are in other places and it is also important that other young people from far away come and take part in it. They bring a special touch, even if at first it is foreign; it ends up being a part of the Mojiganga" (José Baeza, 37).

A second re-encounter is with history and with the transgenerational heritage in three ways. First, it involves a relationship to the past Mojigangas that have been celebrated in Zacualpan for at least 180 years. Second, it implies a relationship with history that is re-signified in the present (e.g. historical representations such as 'Coatlicue'[13] or 'ancient Egypt'). Third, it relates to the transgenerational transmission of cultural heritage inside the families and the troupes. In either of these cases, "resilience is interwoven in a web of relations and experiences in the life cycle and across generations" (Walsh 2005) and that is how it takes root as part of the family, troupe and community's cultural heritage: "This is what I say to them that I will bequeath them. I do not have any money or goods, but they know if they

[13]'Coatlicue' from Nahua mythology is the mother of the gods, dual goddess of life and death, representing Mother Earth and fertility.

want to take advantage of this legacy, that is their choice, if they want to keep together in this, as they wish" (Imelda Ríos, 73).

The Mojiganga entails a third re-encounter, with nature. This is quite possibly strengthened due to a water scarcity crisis and to the weakening of agricultural production in the region. This re-encounter with nature translates into a vision of sustainability and a questioning of the consumerist model. Originally, displays were prepared with cardboard since it is an accessible material, affordable on any budget. Nevertheless, lately an effort has been made by different groups to use recycled materials and sustainable art. Displays also reflect this re-encounter with nature in themes such as 'the men of maize' by the Falfán troupe or 'nature and animal and environmental abuse' which was the first display by the Zacualpan Mágico troupe. Finally, the consumerist model starts to be questioned: "all this we are doing stems from donations. We believe that if you have too much of something it may be useful somewhere else. This is what brings to life our projects and we use the artefacts available. Sometimes we live under the false illusion that the newest things are the best, the most useful. However, as long as something is useful we can make it work and this is something we have to teach children as well" (Esteban Falfán, 24).

The fourth re-encounter is with life and death and it applies to choosing representations of death (e.g. 'resurrecting the Bicentennial') as well as to giving a place at the Mojiganga to people who have passed away (e.g. a Mojiganga display dedicated to Señor Beto Falfán). Linked to this, there is a re-encounter with creative imagination in relation to the way that the universe is interpreted (e.g. the display 'the Martians have landed').

Finally, there is another potential re-encounter that has not yet matured. It is a re-encounter based on a dialogue between civilizations. Currently, families and troupes represent their interpretation of other subjects, other groups, other cultural heritages, and that is how they relate to them. Today, in an era when information technology makes long-distance communication and exchanges possible, it would be fascinating to see how the people of Zacualpan engage in a direct dialogue with these living cultural heritages and their agents. For example, a dialogue about the display of 'Huichol dreams', to see them relate to the Wixárikas, or see Zacualpan interact with its twin cities—Camaguey, Cuba and Pharr, Texas—in the Mojiganga.

4.5.2 Identity

Identity, in the case of Zacualpan, is always forged in the bridge between individual, group and collective relations. On the one hand it responds to the *self*-conception and *self*-recognition of an individual or collective subject and on the other it implies identity assignations in order to situate and differentiate identity traits and the field of action of concrete *other* subjects and being identified by others (hetero-assignation and hetero-recognition). It is pertinent to stress that psychologically our cognition and relational capacities imply information selection processes and thus our knowledge of our self and of others will always be partial. Nevertheless, seen from an anthropological viewpoint, identity does encompass all the elements that make an individual or collective subject, which is not seen as an end result, but rather corresponds to a living being, constantly changing and renewing itself. Identity entails conscious as well as unconscious and semi-conscious elements. The contours of identity are delimitated by forms of thought, communication and practice. Defending identities as dissociated, fixed, or end products stems from essentialist thought, which instead of looking for the relational feedback processes between singular and plural agents justifies in its conception of identity elements such as violence, passiveness and prejudice. Thus, methodologically, the more we look for processes that implicate this relationship between the individual self and the broader self (group, community and societal), and its transitions, the more we will obtain a wider panorama of the integral identity unit or dynamic system of identity. Culture is the framework where identity processes (identification, differentiation) and relations take place; it is the space where knowledge, action, re-signification and transformation occur. Culture is the fertile land where identities take root, nurture and transform. That is the reason for looking at how resilience is possible in the processes of renewal of cultural heritage, since it is this dynamic identity which gives coherence to the self.

A good example in Zacualpan has to do with the nicknames that people and neighbourhoods are given following the Mojiganga. When Rafael Ramírez started to represent the 'circus', many people started dressing up as animals and the people, their families, troupes and neighbourhoods started being referred to by the name of these animals. Visiting Zacualpan today one will notice that many people know each other by nickname rather than by first name or family name, and that these nicknames are the names of animals that are historically related to their participation in the Mojiganga: "for example, imagine that if he could not find a deer, people dressed like a deer, and today there is an entire family that is nicknamed after that animal" (José Baeza, 37). There is a troupe called 'Cacomixtles' (*Bassariscus sumichrasti*, the cacomistle, a famous local animal).

4.5.3 Exchange, Reciprocity and 'Convivencia'

Zacualpan is a social space characterized over the centuries by relations of mutual exchange and reciprocity such as those expressed by the practice of '*trueque*' (barter), which is still practised in everyday life and in Zacualpan has an official annual festival. In the Mojiganga, these exchange and reciprocity relations can be seen throughout the historical evolution of the festival. It is thanks to the generosity with which ideas, knowledge and experience of the practices of popular art and *convivencia* that the Mojiganga has grown and reconfigured itself. "We do this out of joy, without any profit" was repeated over and over again by all the people interviewed. The Mojiganga "is made all together, as a community… we invite and receive our guests, we want them to be happy" (Claudio Falfán, 21). People say that for the Mojiganga they have had visitors from up to eighty different countries, '*Misses*' who are winners of beauty pageants, Chinese lions, Bolivian groups, and other distinguished guests from Mexico and the world over. At the same time, people from Zacualpan have started receiving invitations to participate in cultural exchanges, for example to share their work and experience in France and Cuba. In the words of Juan I. López: "*Convivencia* is beautiful during the Mojiganga. There is a special energy; I would say it is even a mystical question. There is a tremendous energy; people pass it on to others. On that day, the person who does not like to dance starts moving. There is a very positive energy. The whole town makes this festival and generates a tremendous energy that attracts like light people from abroad, from all over the country, to such a small town. The energy that we create is like a giant lamp, a beacon that shines" (41 years).

There is a vision of nurturing relations in which giving to others means that one grows. The people from Zacualpan invite others to integrate into this shared space of *convivencia* and diversity, which in turn provides important feedback and nurtures them. In these mutual nurturing influences and exchanges, security, tranquillity and trust are generated in the face of a very violent and fractured broader social context in the state of Morelos.[14] "It is a way of going beyond the vices and violence prevalent today through culture" (Belem Bonilla, 25); "The axis of the project is solidarity and it is a very important collective thing in which we take part because we have learnt that an isolated person is like an island in the sea of everybody. The same thing does not work for everybody and thus something very important in this cultural centre is collaboration, collaboration in every way. Here all the workshops are collaborations; they are provided for all the people of the town" (Esteban Falfán, 24).

4.5.4 Reconciliation

The Mojiganga is an open, creative and flexible space. Without trying to portray an idealized version that is deprived of social tensions, it does constitute a public space in which private conflicts can be mediated in a ritualistic festive space; this favours their re-signification, mitigation, solution or temporary suspension.[15] This highlights the importance of the potential of the interrelation of ICH and social

[14]Mexico is ranked as the fifth most dangerous country in the Latin American Security Index (FTI 2014). Within Mexico, according to the Citizen's Council for Public Security and Justice (Consejo Ciudadano para la Seguridad Pública y la Justicia 2015), the state of Morelos has the highest violence index in the country, and its capital city Cuernavaca is ranked as the most violent in the country, which puts it among the most dangerous places in the world.

[15]The extensive work on resilience and trauma following violence, abuse and social injustice linked to the importance of including a public ritualistic dimension of therapy by neuropsychiatrist and systemic psychotherapist Jorge Barudy supports this vision (see especially Barudy and Dantagnan 2011).

resilience for peace. Even public historical conflicts have found a solution at the Mojiganga. Despite asking for independence from the municipality of Zacualpan de Amilpas in 1977, the communities of Temoac, Huazulco, Amilcingo and Popotlán have an official place at the Virgin's Feast and they participate in the Mojiganga as troupes and as special guests. This dimension of reconciliation also includes much broader processes, such as the problems and contradictions of the country that are symbolically represented in the public and ritualized space. At the Mojiganga there have been representations of the Zapatista Army of National Liberation (EZLN) and of the silent March for peace. In this sense "the Mojiganga projects everything that the younger people want to convey and the good side is that they can express themselves and their ways of looking at things in a peaceful manner, which is the most important thing" (José Baeza, 37).

4.5.5 Levelling Out Inequality and Promoting Inclusion

The Mojiganga provides a social function of levelling out inequality and promoting inclusion which crystallizes in the metaphor that all displays are different yet everyone dances at the same pace. The Mojiganga is a collective festival, which enjoys the utmost public recognition socially in the community, and so it opens up a public space for social action in the *res publica* where people and groups express themselves beyond the dividing lines that segment social space in everyday life. Although each troupe organizes itself separately, in a polysemic fashion, everyone is valid in the public sphere. In a plural frame and in the meta-displays, tradition and innovation converge, and it is at this level that resilience at the collective level is generated, avoiding, mitigating or overcoming negative conflict. In the words of most interviewees, "a healthy competence is generated in which everyone gives their best for the good of all" (e.g. José Baeza, Imelda Ríos, Esteban Falfán).

We can observe this clearly in the moments that have constituted turning points in the festival. For example, the initiators of the Mojiganga were poor peasants who sought out the Virgin of Rosario as their main religious figure and devoted the festival to her rather than to the religious patron of the town, who was associated more with the elite; they were seeking a more inclusive figure. Another example is the case of Marino Ríos and Jaime García, who sought a space for social recognition and Jaime García, who sought a space for social recognition and public expression by making displays of a higher quality and with greater impact, and had tremendous success. Yet a further example is the inclusion of people of different sexual orientation in the festival, despite it being a religious festivity in a conservative context. Some people participating in the Mojiganga have "had different sexual preferences. Despite that the town accepted them and their innovations. This is the most important" (José Baeza, 37). Also, one could analyse the process of the incorporation of women in the Mojiganga with figures such as Imelda Ríos, who is gradually being recognized for her pioneering role and legacy, even though she had less visibility at the time: "well yes, before we were criticized because the place of the woman was indoors and her activities only beans [cooking]. But we did not care, we always participated as women. Nowadays everybody participates." "Always, every time, I was one of those behind the reflectors. Even if I was not visible, my work was visible… and I did that work, it was my contribution, and that is my greatest satisfaction: that people now keep doing it" (Imelda Ríos, 73). Today women participate in all of the processes linked to the Mojiganga, and they have become troupe leaders as well. A last example could be the Falfán family who returned after migrating with a different education and other resources, and who began to participate by projecting all these resources and creativity into the festival, which in turn started to become more artistic and cultural than religious.

This levelling function is the case with those who organize themselves as troupes or present allegorical displays—given their diversity—as well as for the public. At the same moment and in a framework of equality and inclusion, we observe individuals, families and groups organized as troupes who converge despite their many differences: age; gender; socio-economic status; formal and informal educational levels; economic activities; opposed talents; coming from a more urban or rural context within and outside the community; having distinct technical skills; relating to information technology differently; with experience and life trajectories inside and outside Zacualpan; with friends from other parts of the state, the country, and the world who are also quite diverse (for example, eighty countries converging in a single Mojiganga); knowing how to dance or just walk; being able to walk or not (using horses, carts or wheelchairs); seeking attention or participating in meditative silence; taking part by making displays or as spectators; with dissimilar tempers and personalities; whether introspective or highly expressive; with greater or lower degrees of organization; employing divergent materials and techniques; having a unique discipline and working ethic; whether presenting religious, cultural or historic displays; with different degrees of religious fervour (being practising Catholics, believers, atheists or followers of another creed); having made a particular vow or not; whether participating for the first time, sometimes, or always; choosing a topic that relates to the past, the present or the future; representing living or dead people; consuming water, alcohol or some other substance; wearing a disguise or carrying a monumental figure; acting as performers or as observers for the troupe; whether living in Zacualpa, having family there or just visiting; being migrant; being from Zacualpan, a nearby place, Mexicans or foreigners.

4.5.6 Recognition

Recognition is a central element of social processes, *convivencia* and identity. It is through publicly expressed recognition of an individual or collective subject that knowledge and practice are accepted, reproduced and disseminated until they become part of cultural heritage. In the case of the Mojiganga, recognition was the fertilizer that enabled change to take place and expand from that public announcement of the Virgin's feast to qualitative and quantitative innovation.

Reconfiguring its identity from its own coherence, with feedback provided at a public level, enables the festival and its subsystems to expand, transform and consolidate themselves. The relationship to *be*, to *continue*, to *grow* was possible. Recognition at the Mojiganga is visible in three ways. First, through immediate applause: "here if people like it they will applaud and if they dislike it they will jeer. Here applause is very indicative of whether something is liked and accepted" (Imelda Ríos, 73). "And the fact that at the end they announce your participation, the display you have chosen and people applaud, that is the real payment" (José Baeza, 37). Second, through the reproduction and dissemination of an innovation, for example "the Falfán family started integrating more artistic elements into their work and thought and people liked it" (Juan I. López, 41); "the year after we made the first display others started to do it" (Imelda Ríos, 73). Third, through the participation of and growth in the number of guests and people invited to take part in the Mojiganga: "We want to be seen…. we want people to talk about us… for them to come and take part in it with us" (Juan I. López, 41); "the Mojiganga is beautiful because it enables us to continue with an ancient tradition. I like the participation of many people, especially younger ones, and now a lot of people from many nations come… in other festivals there is no participation like there is in this one… I want to keep inviting people to come, to join us, and to do it in a decent manner" (Imelda Ríos, 73). In this sense, information technology will be another dynamizing element in the Mojiganga in Zacualpan since the festival is already broadcast in real time to audiences throughout the state and the world over. It is important to pay attention to the feedback provided by virtual audiences and their impact on the reconfiguration of this cultural heritage.

4.5.7 Creativity Spiral

Looked at from a systemic point of view, the functioning and growth of a system has to do with the feedback it receives from all of its subsystems. In the case of the Mojiganga in Zacualpan we have already ascertained that we are dealing with a festival that involves both individual and collective subjects, although the system as a whole—the community—is greater than the sum of its parts, and it is at this level that we locate and look at the reconfiguration of both cultural heritage and social resilience. Following the brief historical overview of the festival, and having revised some of the axes of resilience, enables us to see that throughout its history there has been a key element that provides both cohesion and dynamism to the system and is a very important axis of resilience: creativity, which has provided continuous feedback to the system.

This creativity operates at different levels from the individual, family, group and community levels, and creativity has been fundamental in the growth and consolidation of the Mojiganga. It has led to the point we are at now, where the Mojiganga constitutes the most important public event and festival in Zacualpan, and is a pillar of local identity. So we are dealing with a form of feedback that enables the circulation of new meanings, techniques, practices, languages, forms of relationship and *convivencia*, elements and processes of identity that are always being re-signified but that enable growth since they are coherent with the deeper identity of the system, and they reinforce it. In this way we can understand creativity as a spiral rather than as a continuum with a fixed point of departure and arrival. In the case of the Mojiganga, the spiral of creativity has a potential without limits across time. We can see how traditional elements coexist with modern and ultramodern innovations (such as aliens and Hiuchol dreams) which are tested in the public sphere and have continuity once they are accepted.

When we analyse the meaning that 'healthy competition' has for the people of Zacualpan, it does not mean a hostile and negative competitive environment where in order for one to win, another has to lose. This kind of power relationship that favours and devalues at the same time does not lead to the growth of the system as a whole, since it inhibits some of its parts and thus destabilizes it, eclipsing its creativity. There is even a precedent is this regard. A few years ago there was a prize offered for the best displays at the Mojiganga. This prize generated division between families and troupes, and because of these divisions it was got rid of. Rather, the axis of 'competition' in Zacualpan is the cooperation that nurtures creativity: "year after year there were more added, three, five, eight. Today there are between fifteen and twenty allegorical floats and fifteen to twenty troupes, so I think that for some time now we no longer speak of competition between the parties but rather of a lot of creativity. This is the most interesting fact" (José Baeza, 37).

The chief motivation for expression and innovation at the Mojiganga goes way beyond any award, since the festival did not emerge as a result of any prize. The goal is to express oneself publicly and grow, not to compete in order to devalue someone else: "all the people in Zacualpan, and I think all the troupes in general, always find ways of improving year after year. We cannot stand doing things poorly, and the feeling then is that people criticize you. You feel a glance that tells you 'that is not properly done', or something like that, and that is why we do not like to stagnate. This is a healthy competition in which everyone cooperates. When you see something worthwhile, instead of getting angry you are inspired to do things better. So this is not about competing for who is the best. This is more about realizing all that you are capable of doing when you work on a new display. It's a challenge, the main challenge. It is to make new, original, fresh and funny displays. You do not want to hear 'this is the same as last year'. As the human condition, what is at stake here and always is to progress, to advance, to innovate" (Esteban Falfán, 24).

4.5.8 Areas of Opportunity and Danger

In the process of cultural change there are adjustments of form and depth, in such a way that changes in cultural heritage imply a renewal that includes a re-signification (deeper changes, structural changes) beyond mere reorganization (changes in form).

Linked to resilience, there are conciliating transitions (providing feedback to the system) as well as dissociating transitions (that fragment and divide the system), although generally they are not simply one or the other. At present, there are some elements that directly relate to the Mojiganga and may be interpreted as areas of either opportunity or danger, depending on how they are handled. This is why they deserve a mention.

Technology may be an important asset, allowing new dynamizing potentials for the Mojiganga, although it may also mean certain risks. The local population's view is that technology may endanger the Mojiganga if it means the transition from a traditional festival that is 'hand-made' and created by different groups to an event of mass-produced materials, stagnated creativity and clichés (for example using mass-produced plastic disguises).

Alcohol has always had a place in the Mojiganga and in most traditional festivals in Mexican towns since indigenous times. In Zacualpan, alcohol stands out, since '*aguardiente*' or raw rum has been one of the main products; it is called 'Zacualpita'. It has an important place in the Mojiganga; it helps to oil social relations ("a healthy *convivencia*") and to lower inhibitions once people are in disguise; for some it facilitates the process of getting into character; it helps them in the process of making a personal catharsis, and especially helps them to stand and dance for many hours and kilometres during the whole procession: "you want to go on dancing, enjoying, resting, and drinking—yes, you can drink as you go[16]—and that is part of the magic of the Mojiganga. Here we have a saying 'if you don't drink, you don't keep up with the pace.' So you have to drink a bit of 'Zacualpita', not in order to get 'Zacualpitis' disease, but in order to reach your goal" (José Baeza, 37). There are even those who make a special and very original disguise for their alcohol bottle or incorporate it in their costumes. Nevertheless, there are now some people, especially younger people who do not always come from Zacualpan, who use the Mojiganga as a pretext to abuse alcohol and other substances, and although this happens at the individual level, it still impacts on this collective forum of expression and *convivencia*. Many of the stewards at the festival are in charge of preventing incidents caused by people who have had too much to drink.

The fact that the Mojiganga originated as the announcement of the Virgin of Rosario's festival provides an idea of the centrality of religion in the festival. Currently some people think the religious side of the festival gets lost in order to give central stage to more cultural-secular expressions. This view exists despite the fact that collectively the agreement is that themes and displays may be religious, historical or cultural. In strictly religious terms, something to be borne in mind is the nature of changes in the socio-demographic profile of the municipality, since the number of Catholics has decreased but the number of people who identify as Pentecostal, Evangelic or Christians of other denominations has increased (currently 5.2 %). In the face of these changes it will be very important to guarantee that

[16]In Mexico, drinking in the streets is not usually allowed.

the Mojiganga continues to be a plural public forum for all participants, in order to avoid religious conflict.

In examining the axis of creativity as spiral, the importance of the local meaning of 'competition' was stressed, which is more positive and open rather than negative, exclusionary and hostile. This is pertinent because looking at the Mojiganga from the standpoint of an external logic that places emphasis on individualizing and/or free market competition traits, it would be easy to run the risk of thinking that creativity is stimulated only through external incentives that do not respond to the coherence of the system and which might have an undesirable impact in the medium and long term since they destabilize the system's functioning or fragment the system, as happened for example when awards were introduced. Analysing the reconfiguration of cultural heritage in the present context we see that it is thanks to the resilience of the social system that the Mojiganga has grown over such a long period of time. This growth has occurred despite the ambiguous impact of certain elements such as the process of globalization that homogenizes at the same time as it diversifies, of water scarcity and crisis in agricultural production, of employment becoming more precarious, especially for younger generations, and of mass migration.

Nevertheless, the vision of making Zacualpan the third 'Magic Town' of Morelos, of which the state government's declaration of the Mojiganga as 'Cultural Heritage of Morelos' is the first step, means that there are two very important risks that need to be borne in mind. First, it would mean that the main criteria, guidelines, authorities, and evaluation were fixed by people external to the system (community) and its processes (the Mojiganga itself), but especially, by federal bureaucrats who have other visions and interests as priorities in a programme that considers many other elements in many other places. Secondly, it would run the risk of leading to a vision of cultural heritage as primarily a cultural service for tourism. This does not mean that in order to safeguard cultural heritage it should be isolated or fixed, or that cultural heritage does not possess a value that may be quantified or exchanged. Both these risks lead to more questions than answers, and not only must one bear these in mind as an analyst, but they are especially important for the practitioners of heritage, in this case the people of Zacualpan, to consider.

This raises questions about: (i) the deeper logic of cultural services (e.g. Is it internal, external or could it encompass both?); (ii) the autonomy of the system beyond its processes (e.g. Does the system have the possibility of adapting? Can it adapt to externally-induced structural change?); (iii) the management of cultural heritage (e.g. Who has the rights and how do they participate? How are costs and benefits shared, or not?); (iv) the consideration and making visible of cultural services that cultural heritage has provided to the system and of the impact of changes in the vision and use of this heritage; (v) the time frames involved: historical time, the long, medium and short term; (vi) the tensions, divisions and schisms inside the system and how this change would impact on the social tissue—currently not all people and groups are convinced that this is the right moment or the best step to follow (e.g. "Zacualpan is already magical, it does not need an external title" (Claudio Falfán, 21); vii) the traps of cultural heritage as a trademark and as private property; and (viii) making heritage banal and into a simple tourist spectacle. The profound analysis of social and cultural processes across time and using multidisciplinary logic should be the basis of public policies and programmes.

Taking into account these areas of opportunity and risk, it becomes of fundamental importance to support cultural heritage, and the processes of social resilience it contains, through public policies rooted in the deeper culture of the locality and not derived simply from a vision of cultural tourism.

4.6 Concluding Remarks

If one looks specifically at the Mojiganga in Zacualpan from a qualitative standpoint, without trying to overrate this specific festival, important lessons can be learnt that may provide a departure point for more general conclusions about the interrelation of social resilience and intangible cultural heritage. This chapter has stressed that resilience is a wide, dynamic, flexible concept that implies tensions, transitions and competences, paving the way for a holistic vision of development and boundless potential from the individual level up to the collective level (to *be*—to *grow*), and not seeing it as simply coping with adversity in a state of damage, crisis and disaster (to *continue*). Even within such a restrictive definition, to recover means to transform. If it implies regenerating, actively seeking a coherent stability that enables the system to continue, it is a dynamic equilibrium. There is no way of going back to the past, of involution or of staying unaltered; otherwise, the central concept would not be resilience. Much more so when there is a real chance to grow and develop in a myriad ways. The idea is not to exalt resilience as if it were mere rigidity, an idealized past or an evolutionary fixed end point; it is not possible to return to a departure point in the past because stability, just like identity and society, implies a cumulative process of knowledge that is historically reflected in cultural heritage. Is it possible to fix a single departure point when dealing with heritage? Pointing towards one single goal or *telos*, instead of looking at the many possible and creative development options of a system, is restrictive. Of course cultural heritage accumulates across time, becoming richer, but given the inevitability of change heritage is never final. Heritage is always coherent within a given time and space. The same applies to processes of resilience. What has worked in the past does not necessarily work at present or in the future.

In the above discussion, the importance of subjects has been emphasized—both individual and collective subjects—who are protagonists of crises and transformations, of the renewal and reconfiguration of their self and their cultural heritage through agency and action. As Arizpe states (2015: 98), intangible cultural heritage is not an "end point of past practices", it is "the starting point for cultural innovations in plural societies".

Thus, community resilience reflects polysemy—it constitutes a dynamic system of meanings and practices within culture, which may be conflicting or contradictory yet are nonetheless coherent. This enables the incorporation and adjustment of new elements without banishing those formerly existing which are still valid. Cultural heritage constitutes a pillar of the resilience of a system and at the same time resilience as process provides feedback and reconfigures heritage. Rooted in a plural framework of exchanges and relations, creativity leads to innovations and reconfigurations that are coherent with the self. Resilience develops in a meta-systemic identity frame, in a cultural system of systems of meaning and relations which have re-encounters and feedback at their core. It is through these encounters and dialogues that identity and heritage actualize themselves and project themselves to the future in the face of change.

Social resilience in a community setting in Mexico, without seeking to idealize or fix a frame of sociocultural exchanges, organization, institutions, services, values, visions, meaning and belonging, takes us to the 'deep' indigenous legacy and the Colonial period, as well as to the historical shocks in the history of the country such as Independence or the Mexican Revolution with Zapatismo, more recently to the end of the Second World War, and finally to neo-liberal Mexico famous for its violence, deep inequality and exclusion. All of these events have enabled collective subjects to generate a cultural heritage from which to articulate and re-articulate in the face of social change and chronic, generalized and recurrent crises. So, conceptualizing resilience as the result of an isolated event loses explanatory potential. Following on from the study, it is not pertinent to conceptualize resilience only as an a posteriori response to an event, since this view blurs the social and historical capital in resilience, which is part of the cultural heritage of local sites such as the municipality of Zacualpan.

Seen from a historical long-term perspective [*longue durée* (Braudel 1969)], resilience as part of cultural heritage in a social and community framework appears as an important and useful concept, since it enables its characteristics and dynamism to be analysed in a way that avoids the fallacy that agency and resources refer only to the immediate time frame and to the individual level. In addition, resilience as part of heritage situates resilience in a broader political context within a dialogic and participatory democracy, supporting sustainable peace. Linked to this, and before concluding, it is important to state that locally-sensitive government support and coherent public policies may foster resilience and its expression as part of cultural heritage. Lack of support and lack of public policies as part of a laissez-faire strategy, justified in discourses of non-intervention 'favouring endogenous local processes of resilience and cultural heritage', is unacceptable. Localities have an internal coherence and identity, but they are increasingly linked to external feedback and impacts. It is absurd to think that more discrimination, widespread violence and corruption, a higher level of resource extraction and consigning regions and groups to historical oblivion, that is, generally adverse living conditions, lead to the potential for generating a higher level of resilience. The threat of the destruction of the system can be observed throughout history. Adequate public policies that respond to local needs and are framed as part of the internal processes and structures of specific contexts, coherent in systemic terms, are central in realizing the potential of resilience in individual and collective groups, and achieving a positive impact in terms of peace. This in turn is reflected in cultural heritage, and dialectically leads to further resilience and innovation across time.

References

Amescua, Cristina; Arizpe, Lourdes (Eds.), in press): *Renovación y Futuro del Patrimonio Cultural Intangible en Morelos* (Mexico City: CRIM–UNAM).

Arizpe, Lourdes (Ed.), 2011: *Compartir el Patrimonio Cultural Inmaterial. Narrativas y Representaciones* (Mexico City: CONACULTA).

Arizpe, Lourdes, 2014: *Lourdes Arizpe: A Mexican Pioneer in Anthropology* (Heidelberg: Springer).

Arizpe, Lourdes, 2015: *Culture, Diversity and Heritage: Major Studies* (Heidelberg: Springer).

Arizpe, Lourdes; Amescua, Cristina (Eds.), 2013: *Anthropological Perspectives on Intangible Cultural Heritage* (Heidelberg: Springer).

Barudy, Jorge; Dantagnan, Maryorie, 2011: *La fiesta mágica y realista de la resiliencia infantil* (Mexico City: Gedisa).

Berkes, Fikret; Colding, Johan; Folke, Carl (Eds.), 2003: *Navigating Social–Ecological Systems: Building Resilience for Complexity and Change* (Cambridge: Cambridge University Press).

Berkes, Fikret; Folke, Carl (Eds.), 1998: *Linking Social and Ecological Systems: Management Practices and Social Mechanisms for Building Resilience* (Cambridge: Cambridge University Press).

Bonanno, George A., 2004: "Loss, Trauma, and Human Resilience: Have We Underestimated the Human Capacity to Thrive After Extremely Adverse Events?", in: *American Psychologist*, 59,1 (January): 20–28.

Braudel, Fernand, 1969: "Histoire et science sociales. La longue durée", in: *Écrits Sur l'Histoire* (Paris: Flammarion): 41–84.

Consejo Ciudadano para la Seguridad Pública y la Justicia, 2015: *La violencia en los municipios y en las entidades federativas de México* (Mexico City: Consejo Ciudadano para la Seguridad Pública y Justicia).

Dyer, J. G.; McGuiness, T. M., 1996: "Resilience: analysis of the concept", in: *Archives of Psychiatric Nursing*, 10,5 (October): 276–282.

FTI Publishing, March 2014: *Public Insecurity in Latin America* (Palm Beach: FTI).

Guanche, Jesús, 2008: "El imaginado 'patrimonio inmaterial' ¿Un acercamiento a la verdad o una falsedad engañosa?", in: *Perfiles de la Cultura Cubana*, 1 (January): 1–15.

Holling, Crawford Stanley, 1973: "Resilience and Stability of Ecological Systems", in: *Annual Review of Ecology and Systematics*, 4: 1–23.

Knight, Alan, 1986: *The Mexican Revolution* (Cambridge: Cambridge University Press).

Lacarrieu, Monica, 2004: "El Patrimonio Cultural Inmaterial: Un Recurso Político en el Espacio de la Cultura Pública Local", Paper presented at UNESCO's VI Seminar on Cultural Heritage, 21–23 October, Santiago, Chile.

Luthar, Suniya S.; Cicchetti, Dante; Becker, Bronwyn, 2000: "The Construct of Resilience: A Critical Evaluation and Guidelines for Future Work", in: *Child Development*, 71,3: 543–562.

Perez Flores, Edith, in press): "Reciprocidad: el trueque en Zacualpan de Amilpas, Morelos", in: Amescua, Cristina; Arizpe, Lourdes (Eds.): *Renovación y Futuro del Patrimonio Cultural Intangible en Morelos* (Mexico City: CRIM–UNAM): 78–118.

Rutter, Michael, 1987: "Psychosocial resilience and protective mechanisms", in: *American Journal of Orthopsychiatry*, 57,3 (July): 316–331.

Serrano Oswald, Serena Eréndira, in press: "Reencuentro: La Mojiganga en Zacualpan de Amilpas, Morelos", in: Amescua, Cristina; Arizpe, Lourdes (Eds.), in press: *Renovación y Futuro del Patrimonio Cultural Intangible en Morelos* (Mexico City: CRIM–UNAM): 190–230.

Uriarte Arcinega, Juan de Dios, 2013: "La Perspectiva Comunitaria de la Resiliencia", in: *Psicología Política*, 47: 7–18.

Villalba Quesada, Cristina, 2004: "El Concepto de Resiliencia. Aplicaciones en la Intervención Social", Universidad Pablo de Oviedo, Sevilla, January (unpublished).

Walker, Brian; Salt, David, 2006: *Resilience Thinking: Sustaining Ecosystems and People in a Changing World* (Washington: Island Press).

Walsh, Froma, 2005: *Resiliencia Familiar: Estrategias para su Fortalecimiento* (Madrid—Buenos Aires: Amorrortu).

Womack Jr., John, 1968: *Zapata and the Mexican Revolution* (New York: Vintage Books).

Chapter 5
Community Perceptions of Ecological Disturbances Caused During Terrorists Invasion and Counter-Insurgency Operations in Swat, Pakistan

Fakhra Rashid, Feng Feng and Audil Rashid

Abstract This chapter presents primary research that investigates the ecological impact of the counter-insurgency operation in Swat, Pakistan, and the perception among local community of its lasting effects. People in Pakistan have been witnessing violence directed against defenceless civilians in the name of religion. In particular, the Swat district in the north-western part of the country has faced unprecedented terrorism, with militant extremists asserting their dogmatic beliefs stubbornly and with excessive force. The unrest in Swat has not only cost hundreds of innocent lives but also brought destructive consequences for the ecology and environment of the region upon which the local economy was based. Ecological integrity of Swat region was further violated when government launched a military operation in 2009 to counter insurgency and terrorism, which eventually eliminated militants and restored the writ of government. Lasting effects including localized poverty, demographic changes, travel insecurity, damage to schools, health concerns, loss to the landscape and amenity values are comprehensively analysed. In-depth interviews and surveys using structured questionnaires were conducted to gather data. Perceiving their vulnerability in the hands of extremists or ineffective government, respondents displayed a decreased sense of belonging and an increased desire to migrate. The results depicted the possibility of a short-term gain in peace, provided that the local people endorse the options suggested to improve human security in Swat. Imposing alien solutions without considering ecological and geographical norms would prove detrimental to peace efforts. Incongruity between counter-insurgency actions and community's ideology predicted greater failure in peace efforts based on past experiences.

Fakhra Rashid, School of Public Affairs, University of Science and Technology of China, Hefei, Anhui, 230026, China; Email: fakhra99@gmail.com.

Prof. Dr. Feng Feng (China), School of Public Affairs, University of Science and Technology of China, Hefei, Anhui, 230026, China, *Email*: ffeng@ustc.edu.cn.

Dr. Audil Rashid, EcoHealth Research Group, Department of Environmental Sciences, PMAS Arid Agriculture University, Rawalpindi-46300, Pakistan; Email: audil@uaar.edu.pk.

The authors gratefully acknowledge the role of local interpreter Mr. Habibullah for providing assistance.

Ú.Oswald Spring et al. (eds.), *Regional Ecological Challenges for Peace in Africa, the Middle East, Latin America and Asia Pacific*, The Anthropocene: Politik—Economics—Society—Science 5, DOI 10.1007/978-3-319-30560-8_5

Keywords Terrorism exposure · Ecohealth · Peace ecology · Swat valley · Peace dialogue · Conflict resolution · Environmental preservation

5.1 Introduction

Nestled in the north-western part of the Pakistan was the independent Administrative District Swat valley in Khyber Pakhtunkhwa Province of Pakistan. The valley is an integral part of the strategic and significant region where three parts of the Asian continent—South Asia, Central Asia and China—meet (Samad 2011). Apart from its historical significance, Swat valley is reputed all over the globe for its fascinating landscapes, crystal clear water torrents, diverse flora and fauna, hospitality, ancient relics and mesmerizing lakes which attract innumerable tourists and nature lovers from all over the world.[1] Some of the most famous fruits were grown here which is the prime asset for local economy. Almost every family owned some land and indulged in agriculture production. Pears, apricots, apples, cherries, peaches and plums are among famous. All twelve types of peaches are produced here and people in rest of Pakistan wait whole year for the scrumptious strawberries and peaches of Swat (Khaliq 2013; Saqib/Tachibana 2014).[2] The valley is known as "Pakistan's Switzerland", and is the most attractive tourist destination in Pakistan. In addition, mines of Swat are potential resource of gemstones which is another important revenue making business. The ongoing conflict between militants and government forces have not only created havoc with the lives of local people but their ecological resources were badly affected (Ahmad et al. 2014) along with agricultural productivity such as fruit production, which resulted in a severe blow on local economy and earning capacity of Swat population.[3]

It seems obvious that control of this area means complete authority over vast ecological resources. Since 1975, the writ of the Pakistani government was not fully established in the Swat valley because the legal order Frontier Crimes Regulation (FCR) used to govern the area was annulled by court. Hence a political vacuum was created and the whole Swat valley was left without a proper justice and governance system. After the September 11 terrorist attacks in the United States and the subsequent US campaign in Afghanistan, several terrorists and religious extremists were able to cross Pak-Afghan border and occupied numerous borderline areas particularly in Northwest Pakistan. Their concentration began to threaten local population due to increasing incidents of terrorism such as blasting educational institution, destruction of health facilities, beheading, killing of tribal elders and suicide bombing. The failure of government of Pakistan to address the issue of

---

[1]"Welcome to Valley Swat"; at: http://www.valleyswat.net/ (13 June 2015).

[2]Khaliq, Fazal, 2013: "Peaches and plums from Swat, with love"; at: http://tribune.com.pk/story/563154/peaches-and-plums-from-swat-with-love/ (20 June 2015).

[3]Yusufzai, Ashfaq, 2013: "Militancy devastates Pakistani agriculture".

terrorism and provide protection to local populations in a prudent manner transformed the conflict into warlike tension. The situation worsened and finally a full fledge military operation was launched in 2009 by the government. Consequently, Swat valley turned into battle field. As expected like other conflict zones in the world, the war left in its wake not only human casualties but the use of arms and ammunition had also significantly degraded the local environment (Ali 2007). A huge number of internally displaced people took refuge in camps and lived in uncertainty during this entire counter-insurgency operation (Rashid/Adnan 2009). This has created some long-lasting effect on local people as well as their environment.

It is important to note that most often during assessing the impacts of war, the link between human actions that cause not only social violence and severely disturb the ecology of area, is often ignored (Dalby 1992; Deudney 1990). In conflict zones, while initiating peace efforts to improve human security, the restoration of ecological balance is usually not emphasized (Wenden 2012). This is exactly what happened in Swat. In 2009 the local population was forced to leave the area due to the counter-insurgency operation launched by the government. Local people faced a complex situation. Prior to active engagement of government forces, people were terrorized by militants who forcibly occupied their land, killed an overwhelming number of people, and also caused vast destruction to their agricultural land and businesses. Upon the onset of counter-insurgency operation by government forces, local people once again witnessed destruction of their land, orchids, field and other ecological resources but in a much higher magnitude.

An estimation of the ecological potential of conflict zones is an important aspect to be monitored in peace ecology. A 2012 survey by the National Agricultural Research Centre, Pakistan showed that nearly 48 % of Pakistan's total fruit is produced in Khyber Pakhtunkhwa with Swat District being a major contributor with 25 %, which decreased to 10 % when the Taliban ruled Malakand Division from 2007 to 2009. An estimated 60–75 % of the fruits grown in Swat went to waste during the era of Taliban shelling and bombings and the curfews and road blockades that authorities had to impose. An urgent focus is needed to overcome these losses and protect the environment from further deterioration.

Before invasion of terrorists, the Swat was known to be free from all kinds of ecological pollution (Hamayun et al. 2006). To make things worse, the environmental degradation in Swat has not even been considered to be ecological violence. Peace ecology was denied to play its vial role in this conflict zone, a challenging reality for restoring peace in many cases (Galtung 1985). Military solutions that are applied to bring peace not only exacerbate rifts between peoples and cultures, but also severely undermine movements toward environmental sustainability (Conca/Geoffrey 2002).

In this context, upon analysing the Swat region, a key issue that imminently emerges is: how do local communities in Swat perceive environmental changes caused by conflict, terrorism and subsequent military operations to curb insurgency? We assume that when livelihood of communities depends on their local environment, peace ecology and preservation of environment can significantly contribute to peace building in conflict zones. Absence of war is not the only important for peace but is central to ecological balance. Peace with Nature is what constitutes a peace ecology. Swat region confront these eventualities, which are potentially revolutionary for peace ecology. That peace ecology has been inherently denied during the decision-making and planning process, and the community's perception developed during efforts to resolve conflict, demands an in-depth analysis. In order to do that, different research questions were framed such as: to what extent people of Swat realize the detrimental impacts on local environment and ecology in the terrorism arena? Was peace ecology and perspective of environmental integrity given due importance in the peace restoration approach? The study also presents suitability evaluation analysis for the peace approach used to solve the conflict in Swat area, on the backdrop of a delicate link between local populations and their immediate environment. Overall we aimed to investigate the rubrics of peace-conflict-sustainability by analyzing the consequences of a counter-insurgency operation and the resulting perception that developed among the local population regarding losses to their ecological resources and to their personal wellbeing.

5.2 Methodology

The study was confined to Swat, a district of Khyber Pakhtunkhwa province (Fig. 5.1) which stretches nearly 200 km from the Malakand Pass to the high reaches of Swat Kohistan and lies between 34°-40′ to 35° N latitude and 72′ to 74°-6′ E longitude. Preliminary visits to study area (Swat Tehsil) were conducted during August 2009 to March 2010 to gather baseline information and location of houses, schools and health facilities. The response of population exposed to war and terrorism was noted in order to assess prevailing war after-effects, wellbeing and over livelihood vulnerability of people living in Swat area. In country, where communication problem arise, local enumerators were consulted who helped the researchers to collect the data in person. The original sample size was 980 male and female individuals, all of whom were of ages 20 years and above. The lower age limit was set at 18 years assuming that respondents of this age and above would effectively narrate the consequence of ongoing conflict in the area. After excluding those questionnaires which had a high proportion of missing responses, the records of 874 respondents were included in the final analysis.

5.2.1 Questionnaire Design

The survey items of the questionnaire comprised of multiple questions related to personal, demographic and household information was used to collect the first-hand information. The structure of questionnaire was finalized after conducting

Fig. 5.1 Map of Pakistan. *Source* UN. Map No. 4181, Rev. 1, January 2004; at: http://www.un.org/Depts/Cartographic/map/profile/pakistan.pdf. Permission to use this map was granted by the United Nations

preliminary visit to Swat Tehsil and taking into account personal communication with locals. The questionnaire comprised of personal information section and response items related to: demographic changes, localized poverty, travel insecurity, health concerns, damages to educational facilities and ecological & agricultural losses. The household heads and local elders were briefed about the study objectives. A local interpreter facilitated the survey sampling in order to avoid communication difficulties. One of the limitations of study despite travelling to Swat Tehsil was to gain trust of local people as most respondents were unwilling to reveal their experiences in the survey.

5.2.2 *Statistical Analysis*

Principal Component Analysis (PCA) was performed on conflict outcome factors on a six point scale. The strength of PCA lies in the fact that it enables researchers to analyse several variables simultaneously to depict emerging trends and inter correlations. In addition the size effect and magnitude of each significant factor is explained on various axes (Park et al. 2002). Since data was collected on five-point scale (see Appendix 5.1) therefore, prior to run PCA, all such variables were checked for internal reliability. However, the three trend depicting variables were judged on a scale 1–10. The lowest end of the scale is 1, and represents the event never happened or minimum effect and vice versa and were used against the following parameters. *Imposed solutions*: (a) to what extent you were consulted about the counter insurgency operation, (b) in present condition this was best option, (c) your neighbourhood communities were properly informed before the operation was formally launched. *Human security*: (a) logistic facility and ample time was provided to flee the area before the onset of counter insurgency operation, (b) during operation, security and safety of your family was improved than before, (c) to what extent security was provided to children and women. *Ecological norms*: (a) protection of water sources and dense housing areas were ensured, (b) damages to fruit trees, fields and storage items, (c) disturbances in sowing, plucking of ripened fruits and their transportation. The reliability of scale was checked using Cronbach's alpha analysis, which provides a useful measure to determine the internal reliability or consistency of the scale (Hendrickson et al. 1993). The test value is expressed as a number between 0 and 1 that describes the extent to which all the items in a test measures the same concept or construct (Tavakol/Dennick 2011). A Cronbach's alpha value greater than 0.7 is considered acceptable indicator of internal consistency. Linear regression (OLS) ordinary least square was performed to see the effect of insurgency and after effects of military operation on livelihood of people residing in Swat region. The application of OLS is particularly useful as it generates coefficients that enable researchers to determine a low to high status of conditions such as poverty, socio-economic, disturbance, etc.

5.3 Results and Discussion

The demographic characteristic and social information of surveyed population revealed that study group comprised of 55 % male members which appeared significantly higher than the other counterpart (Table 5.1). The age distribution was also distinctly varied among respondents of this study with largest group comprised of ages between 20 and 30 years (37.6 %) whereas 240 individuals out of total subjects (n = 874) included in the analysis had their ages above 40 years and hence it is safe to infer that the information obtained reflects a mature response from population of Swat region. The educational background of surveyed group was also heterogeneous with significantly higher proportion of respondents had obtained either primary or high school education as compared to illiterate people (Table 5.1). Local people expressed their educational concerns during survey. They opposed conflict and war against terrorism because it has hampered most of the educational activities in the area. Teachers in schools were reluctant to serve in the region due to prevailing insecurity, especially for female teachers. In Swat and surrounding areas, more than 200 schools were destroyed and hundreds were damaged out which girls' institutions comprised of a maximum number (Table 5.2).

The results of *principal component analysis* (PCA) has distinctly pointed out two important directions in which the peace-making process was heading based on historic events recorded in this study. The first axis has explained the data with the eigenvalues showing a cumulative variance of 35.4 %, which is considerable enough to be regarded as trend indicator. The variables related to first axis has

Table 5.1 Descriptive characteristics of the surveyed population, data collected from July 2009 to February 2010 by the authors

Variable	N (proportion %)	df	*p*-value[a]
	874		
Gender			
Female	395 (45.2)	1	<0.005
Male	479 (54.8)		
Age			
20–30 years	329 (37.6)	2	<0.001
31–40 years	305 (34.9		
>40 years	240 (27.5)		
Marital status			
Married	388 (44.4)	1	<0.001
Unmarried/widow or divorced	486 (55.6)		
Education			
No education	267 (30.5)	2	<0.05
Primary school	342 (39.1)		
High school and above	265 (30.3)		

Source The authors
[a]Non parametric (chi-square) goodness-of-fit test

Table 5.2 To what extent your following livelihood are affected by insurgency and war on terrorism

Factors	Description of variable	Response (%)
Agricultural and ecological losses	1. Blasting damages to trees and fields	41
	2. Disturbance in sowing/plantation	43
	3. Water courses damages	28
Demographic changes	4. Migration of Earning members	62
	5. Well off families leaving the area	71
	6. Teenage out flux for education	38
Educational damages	7. Primary schools damages	44
	8. Terrorism exposure/fear during school time	69
Health concerns	9. Availability & access to doctors	77
	10. Access to health facilities	72
	11. Extent to which health facilities damaged	70
	12. Functional health services in area	28
	13. Availability of female doctors	59
Localized poverty	14. Income reduction previous years	86
	15. Fulfill family requirements	21
	16. Diet purchase satisfaction	34
Travel insecurities	17. Feel secure in daytime mobility	28
	18. Feel secure in night mobility	26
	19. Feel secure while move with family	32
	20. Can leave home unmanned	47

Source The authors

enabled us to refer as peacebuilding efforts whereas the second axis revealed 19.7 % of variations in whole data set and named as conflict perpetuation (see Fig. 5.2). Since the cumulative variance of both these axes is greater than 50 %, hence it seems reasonable to state that PCA has overwhelmingly quantified all major inherently generated trends and explained most of the complexities that emerged due to simultaneous interactions among conflict actions, peace process and local ecological factors.

A1 = Blasting damages to trees and fields
A2 = Disturbance in sowing/plantation
A3 = Water courses damages
D1 = Earning members migration
D2 = Well off families leaving the area
D3 = Teenage out flux for education
E1 = Primary schools damages
E2 = Terrorism exposure/fear during school time
H1 = Availability & access to doctors

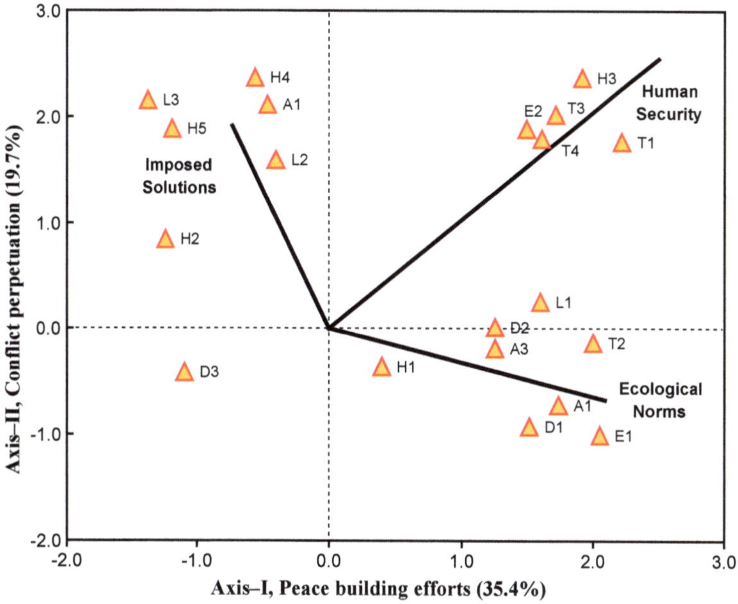

Fig. 5.2 Principal Component Analysis (PCA) for variables related to conflict exposure and resulting perception developed among population of Swat livelihood. *Source* The authors

H2 = Access to health facilities
H3 = Extent to which health facilities damaged
H4 = Functional health services in area
H5 = Availability of female doctors
L1 = Income reduction previous years
L2 = Fulfill family requirements
L3 = Diet purchase satisfaction
T1 = Feel secure in daytime mobility
T2 = Feel secure in night mobility
T3 = Feel secure while move with family
T4 = Can leave home unmanned

There seems a strong perception developed among local population due to prevailing conditions and consequent threats to their family lives, personal belonging and materials associated with their earning. All encompasses into single most important vector emerged as 'human insecurity' in our PCA results (Fig. 5.2). In these results, length of vectors shows the magnitude of the effect while the angle between them states their mutual correlations. A positive relationship was observed for the first two vectors with the PCA axis-I which indicate that human security issues of population in Swat area is directly linked with peacebuilding efforts. The other important factor to be considered for peace efforts related to the ecological wellbeing of the area and integrity of local ecological resources upon which peoples' livelihood relies and is referred to as 'ecological norms'. As conflict perpetuates, there seems a constant negative pressure on ecological norms of the Swat area. PCA results have confirmed this aspect by identifying a relationship between the above two factors, in which the latter appeared to have negative relationship with second axis (axis-II). It seems likely that local conditions demand a thorough understanding of the ecological role in peoples' livelihood, before emphasizing any other conflict resolving solutions. However, third vector (imposed solutions such as counter-insurgency operation) appeared negatively related to PCA axis-I, which is an indication that solutions identified for the area without consulting the local population will not favour to contribute at all in peace building efforts (Fig. 5.2).

Table 5.3 depicts coefficients and significance level derived from ordinary least square regression. All the variables were introduced in three distinct blocks

Table 5.3 Factors affecting peoples' livelihood in Swat during insurgency and after military operation

	Model 1	Model 2	Model 3
	β (SE)	β (SE)	β (SE)
Socio-demographic			
Family size (>4 persons)	−0.113 (0.021)**	−0.072 (0.029)*	−0.021 (0.030)
Gender (male)	−0.382 (0.609)	−1.113 (0.511)*	−0.475 (0.506)
Migration	−4.681 (0.596) ***	−5.003 (0.499) ***	−5.015 (0.487) ***
Poverty	−3.743 (0.604) ***	−3.030 (0.524)**	−3.580 (0.518)**
Conflict based constraints			
Military action		3.624 (0.315)***	3.225 (0.311) ***
Interference in life		0.443 (0.155)**	0.352 (0.151) *
Living conditions		−0.752 (0.060) ***	−0.697 (0.060) **
Life threat		−0.552 (0.090) ***	−0.413 (0.088) **
Economic distress		1.649 (0.169)***	1.580 (0.186) ***
Violence witnessed		0.334 (0.142)**	0.312 (0.147) *
Damages–ecological educational			
Land disturbance			0.114 (0.230)
Plantation hurdles			1.304 (0.197) ***
Revenue decrease from orchids			0.565 (0.121)**
Lack of health services			0.698 (0.045)*
Damages to schools			2.141 (0.523)**
Constant	26.27	29.52	31.27
R^2	0.17	0.36	0.45

Source The authors
Regression coefficients and standard errors performed by ordinary least square (OLS) to predict livelihood dissatisfaction
$*p < 0.05$, $**p < 0.01$, $***p < 0.001$

comprising the respective regression models. In the first model, only socio-demographic variables were analysed. In Model 1 we found that large families with more than three children, along with aged parents, had enormous difficulties in sustaining their livelihood—a significant negative impact was observed among such families. Similarly the other demographic characteristic (gender–female) had revealed rising concerns as in absence of male member. Such families faced a hard time coping with the prevailing conflict situation. In Model 2, both family size and gender continue to have a significant relationship with livelihood conditions. In Model 3, these factors are no longer significant, as the overarching effect of migration and confounded poverty has dominated overall socio-demographic dynamics of the area. In addition, both migration and poverty showed a significant effect in all three models (Table 5.3).

In Model 2, we introduced conflict-based constraints. All of these predictor variables appeared significant in explaining the livelihood dissatisfaction for Swat area population. The families with earning sources dependent on ecological conditions such as fruit crop and their plucking, packaging and transportation to other parts of Pakistan expressed high level of dissatisfaction with life and reported themselves becoming gradually poor. Since the insurgency in the areas was prolonged to several years and to date peace has not yet been fully restored, exposure to terrorism appeared to be a source of major distress for the general population. Consequently, life threat and violence witnessed appeared significant causes of peoples' dissatisfaction in the area (Table 5.3).

The variables pertaining to ecological and educational damages introduced in Model 3 revealed an increase in explained variance to 31 %. Compared to other social and demographic conditions, a different influence on the livelihood was observed upon regressing damage related variables. Respondents in the Swat area who expressed greater dissatisfaction were inclined to protect their crops, orchid farms and plantation timing. In addition, their children were unable to attend school either due to destruction of educational facilities or fear of child kidnapping. The ongoing conflict in the area and resulting military actions to counter terrorism has created an environment in which people's attempt to both protect their earning mechanism and educational future of their children has failed. This is probably the reason that most of the damage related variables showed a significant effect on conditions for livelihood in among the Swat area population.

Serious political interest in sustainable peace efforts has not yet been triggered in Pakistan. It did not take long for attention to focus on local ecological conditions before any concrete steps may be introduced, as it was commonly known that dimensions of ecological landscape are the prime asset of the area that needed to be preserved as a priority. Similar to many conflict prone areas, the findings presented here demonstrate that human equality of Swat community is inextricably linked with environmental quality. Both the PCA and regression results have revealed that repercussions of conflict have a negative influence on environmental degradation and eventually on social conditions. Therefore, to make them sustainable, the population of Swat must be equipped with apparent means of social and environmental justice to resolve the conflict. This concept of environmental peace making

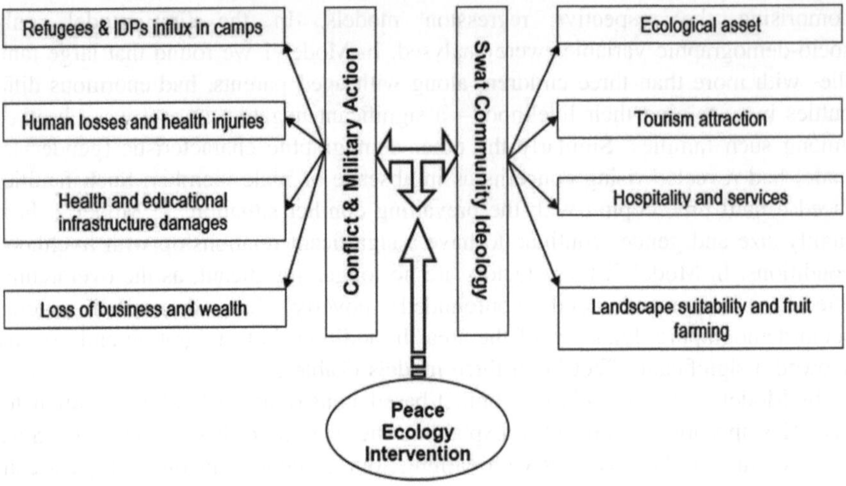

Fig. 5.3 Coherence between peace efforts and public distress issues may prove an effective conflict resolving intervention strategy. *Source* The authors

has echoed worldwide (Agyeman et al. 2003; Amster 2009). In a broader context, the war against terrorism has generated chaos in the whole region, and now many areas in Pakistan including Swat are gripped with terrorism and conflict. However, a critical look at the ecological dimensions of prevailing militancy enables us to understand that both social and environmental systems must be simultaneously restored to make any peace process successful (Fig. 5.3).

There is significant evidence to show that mere claims of peace effort are not enough. There may be something more substantial such as ecological dimensions and human suffering evoked by devastating. The ecology of Swat region must not be overlooked while searching for peace initiatives. Ali (2007) emphasizes that environmental issues can play a role in providing sustainable peace, regardless of whether they are in fact part of the original conflict. Ali observes that positive exchanges and trust-building gestures are a consequence of managing shared environmental threats, and that a focus on common environmental harms can be very successful in leading to cooperative outcomes.

Although numerous reports in media have pointed to grave problems in the Swat region, rarely are the ecological concerns analysed. The post 9/11 era has brought several unprecedented issues to the region which have gradually created unbearable situation for local residents. Our results have summarized these issues and it seems that agricultural based lifelines of the people has severely affected. Regression analysis has confirmed that majority of people who earned money using ecological resources and agricultural productivity are unable to use their land for sowing crops, fruit harvesting and export of their products due to perpetuating conflict. The people have witnessed, on several occasions, complete isolation especially when militants took over the control of this region. The spill over effects were felt in the rest of

Pakistan, for example a massive price hike observed when the arrival of fruits from war-hit Swat and adjacent areas were totally suspended (Ali 2010: 19).

The militants and troublemakers can be indulged by sharing knowledge on how to use vast ecological resources of the area, and offered employment opportunity which will ultimately serve to foster the development of sustainable peace process if both environmental conservation and agricultural production can be facilitated. Such a process would serve to incubate political activities based on equitable social relations (Wittman 2007: 124) and has the potential to (in time) transform into cooperative agricultural initiatives in which local populations may form mutual relation with insurgents on the basis of knowledge sharing to follow an ecological peace plan (Goldman 2007: 336).

It remains to be seen as to whether use of force as a peace initiative taken by the government to curb terrorism and conflict in the area, as an alien solution without consulting the local community and without considering their ecological conditions, can be successful. If not, modifications in the peace plan through considering the ecological environment of the area along with input of local community would be imperative before any counter-insurgency is enacted against terrorism and conflict in other areas. Such an effort to restore peace that might be considered a just treatment, may be all that is required.

5.4 Conclusions

Most of the ecological disturbance indicators obtained in our study were self-reported. Besides being reflective, these indicators were effective in capturing environmental changes perceived by local people during invasion of terrorists, their occupation of Swat and subsequent counter-insurgency operation. There are two distinct facts that have emerged from our study. Firstly, the militants and religious extremists have brought not only a reign of terror in whole Swat valley but also severely undermined the local environment which is closely linked with earning and livelihood of people in the area. Secondly, there is lack of trust by local population on peace efforts carried out by the government. Swat inhabitants were unanimously in favour of conflict resolution. Inevitably, however, their just demand was to avoid warfare and militarization. In their opinion, peace initiatives have so far brought destructive consequences for their environment and to their vast ecological resources. Evidence brought in this study as to the violation of ecological norms during terrorist invasion and counter-insurgency operation in Swat demands that such thought processes and decision-making while tackling conflict resolution be re-considered. Undoubtedly the intentions behind the counter insurgency operation were good, however, the crux of the matter was the sensitive association between people's livelihood and their ecological base, which should have been protected at every cost. We conclude upon analyzing the Swat peace efforts and for future similar scenarios, that environmental preservation should be treated at par to human security as a prerequisite for peace achievement.

Appendix 5.1

On a scale 1–5 (1 = Strongly agree, 2 = slightly agree, 3 = neither agree or disagree, 4 = partially disagree, 5 = strongly disagree) how would you describe the following conditions during terrorists occupation in your area and subsequent counter-insurgency operation.

1. Threats to life increased manifold
2. Economic conditions remained unaffected
3. You had minimum exposure to violence
4. Your land remained undisturbed
5. Plantation schedule remained undisturbed
6. Orchid based revenue increased
7. Health services remained functional
8. Counter-insurgency action was the best strategy
9. Decreased access to health facilities
10. Drastic reduction in functional health services
11. Reduced availability of female doctors
12. Blasting damages to trees and fields
13. Severe damages to water courses
14. Increase trend in migration of earning family members
15. Well off families leaving the area
16. Increase trend in teenage out flux for education
17. Your life remained normal
18. Living conditions disturbed severely
19. Schools remained functional
20. Persistent feeling exposure to terrorism and violence
21. Rising sense of insecurity in daytime mobility
22. Rising sense of insecurity in night mobility
23. Decreased availability and access to doctors
24. Drastic reduction in earning than previous years
25. Inability to fulfil family requirements
26. Inability to purchase adequate food items
27. Rising sense of insecurity while moving with family
28. Situation permits you to leave home unmanned.

References

Agyeman, Julian; Bullard, Robert D.; Evans, Bob, 2003: "Towards just sustainabilities: Perspectives and possibilities", in: Julian (Ed.): *Just sustainabilities: Development in an unequal world* (London: Earthscan): 323–325.

Ahmad, Mushtaq; Sultana, Shazia; Fazl-i-Hadi, Syed; Ben Hadda, Taibi; Rashid, Sofia, Zafar, M; Khan, Mir Ajab; Khan, Muhammad; Yaseen, Ghulam, 2014: "An ethnobotanical study of

medicinal plants in high mountainous region of Chail valley (District Swat-Pakistan)", in: *Journal of Ethnobiology and Ethnomedicine,* 10,36: 1–18.
Ali, H. Saleem (Ed.), 2007: *Peace Parks: Conservation and Conflict Resolution* (MIT Press).
Amster, Randall, 2009: "Pax Gaia: The Ecology of War, Peace, and How to Get from Here to There. In Building Cultures of Peace: Transdisciplinary Voices of Hope and Action", in: Amster, Randall; Ndura Ouedraogao Elavie (Eds.): *Building Cultures of Peace: Transdisciplinary Voices of Hope and Action* (London: Cambridge Scholars Publishing): 39–73.
Conca, Ken; Dabelko Geoffrey D., (Eds.), 2002: *Environmental Peacemaking* (Washington: Woodrow Wilson Center Press and Baltimore: Johns Hopkins University Press).
Dalby, Simon, 1992: "Security, Modernity, Ecology: The Dilemmas of Post-Cold War Security Discourse", in: *Alternatives,* 17,1: 95–134.
Deudney, Daniel, 1990: "The Case Against Linking Environmental Degradation and National Security", in: *Millennium Journal of International Studies,* 19,3: 461–476.
Galtung, Johan, 1985: "Twenty-Five Years of Peace Research: Ten Challenges and Some Responses", in: *Journal of Peace Research,* 22,2: 141–158.
Goldman, Rafi, 2007: "Palestine and Israel: A Co-operative Approach to Conflict Resolution", in: Emmanuel, Joy; MacPherson, Ian (Eds.): *Co-operatives and the Pursuit of Peace* (B.C Victoria: New Rochdale Press): 335–340.
Hamayun, Muhammad; Khan, Sumera; Afzal, Sohn; Eun, Young; Lee, In-Jung; 2006: "Folk Medicinal Knowledge and Conservation Status of Some Economically Valued Medicinal Plants of District Swat, Pakistan", in: *Lyonia,* 11,2: 101–113.
Hendrickson, Anthony, R.; Massey, Patti; Cronan, D.; Timothy, Paul, 1993: "On the Test-Retest Reliability of Perceived Usefulness and Perceived Ease of Use Scales", in: *MIS Quarterly,* 17,2: 227–230.
Khaliq, Fazal, 2013: *Peaches and plums: From Swat, with love.* The Express Turbine.
Park, Hee Sun; Dailey, René; Lemus, Daisy, 2002: "The Use of Exploratory Factor Analysis and Principal Components Analysis in Communication Research", in: *Human Communication Research,* 28,4: 562–577.
Rashid, Audil; Adnan, Mian Nazish, 2009: "Pakistan's Refugees Face Uncertain Future", in: *The Lancet,* 374, 9683: 13–14.
Samad, Rafi, Us, 2011: *The Grandeur of Gandhara: The Ancient Buddhist Civilization of the Swat, Peshawar, Kabul and Indus Valleys* (New York: Algora Publishing).
Saqib, Raheel; Tachibana, Satoshi, 2014: "Contribution of Agricultural and Forestry Extension Services to Inclusive Extension System in North-West Pakistan: A Case Study of Mansehra and Swat Districts of Khyber Pakhtunkhwa Province", in: *Journal of Agricultural Extension and Rural Development,* 6,6: 175–187.
Tavakol, Mohsen; Dennick, Reg, 2011: "Making Sense of Cronbach's alpha", in: *International Journal of Medical Education,* 2: 53-55.
Wenden L, Anita (Ed.), 2012: *Educating for a Culture of Social and Ecological Peace* (New York: Suny Press).
Wittman, Hannah, 2007: "Planting Peace: MST Co-operatives and Agrarian Justice in Brazil", in: Emmanuel, Joy; MacPherson, Ian (Eds.): *Co-operatives and the Pursuit of Peace* (B.C Victoria: New Rochdale Press): 121-146.

Chapter 6
Structure of Discrimination in Japan's Nuclear Export—A Case of Ninh Thuan Power Plant in Vietnam

Michiko Yoshii

Abstract Japan is preparing to export nuclear power plants to Vietnam from 2015 onwards, based on a deal between the Japanese and Vietnamese governments in 2010 that has remained unchanged even after the disaster in the Fukushima Daiichi Nuclear Power Plant in March 2011. This paper highlights the Vietnamese perspective on this project, evidence of discrimination involved in the export of nuclear power plants and the role of researchers studying this issue. This research is based on documentation on Vietnamese homepages and fieldwork undertaken in Vietnam. This study concludes that most Vietnamese have limited access to information on nuclear power plant projects and cannot evaluate such projects. In 2012, some intellectuals promoted the anti-nuclear movement with petitions to the Japanese Prime Minister. Through these exports, Japan has exported a discrimination between big cities and rural areas, between large companies and workers, and between present and future generations. For Vietnam, another structure of discrimination exists against the Cham people, an ethnic minority group in the Ninh Thuan Province. This paper reviews the discriminative structures resulting from the export of nuclear power plants, and places it in the historical context of structures of discrimination between the United States, Japan and Vietnam. The paper discusses the role of Japanese researchers in Vietnamese studies and emphasizes their important role in informing the Vietnamese and Japanese civil societies.

Keywords Nuclear power plant · Vietnam · Ninh Thuan Province · Discrimination · Civil society

---

Dr. Michiko Yoshii, Okinawa University, 555 Kokuba, Naha, Okinawa-ken, 902-8521 Japan; Email: yoshii@okinawa-u.ac.jp.

This work was supported by the Japan Society for the Promotion of Science (JSPS) KAKENHI Grant-in-Aid for Scientific Research (C), Grant Number 26510007 "Studies on earthquake disaster on nuclear power plant and civil society". I express here my sincere gratitude for this support.

Ú.Oswald Spring et al. (eds.), *Regional Ecological Challenges for Peace in Africa, the Middle East, Latin America and Asia Pacific*, The Anthropocene: Politik—Economics—Society—Science 5, DOI 10.1007/978-3-319-30560-8_6

6.1 Introduction

Vietnam's first *nuclear power plant* (NPP) is currently under construction in the southern province of Ninh Thuan. The first two reactors were ordered from Russia. In October 2010, the Vietnamese government decided that Japan should build two reactors for the second site. Japan plans to export the remaining components even after the devastating Fukushima Daiichi NPP disaster in March 2011. This Japanese plant will be constructed in 2015 and 2016,[1] and should be operational by 2021 and 2022.[2]

As Vietnam cannot finance the large costs for the NPP construction Japan will grant an official credit of 1 trillion JPY (nearly 10 billion USD). The Vietnamese staff of the NPP is being trained with funding from the Japanese *Official Development Assistance* (ODA). In November 2012, a portion of the Japanese budget for the reconstruction of East Japan in the event of a big earthquake was spent according to press reports for a feasibility study of the Japanese NPP in Ninh Thuan.[3]

This chapter discusses how the Japanese aid and commerce is been perceived by Vietnamese beneficiaries, and the hidden structures of discrimination exported with this technology. It reviews the nuclear construction project from the Vietnamese perspective, the discrimination exported with it, and the role of researchers investigating this issue. The research relies primarily on websites and blogs accessed from within and outside Vietnam and primarily in Vietnamese; and limited fieldwork with interviews of local residents and intellectuals in big cities was conducted in Vietnam during two trips in 2012. This chapter offers a literature review and case studies on NPPs and exports of nuclear plants (Sect. 6.2), discusses NPP construction from Vietnamese perspectives of three stakeholders: the government, academics, and ordinary citizens (Sect. 6.3), analyses the structures of discrimination associated with these exports (Sect. 6.4) and discusses the role of researchers in this area (Sect. 6.5) (Figs. 6.1 and 6.2).

The analysis presented in this chapter could also be useful for other projects. For example, with regard to the exporting of Japanese NPPs to Turkey. It may also encourage NPP stakeholders to reconsider the validity of such projects, including in other regions of the world where similar projects are being undertaken (Figs. 6.3 and 6.4).

---

[1]Thus initially scheduled, however, Russian project being postponed until 2020 as Vietnamese Prime Minister announced in 2014, Japanese project's schedule also can be changed.

[2]Jiji.dot.com (時事ドットコム), 2012: "Construction of Vietnamese nuclear power plant, maybe postponed = ordered to Japan, worry on security—Minister of Science and Technology".

[3]Tokyo Shimbun (東京新聞), 2012:震災復興予算　原発輸出調査にも流用 (Budget for reconstruction from earthquake—misappropriated for study on export of nuclear power plant); at: http://www.tokyo-np.co.jp/s/article/2012102990071411.html (30 October 2012).

Fig. 6.1 Map of Vietnam. *Source* Author

6.2 Review of Literature and Documentation

6.2.1 Documentation in Vietnam

As no academic research papers were published in Vietnamese on NPPs imports from Japan, this chapter relies on press reports and articles from Vietnamese and non-Vietnamese internet sources. Most reports discuss problems on the introduction of a NPP in Vietnam, without any reference to their import from Japan.

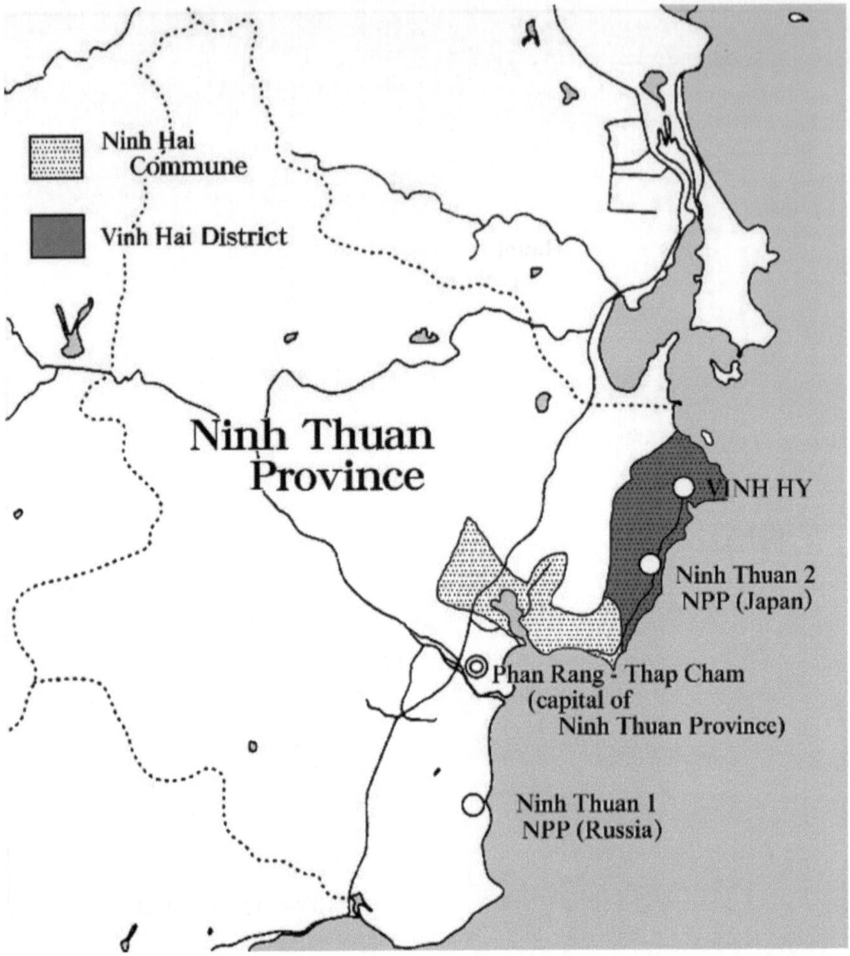

Fig. 6.2 Map of Ninh Thuan Province. *Source* Author

The Vietnamese government's perspective relies on websites of the official press, such as *Tuoi Tre Online*, *Bao Dien Tu Kien Thuc*, *Vietnamnet*, *VNExpress*, *Bao Dien Tu Sai Gon Tiep Thi*, etc. that are all censored. But not all agree with the NPP construction project. Some articles published on unofficial websites and blogs by Vietnamese intellectuals are cautious for or against this project. Among them are Nguyen Khac Nhan, Pham Duy Hien and Hoang Phu Xuan. Two groups, one including Nguyen The Hung, Nguyen Hung and Nguyen Xuan Dien, and another including Nguyen Hung and Tran Hoai Nam published many articles. This study relies heavily on their articles.

Fig. 6.3 Thai An Hamlet, Ninh Thuan, construction site of Japanese NPP. *Source* Tho Mai (2012). Permission to use this photo was granted by Tho Mai

Fig. 6.4 Vinh Truong Hamlet, Ninh Thuan, construction site of Russian NPP. *Source* Inrasara.com. Permission to use this photo was granted by Mr. Inrasara

6.2.2 Documentation in Japan

Similarly, in Japan there are no academic papers, to my knowledge, on the export of Japanese NPPs to Vietnam.[4] Books that discuss NPPs in general dedicate only few lines to the Japanese exports of NPPs. An earlier Japanese version of this text (Yoshii 2013) relied on articles in electronic business magazines, general reviews or newspapers, including websites or NGO magazines that oppose these exports, such as *FoE Japan*, *Mekong Watch*, *No Nukes Asia Forum*, *ODA Reform Network*, etc., on study meetings on this theme by these NGOs, and it referred to their documents. It also reviewed documents by researchers in Vietnam on their government's nuclear energy policy. It analysed documents of public forums after the Great Earthquake in 2011 that discuss the NPP exports to Vietnam where Japanese

[4]During the time the paper was being edited the authors discovered the publishing of important academic studies such as: Sakamoto (2013) and Ito/Yoshii (2015).

researchers argued for or against these exports (Koguchi 2012; 6.4) and it relied on *Asahi Shimbun*, *Tokyo Shimbun* and *Jiji dot com* because of their rapid reporting of information from Vietnam.

6.2.3 Defining Discrimination

The topic of discrimination has been extensively discussed in the academic literature and many definitions are available. UNESCO's "Convention against Discrimination in Education" (adopted in 1960) stated in Art.1,1 that "the term 'discrimination' includes any distinction, exclusion, limitation or preference which, being based on race, colour, sex, language, religion, political or other opinion, national or social origin, economic condition or birth, has the purpose or effect of nullifying or impairing equality of treatment in education and in particular" and that it referred to "inflicting on any person or group of persons conditions which are incompatible with the dignity of man". This definition relies on the French sociologist Memmi (1996). The Japanese sociologist Yamada (1996: 77) stated that: "…discrimination is to put members of one social category into a group and consider them as special persons with an inferior value, to despise or abuse them".

Some Japanese studies refer to specific cases of discrimination involving the construction of nuclear power plants. For example, Yagi (1989: 5–36) claims that "there are four structures of discrimination relating to and involving nuclear power plants, including (1) exposure to radiation of local workers in uranium mines and the inhabitants living in these areas, (2) discrimination of 'under-populated' areas due to the location of nuclear power plants, (3) exposure to radiation of sub-contracted workers in the reactor core, and (4) sacrifice of 'remote [regions]' in relation to nuclear fuel waste". That is, constructing NPPs can be considered an act of discrimination against workers, civilians and land.

Expressions such as "inhabitants living close to uranium mines", "those who live in under-populated areas where nuclear power plants are located", "those who are sub-contracted workers" and "those who live near nuclear fuel waste storage or retreatment centres" refer to the 'social origin' of a people, as defined by the UNESCO Convention (1960). They also refer to "members of one social category", as defined by Yamada. An analysis of these definitions suggests that these people are "despised or abused" (Yamada 1996) by being forced to work in unsafe environments where they are exposed to radioactivity, or by accepting to live in close proximity to a retreatment centre or radioactive waste in their village.

This study discusses this structure of discrimination and transforms it into a structure of opposition: 'those who profit from discrimination' versus 'those who are discriminated against and whose human dignity is damaged'. Thus, Yagi's (1989) second idea of discrimination of 'under-populated' areas due to the location of NPPs, is represented by: 'big cities which consume a high amount of electricity' versus 'communities in remote areas where NPPs are located'. In the same way, Yagi's third point regarding exposure to radiation of sub-contracted workers in the reactor core can be represented by 'big companies making profits from NPP' versus 'sub-contracted workers exposed to radiation'. This text analyses these opposing structures focusing on evident notions of discrimination they represent.

6.2.4 Comparing This Study with Others

This study uses Vietnamese sources translated into Japanese or English. The use of information written in Vietnamese allowed a detailed analysis how the Vietnamese perceive the import of an NPP from Japan. Correspondents from Japanese newspapers have also collected information from Vietnamese sites. Some Japanese NGO staff members have conducted fieldwork at construction sites. As a researcher specializing in Vietnamese studies who speaks Vietnamese, this author could review the material even when translations were unavailable. This study not only to presents the objective facts on this research issue, but it also clarifies the structures that underpin these facts, and attempts to make an ethical and moral evaluation in analysing the role of experts, including the author herself.

6.3 NPP Construction from the Vietnamese Perspective

6.3.1 The Vietnamese Government

The Dalat Nuclear Research Institute in Vietnam was founded in 1961 with US aid to the former Republic of (South) Vietnam. Its research—with government support—has been ongoing since 1976. Economic growth pushed by the *Doi Moi* policy resulted in an exponential increase in the demand for electric energy. In March 2011 the government adopted its "7th National Plan of Development of Electric Power", outlining its position on the development of mixed energy resources such as petroleum, natural gas, nuclear and renewable energies. In line with this Plan, the "Law on Nuclear Energy" was adopted in 2008 and the government continues to establish a system for the construction of NPPs. The government plans to build 14 reactors before 2030, which is projected to supply 8 % of the country's total electricity needs (Endo 2012).[5]

The import of NPPs from Russia and Japan is strongly promoted by Prime Minister Nguyen Tan Dung. He claimed that the "accident in Fukushima has been

[5]Endo (2012) also points out that the population, national economic growth as well as the needs in electricity are all overestimated in the Vietnamese project.

completely concluded. Japan, as well as Russia with its accident in Chernobyl, will export to us absolutely safe NPP, since both of them have learnt important lessons from their accidents."

On the other hand, Nguyen Quan, the Minister of Science and Technology, officially commented in April 2012 that "Vietnam lacks human resources; we will not be able to start the operation of the NPPs as planned earlier." This shows that government representatives are not completely united on the issue of NPP construction. The following is a report of the Minister's statements, as translated into English, on the issue.

6.3.1.1 Perspective on the Ninh Thuan Nuclear Power Plant

"Minister of Science and Technology Nguyen Quan talked with the press about the Ninh Thuan nuclear power plants."… "Do you think that the project will commence in 2014 and be put into operation in 2020 as scheduled?"… "According to schedule, in 2014 we will start the construction of the first plant. However, the starting point depends on preparatory work, including infrastructure. Therefore, we should not decide to commence the project as scheduled. It is more important to prepare well: in terms of legal, regulatory, infrastructure and human resources." … "Human resource development is an important step in preparing the infrastructure for the development of nuclear power in Vietnam. But it seems that at this moment, maybe we have implemented it too slowly?"[6]

The author interprets these statements, as if the Minister prepares some excuses in advance for future delays of the project, and he is not the most convinced promoter of the nuclear project. In October and November 2012, Prime Minister Nguyen Tan Dung apologized to the National Assembly for the failure of his economic policy. It was speculated that he may resign from his duties. These facts allude to the weakening of his political power, and suggest that the import of the NPP is highly contingent on the political environment (Fig. 6.5).

In official media articles pushed for the NPP project. Some articles are not clearly opposed. For example, *Tuoi Tre online*, an official media site, posted an article in August 2012 on "Construction of NPP: let us learn from Fukushima", discussed the advice of the *International Atomic Energy Agency* (IAEA) as being relevant in the Vietnamese context. It argued that it is necessary to create an independent agency for security and learn lessons from the accident in Fukushima.[7] Although the article does not oppose the NPP project, it is still somewhat equivocal. On the same website, another article on "Ninh Thuan NPP: 6 confusing problems"

---

[6]6th Annual Nuclear Power in Asia, 2014: "Ninth Thuan nuclear power plants may not be kicked off as schedule".

[7]Tuổi Trẻ online, 2012a: "Xây nhà máy điện hạt nhân: lưu ý bài học Fukushima(Construction of nuclear power plant: Let us learn from Fukushima); at: http://tuoitre.vn/Giao-duc/Khoa-hoc/508192/Xay-nha-may-dien-hat-nhan-Luu-y-bai-hoc-Fukushima.html (29 August 2012).

Fig. 6.5 Relocation site built for Russian NPP. *Source* Inrasara.com. Permission to use this photo was granted by Mr. Inrasara

that was published in August 2012[8] points to difficulties of moving existing residents to relocation sites. In September 2012, an article on "100 h of Dalat Nuclear Research Institute" was published, showing pictures of research staff working beside nuclear reactors and wearing beach sandals. This article was quoted on many unofficial sites and the government was severely criticized for its lack of security management, e.g. "In NPP of Vietnam, workers should operate with beach sandals on their foot".[9]

6.3.1.2 Vietnamese Intellectuals

Since Vietnam is a socialist country with a single-party dictatorship and has very limited freedom of association, there are no anti-nuclear demonstrations or meetings, as in Japan. However, there are academic scholars who write on unofficial blogs and share research and information on anti-nuclear movements with overseas readers. These unofficial internet sites cannot directly be accessed on the internet in Vietnam, except with a special address (Fig. 6.6).

However, there are still people who oppose NPP construction, including not only anti-communist Vietnamese in the diaspora, such as those who escaped Vietnam during or after the Vietnam War. Opponents can also be found among those close to the Communist Party leadership, intellectuals in Vietnam, and cadet members of the Communist Party. Some senior leaders, already retired, know that

[8]Tuổi Trẻ online, 2012b: "Dự án hạt nhân Ninh Thuận: 6 khó khăn vướng mắc" (Project of Ninh Thuan Nuclear Power Plant: 6 confusing problems); at: http://tuoitre.vn/Chinh-tri-Xa-hoi/505336/Du-an-dien-hat-nhan-Ninh-Thuan-6-kho-khan-vuong-mac.html (8 August 2012).

[9]Tuổi Trẻ online, 2012c: "100 giờ ở lò phần ứng hạt nhân Đà Lạt" (100 h of Dalat Nuclear Research Institute); at: http://tuoitre.vn/Chinh-tri-Xa-hoi/Phong-su-Ky-su/504072/100-gio-o-lo-phan-ung-hat-nhan-Da-Lat.html (19 December 2012).

Fig. 6.6 Nguyen Khac Nhan at Grenoble. *Source* Author

there is no more political danger for them to write in opposition to such projects. Nguyen Minh Thuyet, a retired university professor and ex-deputy of the National Assembly, published a paper on his internet site entitled: "We should not bet people's life on NPP!"[10] He opposed the NPP project while acting as deputy, and then retired after having failed to stop it. In a similar vein, Pham Duy Hien, ex-director of the Dalat Nuclear Research Institute, stated in his article: "Lack of experts becomes an obstacle for the development of NPP." He advocated that the project should be postponed for ten years, as Nguyen Quan, the Minister of Science and Technology, had also advised.[11]

Vietnamese living overseas do not hesitate to criticize the Vietnamese import of NPPs. For example, Nguyen Khac Nhan, an ex-staff member of Electricity Corporation of Vietnam and a former advisor to *Electricité de France*, who is currently an emeritus professor at Grenoble Institute of Technology in France, published a paper entitled: "Do not make Ninh Thuan a second Fukushima."[12]

[10]Nguyễn Minh Thuyệt (2012) Không nên đặt cuộc (cá độ) tính mạng dân tộc (với nhà máy điện nhạt nhân)! (We should not bet people's life to NPP!)http://xuandienhannom.blogspot.fr/2012/05/gs-nguyen-minh-thuyet-khong-nen-at-cuoc.html (26 June 2012).

[11]Phạm Duy Hiền (2012) Tình trạng thiếu chuyên gia sẽ cản trở sự phát triển điện hạt nhân(Lack of experts becomes an obstacle for development of NPP)http://www.viet.rfi.fr/viet-nam/20120521-tinh-trang-thieu-chuyen-gia-se-can-tro-su-phat-trien-dien-hat-nhan (26 June 2012).

[12]Nguyễn Khắc Nhẫn (2012) Không thể để Ninh Thuận trở thành Fukushima(Do not make Ninh Thuan a second Fukushima)http://chimbaobao.wordpress.com/2012/03/16/khong-the-de-ninh-thuan-tro-thanh-fukushima/ (26 June 2012).

These intellectuals have offered five practical reasons to oppose the NPP projects. First, NPPs are not profitable. Importing NPPs from Russia or Japan requires huge loans, aside from waste treatment issues and large amounts of money lost to corruption. Thus, the project cost does not justify the investment. Secondly, developed countries have a tendency to stop constructing NPPs. Thirdly, NPPs are simply too dangerous. The location of the NPP proposed in Vietnam is very close to the city of Phan Rang-Thap Cham, with a population of 180,000. Although the area has very few earthquakes, it is still an area subject to the risks of tsunamis. In the event of an accident, information would not be smoothly communicated to the population. Fourth, there are many possible sources of electricity, such as solar, hydraulic, wind, etc., much better for health and environment and the region of Ninh Thuan has a big potential for such renewable energy resources. Fifth, there is a lack of human resources trained in the construction, operation and security management of an NPP.

In May 2012, intellectuals who were critical of NPPs organized a campaign on the blog of Nguyen Xuan Dien, a researcher at the National Research Institute of Hannom. The campaign sought to collect signatures from persons opposed to the NPP project, in a letter addressed to the Japanese Prime Minister Noda, asking him to cease the export of NPPs to Vietnam. The letter noted that government support for such projects is "irresponsible, inhuman and immoral".[13] The petition was signed by 626 citizens in and outside Vietnam, with their real home addresses and full names, and the letter was sent to Tokyo. The blog organizer, Dr. Nguyen Xuan Dien, received threats from a group of retired ex-soldiers and was forced to remove the letter from his blog. Dr. Dien was also the subject of a criminal investigation from the Public Security Police. In the end, he was required to pay a penalty.

Why was this letter by the petitioners addressed to the Japanese Prime Minister and not to their own government? In the Japanese context, citizens conduct campaigns against the government when they want to stop the import of a product from a foreign country. However, in the Vietnamese context, it is difficult to oppose government policy, considering the limits on freedom of expression. For this reason, the letter was first addressed directly to Japanese stakeholders and was sent to Japanese private companies. These companies, which produce materials for NPPs, stated in response that they only sell such products because Vietnam wishes to buy them. Dr. Dien and others then took the desperate measure of writing to the Japanese government to request an end to the export of NPP materials. Dr. Dien received no reply from Prime Minister Noda.

---

[13]Bảovệtổquốc(Defense of fatherland)(2012a) List of 624 signatories collected from 14 May 2012,.http://baovetoquoc.blogspot.com.au/2012/06/list-of-624-signatories-collected-from.html (12 December 2012).

6.3.2 General Citizens

Media reports concerning the construction of NPPs have stated that all Vietnamese citizens know about the accident in Fukushima, but would argue as follows: "I hear that it was totally conclusive and that Japan will construct an NPP for us that will absolutely never cause an accident, because they learned a lesson from their experience." This opinion is an exact reflection of the government's propaganda. A couple of peasants with two small babies stated that: "we worry about radioactivity, but there is nothing we can do if the government so decided. We will move to a relocated village 1 km from here." We can also observe that the information concerning NPPs is not equally received by the population (Nakai 2012).

A woman aged 40 living 20 km from the NPP in Phan Rang-Thap Cham City said, "When I watch programmes on radioactivity on TV, I worry, but the next day I forget about it. I am so worried about how to earn an income for daily meals for the family." Her husband is a migrant daily worker in a factory and she has six children. Her profession is collecting waste to resell. Her husband will surely go and work at the NPP when construction starts. They have no choice to say whether they agree with the project. With no personal computer at home and no connection to the internet, ordinary citizens are living, for the most part, in similar social situations.

6.4 Structure of Discrimination Involved in the Export of Japanese NPPs

Following the NPP disaster in Japan, a structure of discrimination could be observed between 'big cities which consume large amounts of electricity (e.g. Tokyo)' versus 'communities in remote areas where NPPs were located (e.g. Fukushima)'. In addition, there appears to be a structure of discrimination between 'big companies making profit from NPPs' versus 'sub-contracted workers exposed to radiation'.

It appears likely that these two types of discrimination will be exported to Vietnam from Japan in the same manner. Thus, the export will establish a structure of discrimination between 'big cities which consume large amounts of electricity (e.g. Hanoi or Ho Chi Minh City)' versus 'communities in remote areas where NPPs will be located e.g. Ninh Thuan)', and between 'big companies (and people) making profit from NPP' versus 'sub-contracted workers exposed to radiation'. This author added 'people making profit from NPP' because of the issue of corruption in Vietnam, as the Vietnamese intellectuals quote in Sect. 6.3.2.

In Vietnam, we need to add a new structure of discrimination that is evident; 'the majority Kinh people makes decisions concerning the NPP project' versus 'the minority indigenous Cham people, who are forced to observe the NPP on their former territory'. This structure is very similar to that of US Military bases in Japan and the indigenous Ryuku people, who mainly reside in the Okinawa Islands.

Fig. 6.7 Inrasara, Cham poet opposing to NPP project and the construction plan at Thai An Hamlet. *Source* Author

The total number of Cham people in the whole of Vietnam is 160,000, of whom 70,000 live in Ninh Thuan Province, representing 12 % of the total population of this province (Ito 2012). They are descendants of the inhabitants of the Kingdom of Champa, which prospered in central Vietnam before it was destroyed in the 19th century by the Kinh people invading from the North. With numerous temples and cultural vestiges, Ninh Thuan is an important place for the Cham people. There is even a temple with a god that protects people from tsunamis, located in the exact place where the Russian NPP will be built!

Many Chams were signatories of the petition against NPPs (Sect. 6.3.2). This included both those living abroad and those living in Ninh Thuan Province. Many articles opposing the NPP have been published on their blogs, such as 'Inrasara.com',[14] a Cham poet's blog (Fig. 6.7).

This export shows the structure of discrimination by itself. In the discussion between Japanese researchers, one researcher said: "I am theoretically against NPP. The fact that we have no resolution for waste retreatment is a logical failure" (Koguchi 2012: 201). Thus, all debates starts with anti-NPP opinions. However, the same researcher later stated that "if our policy changes into anti-NPP... who will take the responsibility to conduct our reactors to close with the operation of nuclear

[14]Inrasara; at: http://inrasara.com/ (25 April 2015).

decommissioning?" (Koguchi 2012: 201–202). Thus, for the nuclear decommissioning of Japanese reactors, he cannot assume an anti-NPP position. This is in contrast to the position he initially took. He then said that "the problem of NPP in Vietnam should be decided by the Vietnamese government and citizens together in an independent way" (Koguchi 2012: 204).

Finally, the researcher expressed his objective to keep the technology for Japan's own nuclear decommissioning and insisted on exporting NPPs to Vietnam. I do not discuss here whether the import of NPP is decided by the Vietnamese government and citizens in an independent way. It is evident that the logic of this researcher is based on the structure of discrimination between 'developed countries trying to stop NPPs for the security of their own peoples' versus 'developing countries who start introducing NPPs'.

Therefore, the export of Japanese NPPs to Vietnam consists of the export of machineries and technology, as well as structures of discrimination, between 'big cities versus local communities' and 'profiting companies versus workers exposed to radioactivity'. Moreover, given that this NPP will be located in an ethnic minority area, this export creates discrimination between 'the majority people versus the minority'. Finally, the export itself represents discrimination between 'a developed country versus a developing country'.

The discriminative structures do not stop here. An examination of international relations through a broader lens reveals the United States' role in Japan's decision to export NPPs. "The US-Japan Alliance, Anchoring Stability in Asia", generally known as "The 3rd Armitage Report", published in August 2012 by the *Center for Strategic and International Studies* (CSIS), states that: "the cautious resumption of nuclear generation under such conditions is the right and responsible step in our view" (Armitage/Nye 2012: 2).

The authors of this report are Richard Armitage, former Vice-Secretary of State, and Joseph Nye, a professor from Harvard University. In this report, they advocate the need for Japan to restart its nuclear reactors, while also stating that "as China plans to join Russia, South Korea and France in the major leagues of global development in civilian nuclear power, Japan cannot afford to fall behind if the world is to benefit from efficient, reliable, and safe reactors and nuclear services." (Armitage/Nye 2012: 3). This statement alludes to the idea of Japan exporting its NPP in a bid to fulfil the nuclear energy demands of other countries (Fig. 6.8).

The United States' encouragement of Japan to export NPPs to Vietnam implies a structure of discrimination. The United States has ceased to build nuclear reactors on its own territory due to concerns about safety, cost and radioactive waste. However, they have pushed Japan to continue the construction of NPPs. With recent public opinion in Japan showing increasing opposition to NPPs, the construction of new NPPs is becoming difficult there and Japan is thus in its turn trying to export to Vietnam.

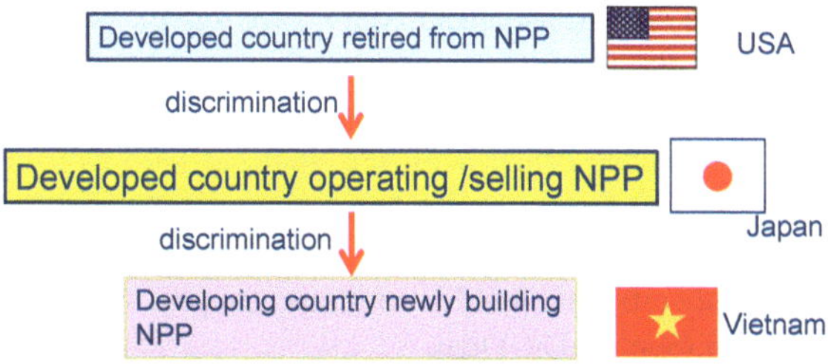

Fig. 6.8 Superimposing structure. *Source* The author

6.5 Role of Researchers

This final section discusses the role of Japanese researchers in addressing the facts highlighted in the above sections. 'Japanese researchers' are referred to as those who know the language and culture of Vietnam well; who can access and understand different internet sites quoted in this study, and are capable of analysing the information in a logical way.

These researchers could assume two main roles, to provide information to Vietnamese citizens and to inform Japanese citizens. This author fully agrees with the scholar quoted earlier that "the problem of NPP in Vietnam should be decided by the Vietnamese government and citizens together in an independent way" (Koguchi 2012: 204). Here, 'independent' means that the Japanese government should not export NPPs to Vietnam by force. The decision of import should come from the free choice of Vietnamese government and its citizens. The problem is that many Vietnamese citizens do not have access to information about NPPs. This NPP project is thus far from "being independently decided by citizens". Moreover, even if citizens have an opinion that diverges from that of the government, the Vietnamese regime does not permit citizens' ideas to be reflected in their policies. Indeed, as we observed above, Dr. Nguyen Xuan Dien, one of the sponsors of the petition addressed to Japanese Prime Minister in June 2012, was punished.

With regard to the second role of researchers to inform Japanese citizens, Vietnamese opinions in opposition to the NPP project are largely published in Vietnamese; they appear on official or unofficial internet sites. There is a need to translate this material into Japanese, thereby enabling Japanese citizens to decide whether their taxes should be used for the export of Japanese NPP technology to Vietnam or for the training of nuclear engineers in Vietnam. They can then decide whether they agree with conducting feasibility studies of NPPs in Ninh Thuan using funding allocated to the reconstruction of East Japan following the Big Earthquake. Thus, it is the researchers' role to provide the taxpaying public with the information needed to make this decision.

In May 2012, as the petition against Japanese NPPs was being circulated in Vietnam, some researchers took rapid action. Campaign letters and calls to sign petitions were translated into Japanese as soon as they appeared on internet sites, and were sent to Japanese NGO, FoE Japan. Dr. Dien was called in by the Public Security Police for an investigation and seemed to be in danger. Meanwhile, another signing campaign was conducted in Japan,[15] with the letter being addressed to the Japanese Prime Minister Noda, as well as to the Vietnamese Prime Minister Nguyen Tan Dung. In the letter, the citizens of Japan expressed their respect and sympathy for the citizens of Vietnam, who had signed the letter with courage. Japanese citizens would continue to pay attention to the affair including the investigation of Dr. Dien.

In Japan, this campaign letter received 1255 signatures in less than two days. Again, a researcher assumed the role of informing Vietnamese citizens about the results. The following reaction of Vietnamese citizens appeared on the unofficial site, "bao ve to quoc":

FoE's support to our campaign of signatures against NPP in Ninh Thuan impressed a large number of our citizens. Mr. Nguyen Hung, engineer, one of the writers of the petition letter to the Japanese government, says in Australia: 'We are so excited to know that Japanese citizens follow our campaign and support us. That was our very objective.'[16]

It can be concluded that researchers have a crucial role to play in connecting the civil societies of both countries. Despite the differences in language and culture, the two civil societies are able to connect if researchers are able to bridge the divide.

6.6 Conclusions

Three main findings emerge from this study. First, views from the Vietnamese perspective regarding the construction of NPPs are from a small group of opposing intellectuals, including those within the government, and a large majority of people without access to adequate information. The opposing intellectuals have attempted to use active campaigns, including using the internet as their main organizing tool.

Secondly, when Japan exports NPPs to Vietnam, it simultaneously exports a structure of discrimination between 'big cities versus local communities' and 'profiting companies versus workers exposed to radioactivity'. This export creates a new structure of discrimination, which may be expressed as 'majority people versus minority people'. Moreover, the export itself involves a structure of discrimination between 'developed countries versus developing countries'. Within a broader

[15]Right for refuge Blog (「避難の権利」ブログ), 2012: "緊急署名:みなさまのお力を!原発輸出にベトナムから抗議" (Emergency signatures: Your cooperation required! Protest from Vietnam for export of nuclear power plant); at: http://hinan-kenri.cocolog-nifty.com/blog/2012/06/post-cd04.html (2 September 2015).

[16]Bảovệtổquốc (Defense of fatherland, 2012b: "Tổ chức Nhật Bản ửng hộ Việt Nam phản đối điện hạt nhân" Japanese organization helps for anti-nuclear movement in Vietnam; at: http://baovetoquoc.blogspot.com.au/2012/06/to-chuc-nhat-ban-ung-ho-viet-nam-phanoi.html (26 June 2012).

historical paradigm, we can situate Japan's export of discrimination within that imposed by the United States, which has pushed Japan to export NPPs. Thus, a superposing structure of a three-way relationship between three nations emerges from this discussion.

Thirdly and finally, Japanese researchers in the area of Vietnamese studies should take on the role of connecting the Japanese and Vietnamese civil societies.[17] Unfortunately, some researchers have assumed the role of encouraging business talks concerning NPP development between the two countries. Such actions are not promoting positive, ethical international relationships, nor promoting international cooperation. Instead, such talks promote the expansion of existing structures of discrimination that this study has sought to critique. These actions, along with the structures of discrimination that are exported along with machineries and technologies, also tarnish the researchers' reputations.

References

Armitage, Richard L.; Nye, Joseph S., 2012: *The U.S.-Japan Alliance—Anchoring Stability in Asia* (Washington, D.C.: Center for Strategic & International Studies, August 2012).

Endo, Satoshi (遠藤聡), 2012:"Vietnamese energy policy in recent years—focused on nuclear power plant project -" (近年のエネルギー政策-原子力発電計画を中心に-).Paper for Japanese Council on Vietnamese Studies (日本ベトナム研究者会議発表資料), Tokyo, 28 July.

Ito, Masako (伊藤正子), 2012: "Rich and natural beach for construction in Vietnam—This is the destination of nuclear power plant" (ベトナムの建設予定地は豊かなビーチここが　原発の輸出先だ),in: *Asahi Shimbun Weekly AERA,* 4 June (Asahi Shimbun Shuppan [朝日新聞出版]): 45.

Ito, Masako (伊藤正子); Yoshii, Michiko (吉井美知子) (Ed.), 2015: *Deception in the Export of Nuclear Technology from Japan to Vietnam: Behind the Scenes of a "Friendship"* (原発輸出の欺瞞-日本とベトナム、「友好」関係の舞台裏)(Tokyo: Akashi Shoten, 明石書店).

Koguchi, Hikota (小口彦太ほか編) (Ed.), 2012: 3.11後の日本とアジア—震災から見えてきたもの (Japan and Asia after March 1—Things appeared from earth-quake)(Tokyo: めこん [Mekong]).

Memmi, Albert (メンミ、アルベール), 1996: 人種差別(Racial discrimination) (Tokyo: 法政大学出版 [Hosei University Publishing House]).

Nakai, Shinsuke (中井信介), 2012: 忍びよる原発～福島の苦悩をベトナムに輸出するのか』 (Nuclear power plant secretly approaching—shall we export suffering of Fukushima to Vietnam? [Documentary film]) (Tokyo: FoE Japan).

Sakamoto, Megumi (坂本恵), 2013: "福島原発事故の教訓からみた、ベトナムへの原発輸出の課題" (Problems of Export of Nuclear Power Plant to Vietnam Viewed from Experiences of Nuclear Disaster in Fukushima), in: 福島大学地域創造 (Fukushima University Regional Creation), 25,1: 44–64.

UNESCO, 1960: "Convention against discrimination in education"; at: <http://www.unesco.org/education/pdf/DISCRI_E.PDF> (25 June 2014).

Yagi, Tadashi (八木 正), 1989: 原発は差別で動く—反原発のもうひとつの視角 (Nuclear Power Plant operates by discrimination—Another view for anti-nuclear power plant) (Tokyo: 明石書店 [Akashi Shoten]).

[17] I do not mention here about the role of Vietnamese researchers, since they have much restriction on their freedom of expression, except those who stay in abroad for life.

Yamada, Tomiaki (山田富秋), 1996: "アイデンティティ管理のエスノメソドロジー"(Ethno-methodology for identity management). in: Kurihara, Rin (栗原彬) (Ed.): 差別の社会理論 (Social logic on discrimination)(Tokyo: 弘文堂 [Kobundo]): 77–99.
Yoshii, Michiko (吉井美知子), 2013 "日本の原発輸出-ベトナムの視点から-" (Export of Japanese Nuclear Power Plant – How it is viewed from Vietnam), in: 三重大学国際交流センター紀要 (Bulletin of Center for International Education and Research, Mie University), 8: 39–53.
Yoshimoto, Yasuko (吉本康子), 2012: "波の神を祀る人々"(People offering prayers for goodness of waves), in: 月刊みんぱく(Monthly Minpaku), 2012, 5: 22-23 (Osaka: 国立民族学博物館 [National Ethnological Museum]): 22–23.

Chapter 7
'Global Hibakusha' and the Invisible Victims of the U.S. Nuclear Testing in the Marshall Islands

Seiichiro Takemine

Abstract Hibakusha is a Japanese term that refers to people who have been exposed to nuclear radiation. This chapter explores what a 'Global Hibakusha' might involve, through the example of invisible victims of United States' testing of nuclear weapons conducted in the Pacific mid-last century. The chapter suggests that the native people's exposure to radiation was fully predictable prior to the 'Castle Bravo' test, thus the effects cannot be considered 'accidental'. The predictability of these effects are arguably the motivation behind the United States conducting the tests in the *Republic of the Marshall Islands* (RMI) rather than near to their homeland. The lingering effects of U.S. nuclear damages in the RMI drawing attention to the long-term effects of nuclear radiation that are often overlooked and which have important implications for ecology and peace. This chapter closes with a call for a new research field of 'Global Hibakusha' within the larger field of peace studies.

Keywords Marshall islands · Bikini · Eniwetok · Rongelap · U.S. nuclear testing · Hibakusha · Exposure to radiation · Radioactive fallout · Nuclear development · The fifth lucky dragon

7.1 Introduction

The year 2015 marks the 70th anniversary of the US nuclear bombings in Hiroshima and Nagasaki. The notion that Japan is the only country to have suffered atomic bombings is often repeated in discussion about nuclear issues. It is true that nuclear weapons have not been used in a direct attack to cities since the atomic bombing on Hiroshima and Nagasaki. This is largely due to 70 years of interna-

Dr. Seiichiro Takemine, Meisei University, 2-1-1 Hodokubo, Hino, Tokyo 191-8506 Japan; Email: seiichiro.takemine@meisei-u.ac.jp, takeminese@hotmail.com.

Acknowledgments: I would like to thank Marshallese for assistance the filed research. This work was supported by JSPS KAKENHI Grant Numbers JP26760013.

Ú.Oswald Spring et al. (eds.), *Regional Ecological Challenges for Peace in Africa, the Middle East, Latin America and Asia Pacific*, The Anthropocene: Politik—Economics—Society—Science 5, DOI 10.1007/978-3-319-30560-8_7

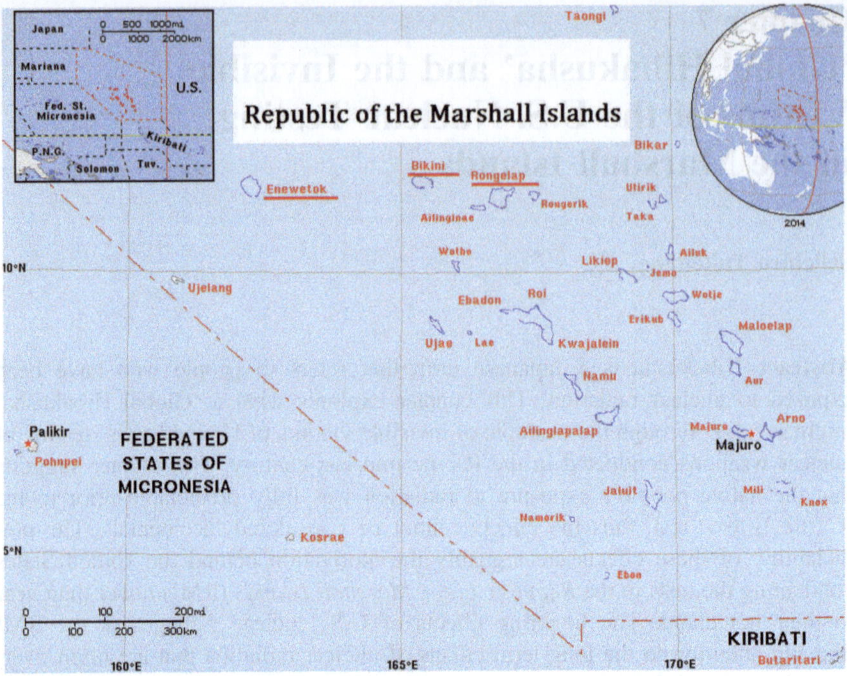

Fig. 7.1 Map of the Republic of the Marshall Islands. *Source* Public domain; at: http://ian.macky.net/pat/map/mh/mh.html. The author made some adjustments

tional community's efforts to build a nuclear free world (Wittner 2009). However, calling for "no more Hiroshima and Nagasaki, no more atomic bomb victims" based only on that perspective ignores the reality of the nuclear disasters that have spread worldwide since 1945.

Paying heed to the nuclear devastation since the wartime atomic bombing, this chapter focuses on the Marshall Islands, in the Middle Western part of the Pacific Ocean where the United States conducted 67 tests in total at Bikini Atoll and Eniwetok Atoll between 1946 and 1958 (Fig. 7.1).

The U.S. hydrogen bomb testing, code-named 'Castle Bravo', took place on 1 March 1954 also in Bikini Atoll, Marshall Islands. The radioactive ash from the H-bomb explosion fell on a Japanese tuna boat, the Fifth Lucky Dragon (*Daigo Fukuryu Maru*) and many others.[1] Therefore in Japan, the H-bomb test is remembered as the 'Lucky Dragon Incident' or the 'Bikini Incident'.

[1]The victims of radiation exposure are not limited to the crews of the Fifth Lucky Dragon. It is estimated that about 1000 fishing boats and ships were exposed to the radiation as a consequence of Operation Castle, a series of nuclear tests including 'Bravo' (Kochi ken bikini suibaku hisai chousadan 2004; Ito 2014).

The fact that the local islanders were also exposed to the significant fallout must not be forgotten. In the Marshall Islands, 1 March is a national holiday called 'Nuclear Victims Remembrance Day'.[2] This is a day to remember not only the Bravo Shot, but also all the 67 nuclear tests conducted by the United States in the Marshall Islands.

The radioactive fallout continues to threaten the basis of daily life in the local communities even up to now (Takemine 2015: 65–111). The far-reaching effects of the nuclear tests are evident not only in islanders' health but also on their culture, life, and psychology. Some people are still forced to leave their home-lands being 'nuclear displaced.' Christopher J. Loeak, President of the Republic of the Marshall Islands (RMI) stated at the commemoration ceremony on 1 March 2014: "We remain the closest of friends with the United States, but there is unfinished business relating to the nuclear weapons testing that must be addressed", "my government will continue to pursue justice for those affected by the Bravo test and the other 66 atomic and nuclear weapons detonated in our atolls" (Loeak 2014).

These nuclear damages are almost totally invisible. In an interview by author on 1 May 2012, Lemeyo Abon, a survivor of the Bravo shot said, "I had an operation on my thyroid, but all of could not have been removed. The sadness still remains in my mind. It cannot be seen from outside".

Visitors of the Marshall Islands today will only see beautiful, tropical scenery evocative of 'paradise,' rather than the former nuclear test site it actually is. It is difficult to grasp the radiological damages not only for scientific but also for political and sociological reasons. On 2 March 2014 in an interview with the author Tony DeBrum, an eye-witness of the nuclear testing and RMI Minister of Foreign Affairs, pointed out that the nuclear disasters "deny, lie and classify. It is nuclear culture. It is repeated in Fukushima".

This chapter analyses why the Marshall Islands people were exposed to radiation and how the invisible aspects of nuclear damages can be approached. This chapter introduces the 'Global-Hibakusha' concept by focusing on the effects of nuclear development and radiation on the people and their society. It then examines the historical processes by which the United States selected Bikini Atoll and Eniwetok Atoll in the Marshall Islands as the nuclear test sites, based on an official report on the Operation Crossroads (Shurcliff 1947) and other declassified U.S. official documents and analysis by Weisgall (1994). Furthermore it questions the U.S. accounts, that the Marshallese people were 'accidentally' exposed to radioactive fallout from the Bravo shot, through an examination of official U.S. statements and archival documents. The official explanation has long been widely accepted even in peace studies.[3] This study assesses whether United States nuclear damages in the RMI might become a starting point for research on 'Global-Hibakusha' in peace studies.

---

[2]The holiday is also called 'the Memorial Day and Nuclear Survivors Remembrance Day.'

[3]For instance, Lawrence S. Wittner states "The AEC had staked out a danger zone roughly the size of New England around the test site. But the blast proved to be more than twice as powerful as planned and generated vast quantities of highly radioactive debris" (Wittner 2009: 52).

7.2 Perspective of 'Global Hibakusha'

'Hibakusha' is a Japanese term that refers to people who have been exposed to nuclear radiation, particularly as a result of the atomic bombs in Hiroshima and Nagasaki. Using the term 'Hibakusha' on nuclear issues prioritizes the existence of victims who are often overlooked. In research on the global expansion of nuclear disasters Dr. Hiroko Takahashi, an American Historian, and this author, in 2004 launched a research project on 'Global Hibakusha'. After that, a research committee on Global Hibakusha was established within the Peace Studies Association of Japan. In Japan, the victims and survivors of Hiroshima and Nagasaki bombings are essential research agendas for peace studies. But it can no longer be claimed that the victims of radiation are only from the Hiroshima and Nagasaki bombings.[4] Therefore this study group created the term 'Global Hibakusha'.

'Global Hibakusha'[5] draws attention to the invisible and unknown victims and survivors of adverse radiation effects caused by various phases of nuclear development, from uranium exploration to nuclear waste. It was created to bring together the experiences of various victims of nuclear disasters, in Hiroshima and Nagasaki, with a global perspective, and to face the facts of environmental pollution on a global scale. 'Global Hibakusha' excavates the victims and survivors from the past—both communities and people who live there—and it creates vertical links across time, connecting historical suffering to present and future issues. It also reviews various aspects of nuclear disasters that are connected by the common denominator of radiation exposure, and assesses them beyond traditional academic borders. By connecting them with the horizontal links, such as radiation exposure, and bringing them into one forum of discussion, 'Global Hibakusha' illuminates the differences and particular characteristics of each issue.

'Global Hibakusha' stresses the need for analysis of nuclear disasters to include narratives of the 'people's peace' in communities which continue to endure radiation. Ivan Illich, an Austrian philosopher and prominent figure in the field of peace studies, cautions that people's peace are overshadowed by the monopoly of the elite, and that peace studies should look beyond issues of economic development

[4]Nuclear devastation has spread worldwide especially since Hiroshima and Nagasaki bombings in the process of nuclear development. Such concerns were shared by pioneers in some media and NGOs. For instance, from a local newspaper in Hiroshima, an enhanced report on the radiation problem with a global perspective was published. The book by Chugoku Newspaper wrote, "in reality, unregulated nuclear testing, the manufacture of nuclear weapons, uranium mining, and accidents at nuclear power plants have caused a steady increase in the number of victims of radiation, or Hibakusha" (Newspaper 1996).

[5]Yoshihiko Uchida, who questioned the way social science was studied, discusses the importance of building our own instrument of conceptualization in his *Dokusho-to-Shakai-Kagaku* (*Reading and Social Science*, Tokyo: Iwanami Shoten 1985). Uchida argues that social science is a field of study that identifies the essence of the matter deep inside phenomenon through an instrument called concept, as in a way people see the world, invisible to the naked eye, through an electron microscope.

(Illich 1992). A great deal of effort has been made in examining of the diplomatic actions and attitudes of the leaders of nuclear countries and would-be nuclear countries. What seems to be lacking, however, are explorations of the people's peace, analysis of the ongoing experiences of the people who face the nuclear dangers. Even in Japan, with their experience of the Hiroshima and Nagasaki bombings, the people's peace has not been comprehensively pursued in peace studies. "There are many people who addressed the issue of nuclear weapons, while not many did so about issues of atomic victims and survivors," sociologist Masaharu Hamatani, pointed out in a presentation to the Peace Studies Association of Japan (PSAJ 2010: 18–19).

Among the different trends in peace studies, the dominant issue in the 1950s and early 1960s was the prevention of nuclear war between the United States and Soviet Union, understood against a backdrop of East and West tensions. From the middle of 1960s, with increased attention to developing countries, peace studies started to address North-South issues. The concept of peace has expanded, from understandings of peace as the absence of war through to understandings of peace as the absence of all violence—that is to say the presence of social justice (Galtung 1996).

If one identifies 'Global Hibakusha' in peace studies, it is to reconstruct the understanding of nuclear issues by expanding the imagination to include the 'people's peace'—including all people who suffered from nuclear disasters regardless of national borders. It also wants to develop existing characteristics of peace studies, with the mission referred to in the charter of the Peace Studies Association of Japan to institutionalize universal peace studies from the standpoint of war victims based on the experience of atomic bombing. From the perspective of 'Global Hibakusha' attention and focus can be shifted to the victims and survivors born in the Marshall Islands.

7.3 Selected Lands as the Nuclear Test Sites

The "choice of site was one of the biggest problems" according to W. A. Shurcliff, a historian of the Joint Task Force One, which conducted the first series of U.S. nuclear tests in the Marshall Islands under the codename of *Operation Crossroads* (Shurcliff 1947: 16). Shurcliff (1947: 16–17) describe the following conditions as requirements for the selection of test sites:

- A protected anchorage at least six miles in diameter. (It must contain not only the enormous target fleet but also the even larger supporting fleet.)
- A site which was uninhabited, or nearly so. (All inhabitants would have to be evacuated.)
- A location at least 300 miles [480 km] distant from the nearest city. (Radioactive materials released in the air might menace persons scores of miles to leeward.)

- A location within 1000 miles [1600 km] of a B-29 base. (The airburst bomb was to be delivered by a B-29 bomber plane.)
- Freedom from severe cold and violent storms.
- Predictable winds directionally uniform at all altitudes from sea-level to 60,000 feet [18 km]. (There must be no chance that the radioactive materials carried high into the air could be wafted back over the task force personnel by a fluke counter-wind.)
- Predictable water currents of great lateral and vertical dispersion; fast currents avoiding important fishing areas, steamer lanes, inhabited shores. (Radioactive materials released in water must be dispersed reasonably rapidly, and without harm to persons or to the fishing industry.)
- Control by the United States.

This evidence leaves little doubt about whether or not radiation-related issues had already been recognized when the United States selected the nuclear test site.

Besides these conditions, the United States had another prerequisite to select the nuclear test site, according to US Navy Rear Admiral William Sterling Parsons's statement in 1946 (Defence Atomic Support Agency 1946). He noted:

> From the experiences in New Mexico […], one firm conclusion was drawn and that was that no more bombings would be conducted in the United States. A further stipulation was made by General Groves that no bomb would be tested within three to five hundred miles of the United States. That eliminated all local areas and all those around Bermuda and the Caribbean area.

"The experiences in New Mexico," the world's first nuclear test, code named 'Trinity,' was conducted by the United States on July 1945, prior to the bombing of Hiroshima. Because of concerns about radioactive fallout, the United States decided "no more bombings would be held in the United States."

Based on the above conditions, U.S. Navy Commander Frederick L. Ashworth presented possible test sites at an informal meeting (The U.S. Joint Chiefs of Staff 1945). He recommended the Bikini Atoll, located in the northern Marshalls, as the location for the tests though the United States had not received the consent of the local people.[6] It was on 20 December, 1945 which was about four and a half months after the bombing of Hiroshima and Nagasaki.

Hiroshima and Nagasaki are deeply connected to the Marshall Islands in the history of U.S. nuclear development. W. S. Parsons armed the atomic bomb on the B-29 bomber, Enola Gay over Hiroshima. Groves served as director the Manhattan Project, a top-secret research project that culminating in the atomic bombings of Hiroshima and Nagasaki. F L. Ashworth was co-pilot of Bockscar dropping the atomic bomb on Nagasaki.

---

[6]Historian Maclellan (2015: 1) has noted that "Many people in the Pacific welcomed the development of nuclear installations across the region, for the economic and employment opportunities created by an influx of military personnel." But the any Marshallese people did not invite the U.S. government to conduct testing on their territory.

The United States started the nuclear testing program Operation Crossroad at the Bikini Atoll in July 1946. In addition, the Eniwetok Atoll, 320 km to the west of the Bikini Atoll, was chosen as the test site for the second series of the U.S. nuclear testing in 1947. According to a press release prepared by the U.S. Department of State and the U.S. National Military Establishment:

> Eniwetok Atoll was selected as the site for the proving grounds after the careful consideration of all available Pacific Islands. Bikini is not suitable as the site since it lacks sufficient land surface for the instrumentation necessary to conduct the scientific observations. Of other possible sites, Eniwetok has the fewest inhabitants to be cared for, approximately 145, and what is very important from a radiological standpoint, it is isolated and there are hundreds of miles of open seas in the direction in which winds might carry radioactive particles (AEC 1947).

Though it is not mentioned above, Bernard O'Keefe, a U.S. Department of Energy prime contractor, explained in his book why the United States established the new site. Eniwetok was used because Bikini Atoll had been contaminated by Operational Crossroad in 1946 (O'Keefe 1983). Later, the United States built a new continental test site in Nevada. It was the site used for atomic bombing test on 27 January 1951. However, the Marshall Islands, continued to be used as the U.S. nuclear test site. "Since larger yield weapons and devices may not be fired within the United States with the requisite degree of safety, continued use of the more isolated Pacific area is essential" (Nevada Test Organization 1957), a bulletin of the Nevada test site explained. An overseas site was considered to be essential. Gordon Dean, the Chairman of the AEC, insisted in a memorandum of 13 December 1950 that:

> it should be noted that development of the Las Vegas range as an atomic weapons test site would not eliminate the current requirement for use of Eniwetok, Amchitka or some other similarly very remote sites for tests where the radiological hazards involved may be beyond the limits acceptable in the United States (AEC 1950).

The United States ended up conducting forty-three nuclear tests in Eniwetok, and twenty-four times in Bikini in the Marshall Islands. Over 7000 Hiroshima-sized bombs, measured in terms of *trinitrotoluene* (TNT), were dropped on the Marshall Islands alone over a 12-year period. So it should be said that the pacific islands did not have a so-called post war period because they were forced to stay on a front line in a new war, that is, the Cold War.

7.4 Predictable Exposed Radiation to the Local People

While U.S. officials recognized the fallout problems, it was hardly a subject of public concern before 1954. At that time, the issue of radioactive fallout remained invisible. Under such circumstances, Japanese media reports on the fact that a Japanese tuna fishing boat named the *Fifth Lucky Dragon* (*Daigo Fukuryumaru*) was exposed to radioactive fallout from the Bravo shot was a shocking revelation.

Thereafter, nuclear testing and the danger of nuclear fallout gained much more public attention. Conversely, indigenous Marshallese victims of radioactive fallout from Bravo were ignored by the Japanese and international media.

On 31 March 1954, after the Bravo shot Lewis Strauss, as Chairman of the Atomic Energy Commission, explained the condition of radioactive fallout on the local people; "the yield was about double that of the calculated estimate … the shot was fired. The wind failed to follow the predictions but shifted south of that line and the little islands of Rongelap, Rongerik, and Uterik were in the path of the fall-out." In addition, Strauss commented "the 236 natives also appeared to me to be well and happy" (AEC 1954a).

The U.S. government has repeatedly claimed the statement and noted that it was an 'accident,' from 1954 to the present.[7] However, prior to the Bravo shot, the Health and Safety Laboratory, an institute under the U.S. Atomic Energy Commission, had established a world-wide network to monitor fallout at 122 points globally (Weather Bureau 1955). In addition, the U.S. Atomic Energy Commission and the U.S. Air Force Project RAND jointly organized a research project named Project Sunshine in 1953 to study the worldwide effects of atomic weapons focusing on Strontium 90 (AEC 1954b). For this project, the Atomic Energy Commission promoted the collection of human tissue samples from all over the world for the research (ABCC 1957).

Although it was clear to U.S. government officials who expected the fallout to spread globally, they did not take any action to prevent local people from being exposed to radioactive fallout. Actually, evacuation of local people was considered but ultimately abandoned. Colonel Vincent G. Huston, the acting director of military application of the U.S. Air Force, argued in a memorandum:

> If the danger area had included such inhabited atolls as Rongelap and Utirik it would have required that the natives of those atolls be evacuated and that a permanent home be found for them elsewhere. … The Department of the Interior was not sympathetic to removing the natives, having experienced considerable difficulty with Bikini natives who were relocated permanently on Ujelang (AEC 1954c).

It was often claimed that the unexpected wind caused the radiation exposure of local people. However, a report prepared by the U.S. Defense Nuclear Agency (1982) actually suggests that the United States pushed the Bravo shot despite knowing that wind predictions were less favourable. According to this DNA report, about thirteen hours before the Bravo shot, "At the 18:00 weather briefing, the predicated winds were less favourable; nevertheless, the decision to shoot was

[7]For example, Embassy of the U.S., Marshall Islands (2012) express the following view about the nuclear tests. "The hydrogen bomb test on March 1, 1954, code-named Castle Bravo, far exceeded the size expected by scientists. This factor, combined with shifting wind patterns, sent some of the radioactive fallout over the inhabited atolls of Rongelap and Utrik.", and "The United States has expressed regret about the Bravo accident when 253 Marshallese were exposed to high doses of radiation from a nuclear test. While international scientists did study the effects of that accident on the human population unintentionally affected, the United States never intended for Marshallese to be hurt by the tests."

reaffirmed, but with another review of the winds scheduled for 24:00". The report included an interesting decision. "The midnight briefing indicated less favourable winds at 10,000–25,000-foot (3.05–7.52 km) levels. Winds at 20,000 ft (6.10 km) were headed for Rongelap to the east … The decision to shoot was reaffirmed".

In addition, Bill Graham, RMI Foreign Affairs Advisor on Nuclear Issues, found a new U.S. official document in 2013 which are largely different from the repeated U.S. official statement that code-named *Castle Bravo*, far exceeded the size expected by scientists. It is a meeting report for chief of staff, Task Group 7.4 which jointed the Bravo shot issued from headquarters Task Group 7.4, provisional dated on 23 February 1954 (Crosby 1954). It is just five days prior to Bravo shot. The memorandum notes "On 20 February 1954, General Estes, Doctor Schwarts and Lt Colonel Crosby attended a positioning meeting for the purpose of determining the final positions of all aircraft participation in Shot BRAVO" and "It was decided that aircraft would be positioned on the basis of a twenty-megaton yield with the exception of the two (2) effects aircraft which will be positioned on the basis". It is surprising that one of the estimation for the Bravo shot was twenty-megaton yield. The United States could adequately predict that the Bravo shot would be on a larger scale of fifteen megaton.

In 1946 the Rongelap people were evacuated in advance of U.S. atomic testing at Bikini Atoll. However in 1954, they were not evacuated at the time of the hydrogen bomb estimated twenty-megaton Bravo shot in Bikini Atoll. Locals, particularly the Rongelap people claim they were exposed to radiation intentionally and treated as guinea pigs.

7.5 Conclusion

This chapter introduced the concept of 'Global Hibakusha', focusing on the areas affected by radiation and the victims of radiation-related effects from the nuclear development who have often been overlooked. It discussed nuclear issues in the Marshall Islands where the United States tested many nuclear bombs.

Why were the local people of the Marshall Islands exposed to radiation? Since the start of nuclear testing in the Marshall Islands in 1946, the United States was concerned with the consequences of radioactive fallout. For this very reason nuclear testing was conducted in the Marshall Islands: they were far away from the U.S. mainland. The native people's exposure to radiation was fully predictable before the Bravo shot test. The references to 'unexpected wind' and "exceeded the estimates" were argued to be an excuse by the United States for the exposure of Marshallese people to nuclear radiation. It is no longer acceptable to claim that it was 'accidental'. Rather, it is obvious that the Marshallese were not treated as human beings and their pain has subsequently been rendered invisible.

The United States has completely overlooked the existence of local peoples and the value of their lives in U.S. nuclear development. It was a typical environmental injustice and a violation of their human rights. The U.S. marginalized security, justice, and human rights of the Marshallese in the nuclear testing. This refers to United States' double standards of security, justice and human rights in the framework of nuclear development.

On 1 March 2014, during the 60th anniversary of the Bravo shot, a U.S. official made a speech in front of the survivors/victims that the nuclear tests are the "historical contributions that the Marshallese people make to help promote peace and stability around the world" (Gottemoeller 2014).

Further research on the reality of damages brought about by U.S. nuclear testing in the RMI is needed. Particularly on the matter of the treatment of local people after the Bravo shot. Also, nuclear damages, beyond those recognized by the U.S., such as in the Ailuk and Likiep atoll, should not be ignored.

This chapter tried to clarify the same facts regarding U.S. nuclear damage to the RMI. For instance, it has argued the reasons that the Marshall Islands were selected as the test site, shedding light on both Bikini Atoll and Eniwetok Atoll. An address of W. S. Parson (U.S. Navy) in 1946 offered new information that the United States had decided, after the first Atomic bomb test, in New Mexico not to hold any nuclear explosions within the continental United States.

This chapter contributes to the emerging research area referred to as 'Global-Hibakusha' in international peace studies, introduced here for the first time in English. This chapter is to enhance the awareness for the overlooked aspects of human suffering due to nuclear developments affecting the victims in the Marshall Islands with the 'Global-Hibakusha' concept.

Acknowledgment I would like to thank Marshallese for assistance the filed research. This work was supported by JSPS KAKENHI Grant Numbers JP26760013.

References

Archival Sources

ABCC (Atomic Bomb Casualty Committee), 1957: *Bone Sample Analysis by AEC-NYOO*, Series 3: *ABCC Program Components*, US National Academy of Sciences Archives.

AEC (Atomic Energy Commission), 1947: Information for the Press Prepared in Collaboration with the Dept. of State + The National Military Establishment to Supplement the Statement of the US AEC on the Establishment of Pacific Experimental Installations, 1 Dec., DOE OpenNet, Accession Number: NV0409585.

AEC, 1950: "Memorandum from Gordon Dean to the special committee of the national security council for atomic energy matters, Subject: Additional Test Site, in Atomic Energy Commission Location of Proving Ground for Atomic Weapons Note by the Secretary", Author: Snapp, R. B., 13 Dec., DOE OpenNet, Accession Number: NV0750356.

AEC, 1954a: Press Release, Subject: "Tests of Thermonuclear Weapons in the Pacific Proving Grounds by L. L. Strauss", 31 March, DOE OpenNet, Accession Number: NV0049192.

AEC, 1954b: "Report on Project Gabriel", 01 July, DOE OpenNet, Accession Number: NV0720894.

AEC, 1954c: "Letter to K. D. Nichols, Subject: Chronology of Establishment of Danger Area around Pacific Proving Grounds", Author: Huston, V. G., 30 March, DOE OpenNet, Accession Number: NV0029635.

Crosby, James E. Jr., 1954: "Memorandum for Chief of Staff, Task Group 7.4, Provisional, Subject: Report of Conference, 23 February".

Galtung, Johan, 1996: "Violence, Peace, and Peace Research" in: *Journal of Peace Research*, 6,3: 167–191.

The U.S. Joint Chiefs of Staff, 1945: "Discussion of Navy Tests, 20 December, 1945", in Folder: Navy Tests, Central Decimal File 1951–53, Entry UD10, Box 162, RG 218, National Archives at College Park, Maryland

Defence Atomic Support Agency, 1946: "Operation Crossroads address by W. S. Parsons at Fort Belvoir, Virginia, 24 September", in: Armed Forced Special Weapons Project Office of the Historian Reports 1943-48, Entry 19, Box 18, RG 374, and National Archives at College Park, Maryland.

Defence Nuclear Agency, 1982: "Castle Series 1954", Authors: Martin, E.J.; Rowland, R. H., DOE OpenNet, Accession Number: NV0407565.

Nevada Test Organization, 1957: "Background Information on Nevada Nuclear Tests", 15 July, DOE OpenNet, Accession Number: NV0410810.

Weather Bureau, 1955: "World-Wide Fallout from Operation Castle", Author: List, R. J., 17 May, DOE OpenNet, Accession Number: NV0051383.

Secondary Literature

Chugoku Newspaper, 1996: *Exposure: Victims of Radiation Speak Out* (Tokyo: Kodansha International).

Embassy of the U.S., Marshall Islands, 2012: "Embassy News: The Legacy of U.S. Nuclear Testing and Radiation Exposure in the Marshall Islands"; at: http://majuro.usembassy.gov/legacy.html (1 May 2015).

Gottemoeller, Rose, 2014: "Republic of Marshall Islands Nuclear Remembrance Day Remark by Acting under Secretary for Arms Control and International Security", 1 March, Majuro; at: http://www.state.gov/t/us/2014/222790.htm (1 October 2014).

Illich, Ivan, 1992: "The De-Linking of Peace and Development", in: *In the Mirror of the Past: Lectures and Addresses, 1978-1990* (New York: Marion Boyars Publishers): 15–26.

Ito, Hideaki, 2014: 放射線を浴びたX年後 (X Years Later: Japanese Fishermen Exposed to Radiation in 1954) (Tokyo: Kodansha).

Kochi ken bikini suibaku hisai chousadan [Research Group for Japanese Fishermen Suffering from Bikini H-bomb Test in Kochi Prefecture, Japan] (Ed.), 2004: もう一つのビキニ事件: 1000隻をこえる被災船を追う(An Alternative History of the Bikini Incident: an Inquiry of over 1,000 Suffering Ships) (Tokyo: Heiwa Bunka).

Loeak, Christopher, 2014: "Speech on Nuclear Remembrance Day by RMI President", 1 March, Majuro (unpublished manuscript).

Maclellan, Nic, 2015: "Grappling with the Bomb: Opposition to Pacific nuclear testing in the 1950s", Proceedings of the 14th Biennial Labour History Conference, Queen's College, University of Melbourne, 11–13 February.

O'Keefe, Bernard J., 1983: *Nuclear Hostages* (Boston: Houghton Mifflin).

PSAJ (Peace Studies Association of Japan), 2010: 日本平和学会ニューズレター (Newsletter, Peace Studies Association of Japan), 19,2 (Secretariat PSAJ).

Shurcliff, W. A., 1947: *Bombs at Bikini: The Official Report of Operation Crossroads* (New York: W. H. Wise).

Takemine, Seiichiro, 2015:マーシャル諸島　終わりなき核被害を生きる (Still Living with Nuclear Fallout in the Marshall Islands) (Tokyo: Shinsen sha).

Uchida, Yoshihiko, 1985: 読書と社会科学 (Reading and Social Science) (Tokyo: Iwanami).
Weisgall, Jonathan M., 1994: *Operation Crossroads: The Atomic Tests at Bikini Atoll* (Annapolis: Naval Institute Press).
Wittner, Lawrence S., 2009: *Confronting the Bomb: A Short History of the World Nuclear Disarmament Movement* (Stanford: University Press).

Chapter 8
The Nigerian Home-Grown DDR Programme—Its Impacts on Empowering the Niger Delta Ex-Militants

Margaret Ifeoma Abazie-Humphrey

Abstract On 25 June 2010 the Federal Government of Nigeria Niger Delta Amnesty Programme under the *Office of the Special Adviser to the President on Niger Delta* (OSAPND) was set up. The aim was to implement the *Presidential Amnesty Programme* (PAP) with a mandate to initiate, plan and implement the *Disarmament, Demobilization and Reintegration* (DDR) programme. The DDR called for 30,000 ex-agitators (822 female) to handed in their weapons, sign up for the PAP, and in exchange they would receive a monthly stipend of N65,000 (US$400) and undergo vocational and academic training in Nigeria and abroad. Livelihood strengthening through training became an essential part of OSAPND's strategy for economic empowerment, for job creation by supporting academic, vocational and entrepreneurial training, and for engaging in business set-ups. This chapter discusses the impact of the DDR programme on the economy and on peace in the Niger Delta region of Nigeria, focusing on how vocational or academic training has improved individual performance and had a positive influence on economic development. Four key questions for assessing this programme are: How did it differ from donor and UN piloted DDR programmes? What did it add? Did it increase the global capacity for a national DDR programme? Has the increase in economic development in the Niger Delta become a transformative mechanism to respond to the long-term structural and historical social exclusion that triggered the conflict?

Keywords DDR · Ex-agitators · Economic development · Niger delta · OSAPND

8.1 Introduction

Local actors' involvement in post-war reconstruction and peacebuilding is receiving global attention as an essential element in *Disarmament, Demobilization and Reintegration* (DDR) programmes and scholars such as Roger MacGinty and Oliver

---

Ms Margaret Ifeoma Abazie-Humphrey, Office of the Special Adviser to the President of Nigeria on Niger Delta, Federal Government of Nigeria Presidential Amnesty Programme, No. 4 Buzi Street, Off Amazon, Maitama, Abuja, Nigeria; email: ifeomaime@yahoo.com.

Ú.Oswald Spring et al. (eds.), *Regional Ecological Challenges for Peace in Africa, the Middle East, Latin America and Asia Pacific*, The Anthropocene: Politik—Economics—Society—Science 5, DOI 10.1007/978-3-319-30560-8_8

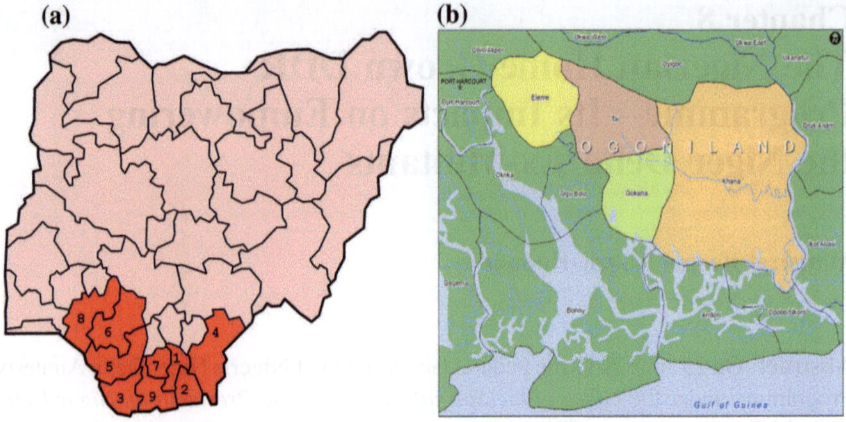

Fig. 8.1 **a** The states of Nigeria in the Niger Delta: *1* Abia; *2* Akwa Ibom; *3* Bayelsa; *4* Cross River; *5* Delata; *6* Edo; *7* Imo; *8* Ondo; *9* Rivers. *Source* Wikimedia commons is in the public domain: NigerDeltaStates.png (29 July 2015). **b** A map showing areas with oil spills and contamination in the Niger Delta in Ogoniland. *Source* UNEP study and map; at: http://www.unep.org/disastersandconflicts/Portals/155/countries/nigeria/imgs/ogoniland_big.jpg (2 November 2015)

Richmond have greatly supported this hypothesis for local actors' involvement in peacebuilding. This home-grown DDR is part of Nigeria's Federal Government Amnesty Programme and through the *Office of the Special Adviser to the President on Niger Delta* (OSAPND) it has become a historic success. Amnesty beneficiaries came from nine states of the Niger Delta region (Abia, Akwa Ibom, Bayelsa, Cross River, Delta, Edo, Imo, Ondo, and Rivers States, see Fig. 8.1a, b).

Among the sub-Saharan African countries Nigeria has experienced many difficulties from oil production, oil companies, and pollution resulting from oil spills, made more difficult to manage in the Niger Delta whose low-lying nature favours a rapid spread of oil spills (Baumuller et al. 2011: 18–19). The vast oil and gas deposits in the Niger Delta region are located in Nigeria's mangrove swamp with creeks, lakes, rivers, forest resources, aquatic life, raffia, oil palm and more (Ariyoh et al. 2013: 14).

According to the *Nigerian National Petroleum Corporation* (NNPC),[1] oil and gas account for about 70 % of Nigeria's fiscal revenue, with about 2.4 million *barrels per day* (bpd). The oil conflict in the Niger Delta region during the 1990s and 2000s has ultimately affected the economy. This triggered the Amnesty programme that was launched by President Umaru Yar-Adua in June 2009. In 2005, Nigeria's crude production was at 2.2 m bpd, but this drastically declined at the peak of the oil conflict in 2009. Statistical records of the *Monthly Petroleum*

[1]NNPC; at: http://www.nnpcgroup.com (29 October 2014).

*Informati*on (MPI)[2] show that between January 2004 and June 2013 Nigeria reached its lowest production level of crude oil and condensates; in April 2009, total monthly production was 55.82 m barrels or 1.86 m bpd. Due to the Amnesty programme hostilities in the region declined, and production again reached 2.4 m bpd. In 2013, the Nigerian government estimated its crude oil production at 2.53 m bpd (Salami 2013: 5).[3]

The *Disarmament, Demobilization and Reintegration* (DDR) programmes were generally managed by donors such as the UN. Nigeria's home-grown DDR was set up for a five-year period, with 2015 as its exit date. Of the 30,000 beneficiaries, over 14,000 were sent to various universities and vocational training centres in Nigeria and abroad. About 5000 were trained in different skills, including marine and automobile technology, boat building, as oil and gas technicians, in agriculture, fashion design, catering, etc. In 2015, about 3330 remain as students in different fields. So far a total of 11,700 have graduated from different training programmes out of which only 238 have gained employment. In addition, 3610 are supported by business set-ups[4] for the 2013 target (Amnesty News 2013a, b). In Africa, most DDR programmes are piloted by the UN or *African Union* (AU), as in Burundi, Angola, Liberia, Sierra Leone, Ivory Coast, Sudan, *Democratic Republic of Congo* (DRC), etc.

8.2 Conceptual Frameworks and Hypotheses

Prior to the PAP/DDR programme, the communities in the Niger Delta were torn apart by armed conflicts resulting from the management of their oil and gas resources. This conflict in the Delta mobilized different groups of ex-agitators through their socio-ethnic networks and this has been a component of social capital. Putnam (cited in Martti 2000: 2) referred to three components of social capital as "moral obligations and norms, social values (especially trust) and social networks (especially voluntary associations)". Martti (2000: 4) further explained that social capital is a sociological essence of communal vitality and its forms are general moral resources of the community through which a solution to the problem of common action and opportunism assume the development of voluntary collective action. Similarly, reflecting the findings on social capital, Francis (2002: 79–88)

[2]MPI; at: http://www.nnpcgroup.com/PublicRelations/OilandGasStatistics/MPIFigures/MonthlyPetroleum/tabid/130/FolderID/52/Default.aspx (18 October 2013).

[3]ICAN Nig; at http://www.icanig.org/documents/Dr-Salami-2013-FGN-BUDGET.pdf (10 October 2013).

[4]With business set-ups delegates are empowered by the provision of shop/business locations and equipped with the necessary business start-up equipment. Such businesses must also be registered with the government regulatory authority and the Corporate Affairs Commission, secure tax certificate/pin, and open a business bank account. All related expenses for this business set-up are paid by the OSAPND and handed over to the delegate without any repayment plan.

suggests that all social structures which contribute to the solution of public or collective action represent social capital. He argued that social capital can be used in the sustainable livelihood approach to rural development policy, as well as in work on conflict and post-conflict situations. The violent activities in the Niger Delta were a public problem for Nigeria. Its Amnesty programme became the social capital to that effect.

Ball/Goor (2006: 1) defined DDR as "the process of demilitarizing official and unofficial armed groups by controlling and reducing the possession and use of arms, by disbanding non-state armed groups and rightsizing state security services and by assisting former ex-combatants to reintegrate into civilian life". Ball and Goor added that DDR can be seen as a five-stage process, namely "weapon surrender, assembly, discharge, short to medium term reinsertion and long term reintegration". Despite the impact of social capital in the conflict mobilization period and the ongoing DDR project, this section focuses on three concepts such as the local actors' participation in peacebuilding, the differences and similarities between donor-funded DDR and Nigerian DDR, and the economic developmental impacts of the amnesty programme in the Niger Delta region.

8.2.1 Involvement of Local Actors in the DDR Project

Let us begin with the impacts of local actors' involvement in the post-conflict consolidation. The involvement of local actors has "hopeful and cautionary implications" because they are seen as "rational economic agents" (Collier 2007: 216). In his analysis, the former sees them as having the "congeniality to respond to incentives" while the latter suggests that it may be of little avail to "buy rebel groups off". However, both implications are not considered here; rather, the positive impacts will be discussed. MacGinty (2010: 402) believes that local actors are capable of influencing the extent to which peace might be "hybridized" since they can resist, ignore, subvert or adapt liberal peace intervention. Theorizing on a hybrid third generation approach to peacebuilding, Richmond (2008: 106) suggested focusing on "self-sustainability" rather than merely on external forms of guarantee. Richmond also stipulated that peacebuilding is "technically feasible" if it is carried out by external actors in cooperation with local ones and thus can eventually stand alone. Following Richmond, the government of Nigeria has funded the DDR programme without the help of external actors.

Building on the goal of a sustainable peace in the Niger Delta, Abazie-Humphrey (2008: 14) stressed that the involvement of both lower stakeholders (local actors) and upper stakeholders (government/oil company officials) would undoubtedly promote peacebuilding. MacGinty equally argued that the ability of local actors to "resist or subvert the liberal peace" include the extent to which they retain power during the liberal peace transition. For Freedman (2007: 248), "interveners pushed in the direction of containing conflict or brokering a settlement" should be dynamic in "interaction with the local people's interests and that intervention should be part of a process with defined stages". Generally, an impactful interest is undoubtedly the interest presented by the owner. In the author's view, a yam ban is best maintained by the farm owner, and harvesting the yam is not enough, but one's style of preservation determines the volume of one's income. It is not enough to have representatives in peacebuilding projects such as DDR; getting the local actors involved in the process will contribute more to the peace finally achieved.

Moreover, Thomas-Larmer et al. (1999: 22) suggest that a credible consensus-building group must involve participants who represent a full range of interests and views on the issue or dispute, and that the stakeholder group must identify their own spokespersons to take part. Thus, the amnesty leaders, delegates, OSAPND staff, and *Ijaw National Congress* (INC) and *Ijaw Youth Council* (IYC) are the local actors in the amnesty project, and the involvement of the OSAPND with these actors in the planning and implementation stages of the PAP is a current trend. Just as MacGinty (2010: 403) stressed that "locally inspired alternative forms of peace do not usually copy approved models from the global north" and are often labelled as "illiberal or illegitimate", the case of Nigeria's home-grown DDR will open up a new discussion on this. Midgley/Hall (2004: 73) argue that community development is based on local people and that they "can implement programmes that significantly reduce the extent of poverty and social deprivation". There was a marked convergence of local actors in Nigeria's home-grown DDR. This text suggests that if local people can implement development programmes to reduce poverty and social deprivation which have been widely argued to contribute to conflict mobilizations in the world, those same local people are vital in the implementation of DDR projects.

A striking example of the involvement of local actors in peacebuilding with a positive impact is featured in the work of Aall (2007: 484) using the Muslim–Christian Dialogue Forum in Nigeria's Plateau State in the Northern region. In this case, the founding fathers of the dialogue forum were militants in the interreligious conflicts and "their interest in the dialogue grew from their religious beliefs" through which they continued to pursue the goal of understanding each other's perspectives and of identifying the common elements of Christianity and Islam. Aall recorded that these dialogue leaders utilized their community relations to "encourage Muslim–Christian dialogue in a highly charged inter-communal conflict" to bring about a peaceful resolution. It is worth noting that the effects of this settlement yielded further peace accords in other Northern states, thereby increasing the local capacity for conflict resolution. The success of this Muslim–Christian dialogue is one of the most evident proofs that peace cannot be forced on others by external actors. This text seeks to assess Richmond's (2008: 113) view on whether a "liberal peace allows for local participa-tion or leads instead to the cooption of local actors". Richmond supports "indigenous peace practices and processes, working from the bottom up, and based on local cultures and traditional practices". Moreover, in Sierra Leone, a rebel leader was appointed to the government as minister of mining in an effort to give rebels a greater interest in peace (Collier 2007: 215). Furthermore, the involvement of leaders in the design of the amnesty programme and the implementation packages of the Nigerian DDR programmes for ex-agitators supports Richmond's (2008) hypothesis that the involvement of local actors in peacebuilding evolved around a tendency to romanticize the indigenous contribution, hence their consent, participation and cooperation are vital to peace.

8.3 Background of Nigeria's DDR Programme

In which regard has the Nigeria DDR programme been home-grown?[5] The development of the amnesty programme emerged from the pronouncement of the amnesty programme by the then president of Nigeria, which was followed up by the launch of a planning and design committee. This committee comprised a pool of consultants from different backgrounds with skills in development and security projects, key stakeholders, and government officials. The *Special Adviser to the President on Niger Delta* (SAPND) has been the Chairman of the Amnesty Committee. Through this committee, a working plan was developed and the project is designated as an intervention project where amendments to its components are regularly reviewed and updated as part of its *standard operating procedures* (SOP). This committee has been the consensus-building platform of the DDR project. Ejovi/Ebie (2013: 132) recorded that the presidential panel on amnesty and disarmament of militants/agitators in the Niger Delta was held on 5 May 2009; and the panel outlined the terms, procedures and processes for the implementation of amnesty. The amnesty granted by former President Yar'Adua was based on Sect. 175 of the 1999 constitution of Nigeria (Fig. 8.2).

According to the OSAPND (2014), the objective of the Niger Delta DDR programme instituted by the *Federal Government of Nigeria* (FGN) has been to institute programmes to rehabilitate and reintegrate ex-militants under a structured *Disarmament, Demobilization and Reintegration* (DDR) programme. OSAPND furthermore stated that the key components of the Niger Delta Amnesty programme stipulated by the FGN were structured under the following bureaux with key functions as follows:

- OSAPND: amnesty programme implementation;
- *Office of the Special Adviser to the President on Petroleum Resources* (OSAPPM): oil assets redistribution;
- Ministry of Niger Delta Affairs: infrastructure development;
- Ministry of Environment: environmental remediation such as environmental clean-up, land reclamation and shore protection.

The OSAPND components can be further clarified as follows. The terms of the Amnesty include the willingness and readiness of the militants to surrender their arms, and unconditionally renounce militancy and sign an undertaking to this effect.

[5]That is, initiating, planning and implementing the DDR programme in the Nigerian way.

Fig. 8.2 Disarmament exercise of the Nigeria DDR programme. *Source* OSAPND records

The disarmament (D1) entails collection and surrender of small arms, ammunition, explosives, light and heavy weapons; and documentation spanning a period of sixty days from 6 August to 4 October 2009. It also included the destruction of these weapons; this took place on 25 May 2011. In the demobilization (D2), the ex-militants (also referred as ex-agitators) were subjected to verification and documentation, wellness assessment, transformational non-violence training, counselling and career guidance, as well as reintegration classification. In the accounts of the OSAPND on the D1 and D2 status for a total of 30,000 of the ex-agitators, only 20,192 were involved in the first phase while totals of 6166 and 3642 were recorded in the second and third phases of the exerçise respectively. The reintegration phase comprises training in education, vocational skills acquisition, and entrepreneurial skills building. In addition, the target group for the amnesty as stipulated by the presidential proclamation involves those who have directly or indirectly participated in the militancy. During the D1 and D2 phases, selection involves the core militants and their wives/concubines, cooks, chores-workers, spies and so on. Surrender of weapons was part of the evidential criteria for inclusion as well as identification by the camp warlords (Figs. 8.3, 8.4, 8.5, 8.6, 8.7, 8.8, 8.9, 8.10 and 8.11).

One of the interesting elements that make up this committee is what the OSAPND calls "the leaders". Those identified as leaders are the key stakeholders, and also included are warlords and militia commanders. Inherently, there is a typical form of social capital on which the members of the Niger Delta youths base

Fig. 8.3 Beneficiaries of the Niger Delta Amnesty Programme arriving at the camp for D2 programmes during the campaign. *Source* OSAPND records

Fig. 8.4 Beneficiaries of the Niger Delta Amnesty programme participating in the biometric documentation programme during the D2 campaign. *Source* OSAPND records

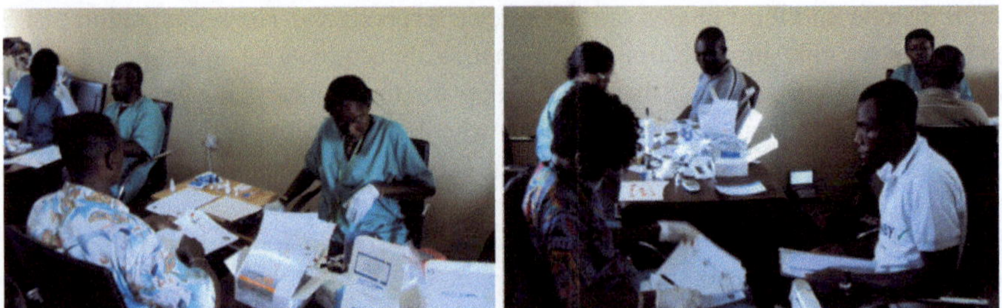

Fig. 8.5 Beneficiaries of the Niger Delta Amnesty Programme participating in the health and wellness check during the D2 campaign. *Source* OSAPND records

Fig. 8.6 Beneficiaries of the Niger Delta Amnesty programme attending the transformation classes of non-violence during the D2 campaign. *Source* OSAPND records

Fig. 8.7 Beneficiaries of the Niger Delta Amnesty Programme participating in physical exercise during the D2 campaign. *Source* OSAPND records

Fig. 8.8 Beneficiaries of the Niger Delta Amnesty programme participating in the reintegration training classification programme of the D2 campaign. *Source* OSAPND records

Fig. 8.9 Beneficiaries of the Niger Delta Amnesty programme attending a career fair (skill sets) during the D2 campaign programme. *Source* OSAPND records

Fig. 8.10 Beneficiaries of the Niger Delta Amnesty programme participating in the passing-out parade from the D2 programme of the campaign. *Source* OSAPND records

Fig. 8.11 Beneficiaries of the Niger Delta Amnesty programme departing the D2 campaign programme. *Source* OSAPND records

Table 8.1 Nigeria's DDR budget description

	Amnesty 2014 budget proposal with description		
S/N	Project description	Naira	USD$
1	Stipends and allowances of 30,000 ex-agitators	23,625,000,000	$144,098,813.25
2	Operational cost	3,699,933,814	$22,567,452.77
3	Reintegration of transformed ex-agitators	35,409,859,972	$215,979,631.72
4	Reinsertion/transition safety allowances for 3642 ex-agitators (3rd phase)	546,300,000	$3,332,113.51
	Total	63,281,093,786	$385,978,011.25

Source Federal Government of Nigeria Budget Office for 2014; currency conversion by the author Budget Office. Currency conversion rate on 3 March 2014 based on US$1 = N163.95 (Naira). On 29 July 2015 it was: US$1 = N198.9

their positions and this is referred to as the *Ijaw National Congress* (INC) and *Ijaw Youth Council* (IYC). INC and IYC play dominant roles in the amnesty programme, hence the majority of the delegates or leaders are also strong members or previous office-holders of the INC and IYC. INC and IYC provide a playground for future Ijaw leaders as well as offering access to a wider circle of influential people and their impact on the amnesty consensus-building committee must be acknowledged. It is important to note that the home-grown DDR programme development originated from the mutual cognition and recognition of inputs from different key stakeholders and ministries in the PAP committee to form the SOP.

The emphasis is on Nigerians designing the DDR project for fellow-Nigerians. The DDR project is currently managed by Nigerians with 80 % of the staff coming from the Niger Delta states—a strategy of owner-based models in the implementation style. The SOP forms the baseline for the amnesty implementation. Nigeria's home-grown DDR programme is completely funded by the *Federal Government of Nigeria* (FGN) and comes under the projects and budgets of the Presidency. However, the OSAPND through the SAPND will directly defend the amnesty budget before the National Assembly to obtain approval as part of the annual federal budget; its disbursement is made directly from the Central Bank of Nigeria to OSAPND. At a recent press briefing by the SAPND, the Hon. Kingsley Kuku stated that a total of N234,133,917,560 (US$1,428,081,229) budgetary allocation has been spent since its actual implementation programme began in March 2010 (Kuku 2014a, b). This budget spending involves overhead costs for staff, delegates' stipends, and DDR project costs. A typical example of a 2014 budget summary is illustrated in Table 8.1.

From the outset, it is important to acknowledge that the Government of Nigeria decided to manage the DDR programme by itself. The possible reason might be that experiences from the DDR programmes of African countries is a case study in itself for review and analysis, and it has not been so good. In addition, there were already emerging researchers with strong arguments for local actors' involvement in peacebuilding. Another possible reason might be that the FGN has already established sustainable structural transformation agencies or Acts at different periods and these include:

(a) *Niger Delta Development Board* (NDDB) in the 1960s;
(b) *Niger Delta Basin Development Authority* (NDBDA) in the 1980s;
(c) The Revenue Act passed by the National Assembly in 1991. This law made provision for more funds for the region for development, with a 1.5 % derivation fund (Eteng et al. 2013: 423);
(d) *Presidential Implementation Committee* (PIC) in 1987;
(e) *Oil Minerals Producing Areas Development Commission* (OMPADEC) in 1992;
(f) 13 % Revenue Derivation principle enshrined in the Nigeria 1999 Constitution;
(g) *Niger Delta Development Commission* (NDDC) in 2000;
(h) Federal Ministry of Niger Delta Affairs in September 2008.

The programme structures of these agencies provided a backlog of experiences and lessons learnt which will obviously play a dominant role in the amnesty decision-making and -framing of the DDR project in 2009. Relevant to this discussion is that these development agencies operate with different mandates and responsibilities in the Niger Delta region. Given the implication of the likely DDR project cost and the issues of the conflict, the FGN is confident of funding the DDR programme without assistance.

It is particularly interesting to note the introduction of a new trend in the Nigerian DDR project—that is, the incorporation of 1000–3000 people from the *Impacted Conflict Communities* (ICC) into the DDR training programmes. The local actors and implementers extended training opportunities to people whose communities were seriously affected by the decades of oil conflict in the region. These categories of people form the second cohort of amnesty project beneficiaries. It is important to note that these 3000 people never carried arms during the conflicts but were directly affected by the destruction of lives and properties.

A question of importance to this study is, what were the social and political factors that inspired the oil conflict in the Niger Delta? In the account by Kuku (2012: 21–22), the factors of interest include poor oil and gas operations (such as oil spillages and gas flaring); environmental problems (such as the low level of involvement of host communities in oil and gas work/business); and the loss of traditional occupations (such as loss of farming, fishing, and other natural capital). Also in line with the account by Rowell et al. (2005: 67–8), from 1958 to 2003, Nigeria produced a total of 22.8 billion barrels of oil, and on average 1000 cubic feet of gas is flared per barrel of oil, which equals 22.8 trillion cubic feet total of gas flared. Rowell Moreso estimated this figure as slightly more than the UK's total gas reserves in the North Sea in 2004. Moreso (Ukiwo 2007: 590) added that contemporary violent conflict and insurgency in the Niger Delta are linked to injustice, intergroup inequalities and political and socio-economic marginalization (Fig. 8.12).

Fig. 8.12 Images showing the level of oil spillages in Niger Delta. *Source* OSAPND records

8.4 Challenges Faced by the DDR Programme in Nigeria and Possible Overcoming Strategies

The Office of the Special Adviser to the President on Niger Delta (OSAPND 2014) reported the most significant examples of the challenges faced by the DDR programme in Nigeria, and identified possible overcoming strategies as including (but not limited to) the following:

1. Payment of US$400 monthly stipends to ex-agitators by the Federal Government. The question that remains unanswered is, what happens with this payment after the expiration of the DDR project? Will these ex-agitators accept the fact that this stipend was not meant to be a lifetime salary? Will the government be able to overcome the after-effects of the drama that might come out of it? Obviously, many ex-agitators now live on this stipend as lifeline wages and the issue of adjusting to its shortfall for their basic needs after DDR might pose problems. Nevertheless, there has been substantial change in the empowerment packages of the ex-agitators by the OSAPND. The purpose is to create enhanced economic opportunities for the delegates that will sustain their needs at the expiration of the project.
2. Delegates exiting the Programme based on social ills. There have been a small proportion of the ex-agitators who have been exited from the DDR programme due to gross misconduct. For instance, on 2 October 2013 the PAP, through the

OSAPND, announced the withdrawal of six out of twenty-four delegates who were studying at the People's University Russia. This action made news headlines. The OSAPND said that by going on a rampage and violently attacking the Nigerian Mission, these students had breached the Code of Conduct for delegates on scholarship that they had all signed before their departure from Nigeria. The Nigerian government could not tolerate such gross misconduct, and SAPND expressed shock that the delegates had invaded the embassy, destroying properties and attacking the Mission officials over the question of unpaid allowances. SAPND described the action as totally unacceptable. This kind of social ill does not favour the DDR project because all the ex-agitators are legally expected to be reintegrated and failure to incorporate all of them will pose a limitation on the project's overall output. Despite the exits, the OSAPND has maintained strict adherence to the code of conduct in the programme.

3. Engagement/employment opportunities. There are issues with the stereotyping of ex-agitators by society during engagements. Even after their training, prospective employers still look on these ex-agitators as militants, ex-convicts, etc. This invariably hinders their possible chances and opportunities in the crowded Nigerian labour market. In this regard, the OSAPND employs town hall meetings and briefings to inform the public of the transformation that has taken place among the ex-agitators. Labelling is always preached against. For instance, in the past, they were usually labelled as ex-militants but currently they are referred to as ex-agitators. In addition, OSAPND organizes job fairs and also participates in public and private job fairs in the country, where our trained delegates are showcased.
4. Continuous agitation for new list inclusion in the DDR programme. In this regard, there have been some court cases against the Federal Government of Nigeria/OSAPND, seeking to include new delegates in the DDR programme. These groups of people did not sign up during the amnesty registration period. Their argument was that, initially, they did not trust the sincerity of the government at the time of amnesty registration. OSAPND has refused to accept their inclusion appeal, arguing that the time limit had lapsed, that is, the sixty-day sign-up period from 6 August 2009 to 4 October 2009. In view of this, the FGN has remained adamant in its decision not to accept further inclusion. The FGN insists that this is a precaution against further agitation.
5. Luxury expectation by the ex-agitators from the OSAPND. Most ex-agitators see the DDR programme as their own personal share of the national cake. They came into the programme with very high expectations (from the FGN). The pre-amnesty period witnessed large sum of money being transferred from the oil companies to the environmental activists. With this in mind, those ex-agitators who may have received thousands of dollars from the multinational companies believe that the FGN should similarly lavish such luxury provision on them. Unfortunately, government spending is accounted for in approved expenses. In contrast to their expectations, the OSAPND has continued to utilize its benchmark for project budgets and execution.

6. Project end-time. There has been a wider argument about when the amnesty programme should end. The SAPND gave the project limit as 2015, based on the current programme outline. However, there are numerous ex-agitators and scholars from the impacted community project who will be undergoing their programmes beyond 2015: therefore, what will be their fate? Moreover, there will be a need to produce a final report on the Nigerian DDR project and an overview of its programme achievements. This can only be possible when the exit time is confirmed. From the preceding analysis of the DDR programmes, it is evident that there will be a need for an extension of the project.
7. Politicking of the amnesty project by opposition members. Indeed, differences were often evident in how opposition politicians tended to talk about the amnesty project within Nigerian society. Queries are always raised about the project's spending. The SAPND recently gave a press briefing of the spending of the amnesty project since its inception, as shown in Table 8.1. The statistics differed from what was stated by the opposition politicians. Therefore, regular press briefings have been adopted in order to inform the public. In addition, the FGN budget is now published online for public access.
8. The question of whether violence will become the new trend in agitation for economic needs in Nigeria. Given the implications of the amnesty offer for society, and the fact that youth unemployment is at a high level, as well as the noticeable media showcasing of the amnesty training programmes, certain groups are reviewing the option of violence as a way of attracting sympathy and attention from the FGN. Recently, the terrorist group *Boko Haram*, which is operating in northern Nigeria, has raised the question of whether an amnesty should be given to its members as a way of ending their deadly bombings in the region or not. This suggestion was rejected by the society. These dynamics can help to explain the challenges that the country may face in the future.

8.4.1 Partner Organizations in the Nigerian DDR Project

To continue the entrepreneurial skills-building of the post-training and engagement package of the DDR project, twelve multinational companies in the oil and gas industry set up the "Post Amnesty Oil and Gas Industry Foundation" (OGIF). OGIF came to an agreement with the OSAPND to train a small proportion of the delegates in specific skills. This is a project similar to OSAPND's empowerment/business set-up programmes for ex-agitators. OGIF is funded by the following oil companies: NAOC, Addax, Oando, Niger Delta Petroleum Resources, Chevron, Exxon Mobil, Shell, Total, NLNG, SLB, Pan Ocean, and NPDC. The project is managed by the donors. There are programme evaluation meetings between the OSAPND and OGIF staff on a regular basis to review and monitor the progress of activities. OGIF was established by these companies and not through compulsion by the FGN. Thus, OGIF is regarded as a vendor in the empowerment project. The difference is that they do not receive funding from the OSAPND budgets. However, the OSAPND provides laptops for all ex-agitators, including the OGIF trainees, as a working tool.

8.4.2 The Nigerian Home-Grown DDR Project and the Work of Donor- or AU/UN-Piloted DDR Programmes

According to OSAA/GSL (2005), about "twenty-five Africa countries" were engaged in armed conflict or were experiencing political crisis. Most of these countries have experienced UN/AU-led DDR programmes and this includes countries such as Angola, Burundi, the Democratic Republic of the Congo, Liberia, Mozambique, Rwanda, the Republic of Sierra Leone and Zimbabwe. To the UN, each of the DDR processes is unique especially in the *reinsertion, reintegration, resettlement, and repatriation* (Rs) programmes (OSAA/GSL 2005: 11). Furthermore, about seven African countries in the Great Lakes Region benefited from the *Multi-country Demobilization and Reintegration Programme* (MDRP) with a target of 400,000 combatants, and the project was financed by the World Bank and thirteen other donors, namely twelve European countries and the EU. The MDRP project closed in June 2009 with about 300,000 ex-combatants demobilized and 232,000 ex-combatants reintegrated.[6] Nigeria's DDR project had not commenced during the period of operation of the MDRP (2002–2009), so the author cannot suggest if Nigeria would have participated in the project or not. However, this section will examine closely the differences and similarities between Nigeria's DDR programme and Angola's; both countries share similarities in oil conflicts.

In the Angolan DDR programme, for instance, its reintegration implementation, which started in 2003, was through the *Institute of Socio-Professional Reintegration for Ex-Combatants* (IRSEM) and its programme execution was carried out by *non-governmental organizations* (NGOs) both national and international; whereas the Nigerian DDR is being implemented by OSAPND under the Presidency. It will be of interest to note that the Nigerian DDR project is characterized by learning-by-doing, with regular amendments to the SOP as a result of lessons learnt. But OSAA/GSL (2005) hinted that lessons learnt in most of their DDR projects are not always incorporated into the planning and design of subsequent DDR programmes. This is a pitfall for the sustainability of donor-funded projects. In similar terms, in May 2001 in Nigeria the then President Obasanjo supported the DFID, the World Bank, USAID and UNDP in producing a national *strategic conflict assessment* (SCA). In this project, OECD (2007: 57) reported that this multi-donor approach experienced challenges for more effective "co-ordination

[6]MDRP, at: http://www.mdrp.org/ (14 March 2014).

in harmonising disbursement; accounting and reporting systems", since donors used different funding regulations and procedures.

Table 8.2 shows the major similarities and differences between the Nigerian home-grown DDR and the UN/AU/MDRP-funded Angola DDR for our clearer anlysis.

Reporting lessons learnt, MDRP (2010: 43) reported that the experience of the MDRP affirms that a regional multi-partner coordinated response to DDR was the most appropriate; "the counterfactual and fragmented response would likely led to duplication, inefficiencies, and gaps in programming". This view gained support from Lamb (2013: 3) and OSAA/GSL (2005: 13). The former (MDRP) found that a large number of individuals who underwent demobilization in Angola were actually surrogates for authentic UNITA combatants; and the latter (Lamb) stipulates that recycling of ex-combatants disarmed and demobilized in previous DDRs was a challenge to the Angolan DDR. In these circumstances, while these social indicators reveal the extent of the problem with the Angolan DDR, the author argues that the commitment of local actors' involvement in the DDR will minimize the issue of duplications and surrogates; hence the interveners will be able to identify such issues more quickly than external actors. There is a common saying in Nigeria that "we know ourselves"; this phrase will continue to play a dominant role in local participation in peacebuilding. Generally, in Africa, people seem more careful with their own inputs than with aided inputs; that is, local funding is better managed and accounted for than foreign aid.

Narrowing the DDR implementation to local actors in Africa will be the most ideal solution. For instance, OECD (2007: 58), reporting lessons learnt from implementing the Nigerian SCA, said that international actors (donors) need to "leave room for local ownership"; hence, the experience gathered demonstrated the need to leave room for ownership by in-country partners. It is therefore necessary to consider the options of liberal peace thinking, which emphasizes peacebuilding from the bottom up rather than from the top down. Most relevant to this analysis is the work of Richmond (2008: 106), who sees orthodox international relations as combining the outside-in construction of peace, where outside actors "import specialised knowledge, procedures and structures", with an inside-out approach, where "disputants' attempts to re-negotiate" this process follow their own interests, culture and frameworks. The MDRP project is one such example, with various imported specialized skills and procedures. As we have seen with the example from the work of MDRP (2010: 1) in their final report, over forty national and international partners were involved over a period of seven years, and they succeeded in demobilizing 300,000 and reintegrating 232,000 ex-, giving an average of 7500 and 5800 ex-combatants per nation respectively. When you compare their success rate with that of only one nation—Nigeria demobilizing 30,000 and reintegrating 14,029 ex-agitators in three years—the latter success far outweighs the former. Therefore, the author strongly suggests that local actors' involvement is indeed a welcome trend in DDR projects.

Moreso, the operational budget of the Nigerian DDR project in its 2014 proposal is US$22,567,452, and with 80 % of the staff coming from the Niger Delta region,

Table 8.2 Differences between the n and Nigeria DDR programmes

Differences between Angola DDR and Nigeria government/donor piloted DDR projects	
Angola	Nigeria
DDR features	
Negotiations concluded in New York plus subsequent agreements/accords	Previous Negotiations included the 2002 Lt Gen. Alexander Ogomudia Committee; 2006 Dr Goodluck Jonathan Committee on Empowerment
Accords included a DDR programme	Still on the 2009 proclamation agreement
DDR program failed with resumption of war triggered by 1992 election outcomes	Still on-going and active
Agitators were integrated into national army	None integrated directly to national Army
General amnesty to all UNITA soldiers in 2002 after death of leader	Amnesty to all who signed up within 60 days period
35 Quartering areas set up for the project	Only in 1 quartering area in Obubura
Reception for both UNITA soldiers and dependents	Reception to only ex-militants and leaders dependents
91,127 agitators registered	30,000 ex-militants
288,756 family members registered	
5000 integrated into National Army	No automatic entrance but ex-agitators can apply to enrol into the Army
Main DDR started September 2003	Main DDR commenced in March 2010
Training types	
Vocational training	Yes
Traditional apprentices hips and on-the-job training	Yes
Community works	
Access to took-kits	Yes
Micro-business training, advisory services and microcredit	Yes
Not recorded	Specialized program training in aviation, maritime
New trend	
Not recorded	Inclusion of 1000–3000 delegates for training from the conflicted impacted communities (who never bore arms but were direct and indirect victims of conflict)
None	Academic training for degree qualification
Duration and speed	
Between 2003 and 2005: Over 20,000 ex-combatants benefiting from reintegration	11,700 have received reintegration packages between 2010 and 2013
Factors	
Recycling of ex-combatants in previous DDRs	No official record
Large number of war-disabled ex-combatants	No official record

(continued)

Table 8.2 (continued)

Differences between Angola DDR and Nigeria government/donor piloted DDR projects	
Angola	Nigeria
Funding	
Donor and national government funding: received USD$22,950,865 from MDRP & UNDP as of July 2008	Only Nigeria Government funding: USD$14, 233,064,89.72 (2009–2014)

Source Author's compilation based on OSAA/GSL (2005), MDRP (2008), Amnesty News Publications (2013a, b), Amnesty News (2014a, 2014), OSAPND (2014), and Lamb (2013)

this will inherently contribute to the economic development of the region through employment generation. It is important to acknowledge that the *Presidential Amnesty Project* (PAP) also has created employment opportunities for over a hundred staff working as consultants/interveners in the DDR project. It could be argued also that the high running costs as well as expatriate fees associated with external actors in DDR projects could have huge implications for the project cost. Making reference to this discussion, previous studies on MDRP (2010:10) have reported that the project budget cost was US$500 million. Out of this total, US $446.5 m was budgeted for national programmes, and US$37.5 m for special projects. In addition, the secretariat's management cost totalled US$24.9 m or approximately 9.9 % of the *Multi-Donor Trust Fund* (MDTF) (MDRP 2010: 33). Such findings, identifying huge management costs, are consistent with those by Winter (2010: 36–7) that in aid programmes, a relatively small portion of *Organisation for Economic Co-operation and Development* (OEDC) *gross national product* (GNP), usually "less than half a percent, and much less than private sector flows to a handful of middle-income countries", hence the donor countries are also "building supranational bodies" (WTO, EU, NAFTA, NATO, etc.) to "maintain prosperity, setting the pace of globalization and writing rules of intervention of the Security Council". Winter added that donor countries are committed to the "relief of the victims of war" without a more serious commitment to discourage wars and control the arms trade and build peace. It can be argued that 9.9 % of the MDRP's US$500 million would have contributed to pilot countries' feasible human and economic capital if local actors/implementers were the beneficiaries of the management cost indicated in the project, an approach that is the opposite of the Nigerian home-grown DDR project.

8.5 Economic Impacts of the Amnesty Programme in Nigeria

For Midgley/Hall (2004: x), empowerment refers to "the acquisition of power to control or influence the course of events, often assumed to be a *sine qua non* of authentic development, especially at grassroots level". The value that the Nigerian amnesty business set-ups attach to increased industrialization in the region is assumed by the OSAPND to reduce poverty, dependence on subsistence agriculture, and social ills.[7] Furthermore, Winter (2001: 37) describes empowerment as a component of education which is likely by "its nature to subvert established interest". Winter added that project implementers could try empowering communities by funding local assemblies, training local leaders and holding warlords to account, investing in schools, starting adult education classes, and so on. Generally, DDR is a development intervention that is meant to transform the Niger Delta oil conflicts, build sustainable peace, and foster resilience.

One striking benefit of the amnesty programme is stability in the oil and gas revenue as against the pre-amnesty period. Stability brought oil production back up to 2.4 million bpd, which is the main source of revenue in the country. Decreasing militancy, as demonstrated in Ariyoh et al. (2013: 15), remains a vital economic element, which assumes far greater importance in the post-amnesty period in Nigeria. Ariyoh et al. found the Niger Delta to "appear peaceful" and this is a "pre-condition for sustaining a long term and sustainable growth in the artisanal fishing business". In addition, this stability has also brought about speedy completion of infrastructures by both the Federal and State Governments in the region. This process brings about industrialization and the creation of jobs, which in turn brings about wealth generation and employment, thereby impacting on the economy of the region. Similarly et al. (2013: 424) found that issues "post-amnesty in Nigeria have led to some developmental activities" around the Niger Delta states; hence a peaceful state has improved oil exploration, which brings in revenue to the government.

According to Ariyoh et al. (2013), the "amnesty policy intervention has yielded progressive impacts on artisanal fishing agribusiness" based on fieldwork conducted in ten different rural riverine communities in the Niger Delta region, where data collected was distinguished between pre- and post-amnesty periods. For Ariyoh et al. (2013: 14), fishing production among fish farmers increased significantly, with average income rising from US$17.46 (pre-amnesty) to US$63.23 per week.[8] This means that fish farmers could earn an average of US$242.51 per month instead of US$69.84, leaving a generous surplus of US$172.67. Linking this fish-farming business finding to the economic developmental impact of the PAP, one could argue that the amnesty programme contributes to an increase in productivity. Given the more encompassing analysis that fishing is an important livelihood activity in most villages in the Niger Delta region because of its geographical nature that favours small-scale fisherfolk, its impact on local community internal revenue cannot therefore be overemphasized. Setting up a five-point training agenda, Kuku listed agriculture as among his priority areas (Amnesty News 2013a: 1). To emphasis this, Amnesty News (2013b: 9) reported that skills

[7]Such as kidnapping, oil theft, violence/conflicts, etc.

[8]Currency conversion by the author at US$1 = N164.94 (Naira): accessed on 12 March 2014.

acquisition in the field of agriculture is part of the training programmes for the 4608 delegates, both onshore and offshore. This demonstrates the position agriculture occupies in the country.

Nagpaul (1991: 189) suggest that "it has become a universally accepted fact that vast inequalities in incomes, opportunities and levels of living continue to exist between the rural and urban sectors in almost every society in the Third World". Nigeria happens to be among the Third World countries, and large numbers of the beneficiaries of the Nigerian Amnesty project dwell in the rural areas, where its ultimate impact will contribute immensely to the rural reconstruction of the Niger Delta region. The Amnesty programme sees education and training, as well as engagement and empowerment, as primary toolkits for the reintegration of ex-agitators. This approach agrees with Nagpaul (1991: 193), who stipulates that "human development and mobilization through education and employment" is one of the strategic programmes that will promote reduction and resolution of conflicts.

A strong livelihood activity is most likely to improve community development. If the communities in the region are witnessing through the amnesty programme a relatively peaceful environment for their daily economic activities, ultimately business output will increase, and this will obviously strengthen livelihood activities. There has been relatively systematic research on community development by Midgley/Hall (2004: 73–6), who present "local community as a vital resource for development effort". They also posit rural community development programmes as making a major contribution to agricultural production, and that "small scale community development projects also contributes to poverty eradication because they generate human capital through development of skills, literacy and job experience". According to Amnesty News (2013b: 9), 4608 delegates are engaged on skills acquisition, 2500 delegates on formal education, 2000 delegates on entrepreneurial skills/business empowerment, and 222 delegates on direct employment, a total of 9330 delegates. This figure represents 31 % of the 30,000 delegates who have received a reintegration package, and this generally reinforces the human and socio-economic capital of the beneficiaries' communities. Ejovi/Ebie (2013: 136) argue that the "Amnesty programmes skill acquisition packages promises a better future for both local populations and the oil companies". Looking at the 2014 budget, for instance, a total of US$385,978,011 has been budgeted for the 2014 amnesty programmes, a sum most likely to impact on the development of skills and wealth creation in the region.

Kuku (2014a, b),[9] in a press briefing, stated that OSAPND is currently "setting up 2000 of the graduates of the skills acquisition programme in small scale businesses". It should be noted here that small-scale businesses are elements of the private sector. According to Hall/Midgley (2004: 17), the private sector comprises

[9]Kuku Kingsley (2014a), "Press Briefing on the Amnesty Budgetary Allocation since inception", in: *ThisDay Live Newspaper publication* (18 February); Kuku Kingsley (2014b), "Press Briefing: Amnesty Office sheds light on controversial Budget figures", in: *The Guardian* (19 February).

areas of activity in the formal economy of firms and enterprises, and the informal sector in the south has “social policy implications to the extent that [it] creates employment, generates wages, salaries and other benefits”. Hall and Midgley added that people in the private sector engage in activities that have other “profound economic, social, and environmental impacts”. Therefore, the outputs of the PAP help to engage people on activities that have profound economic, social and environmental impacts in the Niger Delta region. In addition, Ejovi/Ebie (2013) add that the ex-agitators trained in oil-related skills should be engaged in the oil industry through the “reservation of employment quotas”, as this will make the locals operating in the region feel themselves to be stakeholders. Obviously, this is favourable to conflict prevention. There is much to believe that constituting the ex-agitators as part of the oil company workforce will create a company-ownership mentality among them, thereby reducing the issues of conflict escalation that are associated with the precarious relationship between the oil companies and local communities.

There has, thus, been a shift in the thinking of Nigerians towards what some see as a new economic development in the Niger Delta region aiming at achieving amnesty programme objectives that will strengthen social and cultural capacities to economic empowerment. The varied training programmes in the reintegration packages are linked to developing trust, safety, and social cohesion within and between communities, which will improve business relations in the region. Furthermore, the business set-ups by the OSAPND are structured in such a way that once an ex-agitator is empowered, there is a tendency that this will create jobs for at least five apprentices or family members.

Figures 8.5 and 8.6 illustrate the spending pattern by the amnesty office and the nine Niger Delta states on education, while Tables 8.3 and 8.4 give statistical descriptions of the data (Figs. 8.13, 8.14 and 8.15).

This article brings together information gathered on the budgetary allocations on education by the nine Niger Delta states in 2012. The reason is that the amnesty project is a classified social service programme specializing in the education of the amnesty delegates. Perhaps the description of education by Peters will widen our understanding of the term ‘education’. Peters (2010: 1) describes education as a “reform with no particular process” and that it is also an initiation of a process whose task is relative to achievement. In Amnesty News (2013b: 25), Kuku stated that all the amnesty delegates have been “fully disarmed and demobilized, and that they are currently in training or have been trained” with a view of adding to the national GDP and improving themselves and their families. It was recorded that over 14,000 delegates have been deployed to either academic or vocational certified training. Most relevant to this analysis is that in 2012, a total of US$1,180,540,975 and US$403,637,774 was spent on education by the nine Niger Delta states and the Amnesty Office respectively, a grand total of US$1,584,178,749. The implication of this is that an additional average of US$44,848,641 was added to human capital development spending in the year 2012 per state educational sector through the

Table 8.3 Statistical description of FGN presidential amnesty budget allocation (2010–2013)

	Amnesty budget summary from 2010 to 2013				
2009	2010	2011	2012	2013	Total
Take off grant					
10,000,000,000[a]	8,000,000,000	102,176,411,902	66,176,411,902	66,781,093,786	243,133,917,590
USD$	48,795,365.33	623,216,918.4	403,637,774.4	407,325,983.6	148,297,6042

[a]Announced as take-off grant but actual spending started in 2010 where only 8,000,000,000 was expended

Source Author's compilation from Kuku (SAPND) press briefing (2014a, b) and Federal Government of Nigeria Budget Office. Currency conversion by the author at US$1 = N163.95 (Naira) on 3 March 2014

Table 8.4 Statistical Description of 2012 Education Budget Allocation by nine Niger Delta States

	Nine Niger delta states education budget 2012		
S/N		USD$	Nigeria Naira
1	Abia	$141,234,031.53	23,254,182,444.80
2	Alkwa Ibom	$119,040,393.04	19,600,000,000
3	Bayelsa	$127,543,278.26	21,000,000,000
4	Cross River	$147,836,396.67	24,341,261,824.88
5	Delta	$157,330,222.80	25,904,420,240
6	Edo	$46,765,868.69	7,700,000,000
7	Imo	$166,164,348.48	27,358,958,980
8	Ondo	$163,785,253.37	27,000,000,000
9	Rivers	$110,841,182.30	18,250,000,000
	Total	$1,180,540,975.14	194,408,823,489.68

Source Author's compilation from the eight Niger Delta government websites and Niger Delta Citizen Platform websites. Currency conversion by the author at US$1 = N163.95 (Naira) on 3 March 2014

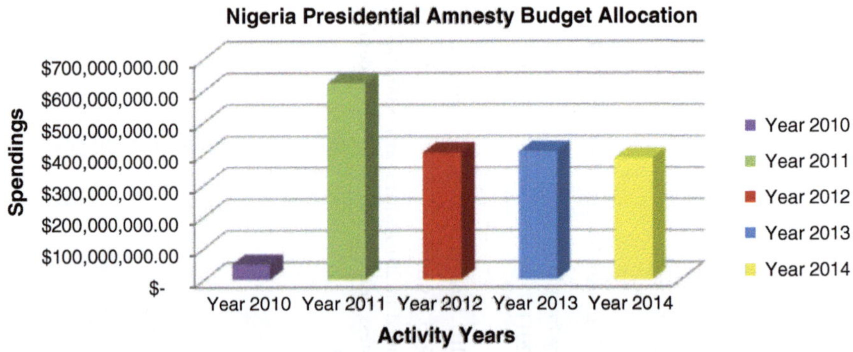

Fig. 8.13 Federal Government of Nigeria budgetary allocation from 2010 to 2014. *Source* Author's own compilation from Kuku (SAPND) press briefing (2014a, b), and Federal Government of Nigeria Budget Office. Currency conversion by the author at US$1 = N163.95 (Naira) (3 March 2014)

DDR programmes. Obviously, the social and economic effect of the input of US $44,848,641 into a state is undoubtedly positive. This view accords directly with Ejovi/Ebie (2013: 133) who argue that the "Amnesty programme is expected to improve the human capital development of the country". An exploratory interview study of the impacts of amnesty programmes as narrated by amnesty delegates in Amnesty News (2013b: 12–13) describes the benefits of acquiring one's own livelihood activity, demonstrating that delegates interviewed have received training and are currently engaged with economic activities.

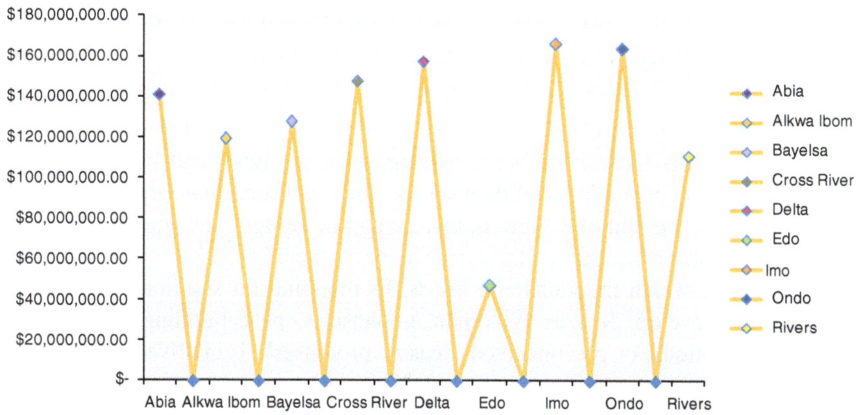

Fig. 8.14 Showing the 2012 Education Budget Allocation by the nine Niger Delta States. *Source* Author's compilation from the eight Niger Delta government websites and Niger Delta Citizen Platform websites (Abia State, at: http://www.abiastate.gov.ng/news/the-governor-chief-t-a-orji-presented-the-abia-state-budget/ and http://www.abiastate.gov.ng/wp-content/uploads/2011/12/2012-Budget-Speech-by-Ochendo-2.pdf (12 March 2014); Alkwa Ibom State; Bayelsa State; Cross River State, at: http://crossriverwatch.com/2013/10/austerity-cross-river-slashes-2013-budget (12 March 2014); Edo State, at: http://website.edostategov.ng/ministries/finance; Imo State, at: http://www.imostateblog.com/2012/12/03/imo-state-budget-governor-rochas-okorocha-presents-a-n197-7-billion-proposal-for-2013 (6 February 2014); Niger Delta Citizen Platform, at http://www.citizensbudget.org/citizens_image/Spend_and_Borrow_2011.pdf (4 February 2014); Ondo State; Rivers State.). Currency conversion by the author at US$1 = N164.65 (Naira)

Fig. 8.15 Reintegration activity photos. *Source* OSAPND Records

8.6 Conclusion: Successes in the Home-Grown DDR and Its Impacts on the Nigerian Economy

Research by Waldman (2008: 13) revealed that people in Afghanistan ranked "community *shura* second as agents to employ in resolving and managing their conflicts". The people understand themselves—their culture, economy, politics, and their identities. The author's view is that as conflict erupts, the immediate population are the first recipients of the consequences; therefore, they will strategize a way out if they weigh the gains and losses. In shopping for solutions, new trends are likely to develop. Just as Waldman emphasizes, peacebuilding is not about "imposing solutions, or preconceived ideas or processes". It involves self-analysis and helps support communities to develop their own means of "strengthening social cohesion and of building capacities to reach solutions that are peaceful and just" (Waldman 2008: 15). Similarly, Ball/Goor (2006: 7) suggest that "DDR should be approached as a process, not a programme, and these programmes should be embedded in a broader dynamic, integrated process such as developing adequate human and institutional capacity". In this context, it is instructive to note that OSAPND thematic activities are based on different integrated processes that will develop human and institutional capacities in the Niger Delta region. As a backup analysis, over 14,000 trained delegates have been equipped with different human capital, and over 2000 delegates empowered in different small-scale businesses. All these categories of people possess the potential for the socio-economic development of the region through their individual skill-set contribution to regional institutions.

Therefore, the opportunity to encourage peacebuilders to start developing solutions in their own ways should be a welcome trend. As already indicated, MacGinty (2010: 404–5) cited instances of "European newcomers conforming to local methods of peacemaking and dispute resolution in North America in the 16th–17th centuries", as well as the incorporation of "warlords and militia commanders in the government in post-Taliban Afghanistan". These are forms of hybridized peace and a success record in our DDR discourse.

The case of Nigeria's DDR programme has provided the DDR community with the inclusion of people from conflict-impacted communities in the reintegration packages. Addison (2003: 1) posits that "community needs must be a focus of attention hence war fractures communities, destroying human and social capital". Generally, the focus of DDR projects has been on the primary stakeholders, who are usually the combatants/agitators and their dependents. There has been an obvious neglect of the people living in the war-torn communities who did not carry arms but lived in fear and experienced the destruction of their family lives and properties. They are indirect primary stakeholders of conflict and should be attended to. The inclusion of 1000–3000 people from the impacted conflict communities in the Niger Delta DDR programme is a success to reckon with.

It is also important to note that the inclusion of 3000 people from the impacted communities is only achievable because local actors were involved. Take, for instance, the issue of duplication and surrogates that was highlighted in the Angolan

DDR; this would not arise in the Nigerian DDR because the local implementers would discover such anomalies. Thus, external implementers will find it difficult to select the recipients of the impacted communities without duplications and surrogates.

According to Ubhenin (2013: 182–3), the FGN lost N500 billion (Naira) in 2006 on account of "restiveness in the Niger Delta", US$6.3 billion in 2008 in oil stolen, and another US$28 billion in oil not explored, which translates to a revenue loss of US$40 million per day in the region. These losses were due to the high level of oil conflicts which triggered a high level of oil theft in the region, thereby reducing oil exploration and production. Nigeria depends more than anything else on oil income and an attempt to limit its production is an attack on the national economy. Moreso (Ejovi/Ebie 2013: 132) reported that the "pre-amnesty period which was filled with conflicts brought about a total loss of US$21.5 billion from the multinational oil companies' outputs in 2003". Therefore, to have the amnesty programme in place is a major factor in national stability.

It is important to acknowledge the work of De Zeeuw (2001: 21) on DDR experiences from Bosnia-Herzegovina, Somalia, and Angola, which demonstrate that full-scale enforced disarmament is only "feasible if the security concerns of the parties are credibly assessed and met by the monitoring mission". De Zeeuw added that there have to be sufficient "economic and political incentives" to encourage the former combatants to look for alternative means of employment. Drawing on De Zeeuw's findings, the Nigerian DDR took into consideration the financial importance attached to arms by ex-agitators and negotiated a monthly stipend of US$400 per ex-agitator as their economic gain—an amount which is higher than a graduate civil servant's monthly earnings. The author suggests that this monthly stipend was perhaps a consideration that paved the way for the success of the amnesty DDR implementation packages. Considerations were also given to higher sustainable livelihood packages by the OSAPND through sustainable training and empowerment packages. Lamb (2013: 3), however, reported that the reintegration packages for the Angolan ex-combatants was "pegged at US$700 per ex-combatant"—an amount which is less than two months' stipend for the Nigerian ex-agitator. Possibly, if this financial package had been similar to that of the Nigerian DDR, it would have led to strong challenges and shortfalls. Therefore, the huge sum spent by the Nigerian government, as well as the use of local actors as part of its implementation mission, contributed to the success of the amnesty DDR programme.

References

Aall, Pamela, 2007: "The Power of Nonofficial Actors in Conflict Management", in: Crocker C. A.; Hampson, F. O.; Aall P. (Eds.): *Leasing the Dogs of War—Conflict Management in a Divided World* (Washington DC: United States Institute of Peace Press): 477–494.

Abazie-Humphrey, Margaret, 2008: "Building Sustainable Peace in the Fragile Niger Delta of Nigeria", Paper for the 12th General Conference of the European Association of Development Research and Training Institutes (EADI), Geneva, 24–28 June.

Addison, Tony, 2003: *Africa's Recovery From Conflict: Making Peace Work for the Poor.* (Helsinki: UNU World Institute for Development Economics Research [UNU/WIDER]).

Amnesty News, 2013a: "Kuku sets five-points training agenda", 1,2 (Abuja: monthly newsletter published by the Presidential Amnesty Office, May ed.).

Amnesty News, 2013b: "Amnesty Programme @ 3—The Facts, The Figures". Anniversary Edition, 1,3 (Abuja: A quarterly newsletter published by the Presidential Amnesty Office).

Ariyoh, L. E.; Achoja, F. O.; Idoge, D. E.; Ukwaba, S. I., 2013: "Economic Impacts of Amnesty Policy Intervention on Artisanal Fishing Agribusiness in Niger Delta, Nigeria", in: *Journal of Agriculture and Veterinary Science* (IOSR–JAVS), 2,6 (April): 12–16.

Ball, Nicole; van de Goor, Luc, 2006: *DDR: Mapping Issues, Dilemmas and Guiding Principles* (Clingendael: The Netherlands Institute of International Relations, Conflict Research Unit, August): 7.

Baumuller H.; Donnelly E.; Vines A.; Weimer, Markus, 2011: "The Effects of Oil Companies' Activities on the Environment, Health and Development in Africa" (Luxembourg: EU Parliament, Policy Department, DG External Policies, EXPO/B/DEVE/FWC/2009-01/Lot5/11 August 2011 PE 433.768 EN).

Collier, Paul, 2007: "Economic Causes of Civil Conflict and Their Implications for Policy", in: Crocker, C. A.; Hampson, F. O.; Aall, P. (Eds.): *Leasing the Dogs of War—Conflict Management in a Divided World* (Washington DC: United States Institute of Peace Press): 197–219.

De Zeeuw, Jeroen, 2001: *Building Peace in War-Torn Societies: From Concept to Strategy* (Clingendael: The Netherland Institute of International Relations, Conflict Research Unit, August).

Ejovi, Austine; Ebie, Sunday, 2013: "Niger Delta: A Critical Appraisal of the Amnesty Programme and Social Political Development in Nigeria", in: *Journal of Research on Humanities and Social Sciences,* 3,22: 130–137.

Eteng, Bassey; Odey, Enng; Levi, Odike, 2013: "The Niger Delta Crisis in Nigeria: Pre and Post Amnesty Situation", in: *Mediterranean Journal of Social Sciences,* 4,6: 421–427.

Francis, Paul, 2002: "Social Capital, Civil Society and Social Exclusion", in: Kothari, Uma; Martin, Minogue (Eds.): *Development Theory and Practice* (Basingstoke: Palgrave).

Freedman, Lawrence, 2007: "Using Force for Peace in an Age of Terror", in: Crocker, C. A.; Hampson, F.O.; Aall, P. (Eds.): *Leasing the Dogs of War—Conflict Management in a Divided World* (Washington DC: United States Institute of Peace Press): 245–263.

Kuku, Kingsley, 2012: *Remaking the Niger Delta—Challenges and Opportunities* (Jacksonville, AR—Croydon, Surrey: Mandingo Publishing).

Lamb, Guy 2013: "DDR 20 Years Later—Historical Reviews of the Long-term Impacts of Post-independence DDR in Southern Africa", in: *Transitional Demobilization and Reintegration Program (TDRP)* (Washington: The International Bank for Reconstruction and Development/The World Bank, June).

MacGinty, Roger, 2010: "Hybrid Peace: The Interaction Between Top-Down and Bottom-Up Peace", in: *Security Dialogue,* 41,4 (August): 391–412.

Midgley, James; Hall, Anthony, 2004: *Social Policy for Development* (London: Sage).

Multi-Country Demobilization and Reintegration Program (MDRP), 2008: *Facts Sheet on DDR Programs Overview in Africa* (Washington: The International Bank for Reconstruction and Development/The World Bank)

Multi-Country Demobilization and Reintegration Program (MDRP), 2010: "*MDRP Final Report: Overview of Program Achievements*" (Washington: The International Bank for Reconstruction and Development/The World Bank, July).

Nagpaul, Hans, 1991: "Urban–Rural Relationships and Social Conflicts in India", in: Vayrynen, Raimo (Ed.): *New Directions in Conflict Theory—Conflict Resolution and Conflict Transformation* (London: Sage).

Office of the Special Adviser to Nigeria President on Niger Delta (OSAPND), 2014: *Challenges of the Nigeria DDR Programmes* (Abuja: Government Registry/Documentations).

Organization for Economic Co-operation and Development (OECD), 2007: *The OECD DACH Handbook on Security System Reform (SSR)—Supporting Security and Justice* (Paris: OECD).

OSAA & GSL (UN Office of the Special Adviser on Africa & Government of the Republic of Sierra Leone) 2005: "Disarmament, Demobilization, Reintegration (DDR) and Stability in Africa: Conference Report, Freetown, 21–23 June" (New York: United Nations AFR/1195-PKO/119).

Peters, R. S., 2010: "What is an Educational Process?", in: Peters, R. S. (Ed.): *The Concept of Education* (London: Routledge & Kegan Paul): 1–16.

Richmond, P. Oliver, 2008: *Peace in International Relations* (London: Routledge).

Rowell, Andy; Marriot, James; Stockman, Lorne, 2005: *The Next Gulf: London, Washington and Oil Conflict in Nigeria* (London: Constable & Robinson).

Siisiäinen, Martti, 2000: "Two Concepts of Social Capital: Bourdieu vs. Putnam"; in: "The Third Sector: For What and for Whom?", Paper for the ISTR Fourth International Conference, Dublin, 5–8 July.

Thomas-Larmer, J.; Susskind, L.; McKearnan, S., 1999: *The Consensus Building Handbook—A Comprehensive Guide to Reaching Agreement* (London: Sage).

Ubhenin, Oscar Edoror, 2013: "The Federal Government's Amnesty Programme in the Niger Delta: An Appraisal", in: *Yönetim Bilimleri Dergisi*, 11,21: 179–203.

Ukiwo, Ukoha, 2007: "From Pirates to Militants: A historical perspective on anti-state and anti-oil company mobilization among the Ijaw of Warri, Western Niger Delta", in: *African Affairs: The Journal of the Royal African Society*, 106,425 (October): 587–610.

Waldman, Matt, 2008: *Community Peacebuilding in Afghanistan. The Case for a National Strategy*. Oxfam International Research Report (London: Oxfam, February).

Winter, Philip, 2010: "A Glossary for New Samaritans", in: Barrow, Ondine; Jennings, Michael (Eds.): *The Charitable Impulse—NGOs and Development in East and North-East Africa* (Oxford: James Currey): 31–44.

Chapter 9
Reflections on Moving Toward Ecological Civilization and Positive Peace

Juliet Bennett

Abstract This concluding chapter points to the alignment of positive peace with emerging ideas about 'ecological civilization', both which entail the aim of bringing about a more socially just and ecologically harmonious global society. It surveys initiatives that are working to bring about change on structural, cultural and direct levels, corresponding with Galtung's (1996) notions of structural peace, cultural peace and direct peace. Under these headings, Bennett presents a small selection of initiatives that she personally finds hope for humanity. For example, she considers the research and action being done in the interdisciplinary fields of process philosophy and ecofeminism, to bring about deep cultural change toward a more peaceful and ecological civilization. On a structural level, the author considers changes in technology, business, laws and economic systems. She links these changes to direct changes that individuals can make within their realms of influence to encourage the broader structural and cultural change, for example, choosing to invest in renewal technologies and divest from fossil fuels, and building the political will to support governments to do the same. Within this framework one can consider how issues discussed in the other chapters of the two volumes fit into the matrix of structural, cultural and direct violence, and what kind of changes and actions at each of these levels can help contribute to positive peace. Overall this essay will leave readers with a sense of hope, that humanity can together work to change their habits and structural constrains and move toward a more peaceful and ecological civilization.

Keywords Positive peace · Ecological civilization · Social justice · Process philosophy · Ecofeminism · Structural change · Cultural change · Direct action

Juliet Bennett, Ph.D. candidate, University of Sydney; co-convenor, IPRA's Ecology and Commission (2014–2016); Email: juliet.bennett@sydney.edu.au.

Ú.Oswald Spring et al. (eds.), *Regional Ecological Challenges for Peace in Africa, the Middle East, Latin America and Asia Pacific*, The Anthropocene: Politik—Economics—Society—Science 5, DOI 10.1007/978-3-319-30560-8_9

9.1 Introduction

This chapter looks to the future with a sense of hope, pointing to some of the many aligned activities of people and groups around the world working toward positive peace. It is a short chapter, with space to reflect on only a small sample of the scholarship and initiatives that the author is most enthusiastic about. These are particularly focused on working to bring about deep cultural and structural change, as well as more immediate direct actions that are and can be taken to contribute to achieving these deeper shifts. These categories of cultural change, structural change and direct action correspond with Galtung's (1996) triangle of violence, which distinguishes structural violence (indirect forms of violence resulting from structures such as poverty and environmental destruction), direct violence (such as war, bullying, and other easily observable forms of violence) and cultural violence (that can make structural and direct forms of violence seem right). All of the chapters in this volume can be seen to deal with issues of structural, cultural or direct violence, or a mixture of the three. Giving consideration to these interlinking factors can be helpful for deepening understandings of conflicts, regional and global, and to exploring who has the power to help resolve it. This chapter proposes that everyone reading this book has some power, within their varying realms of influence, to help contribute to positive change. The chapter closes by considering the potential directions that conversations in ecology and peace might be taken in working toward more desirable futures.

9.2 Context and the Future

The two volumes resulting from the *Ecology and Peace Commission* (EPC) at the 2014 *International Peace Research Association* (IPRA) conference explore many interconnections between environmental issues and issues of peace and justice. Be it the ecological and social impact of nuclear testing in the Marshall Islands, or the control over water between Israel and Palestine, environmental issues are human issues. They are also political, cultural, social, economic and ecological issues.

At the junction of ecology and peace studies is a simple and potent concept worth pausing to consider: *context.* In emphasizing the inseparability of organisms from their relationships and environments, ecology draws attention to the context in which the lives of organisms and ecosystems unfold. Studying ecology from a humanities perspective draws attention to the webs of relationships that humanity is embedded within, both as part of Earth's ecological systems as well as some 13.8 billion years of cosmic evolution.[1] Swimme/Berry (1992) call this whole context of

[1]NASA, at: http://science.nasa.gov/science-news/science-at-nasa/2013/21mar_cmb/ (31 October 2015).

human and nonhuman life "The Universe Story", a story that each creature's personal biographies is each a part.

An ecological understanding of one's self and the world has profound implications for the pursuit of peace. Resolving conflicts nonviolently calls for an empathic appreciation of the context in which people and groups have come to think, learn and act. This understanding of the context of people's lives and decisions can be expanded in appreciating the diverse contexts that other people and groups may live, as well as the shared ecological and cosmological context (or story) in which various forms of life are experiencing the world. It is in this broader context that one can come to understand the implications of their everyday actions for the global Earth community and for future generations.

In exploring the context, influences and potential solutions for conflicts, peace research does not limit itself to looking backward and analysing what has been, it also looks forward. It asks what kind of future is desirable? One way of articulating such an aim is Galtung's (1996) conception of "positive peace", a vision of the world at peace and with social and ecological justice. Positive peace envisages the end of all forms of violence including direct violence (such as war, physical or mental abuse, with easily visible actors), as well less visible indirect forms of cultural and structural violence, such as racism and poverty. Put another way, Galtung says that positive peace aims for direct peace, cultural peace, and structural peace. Furthermore, Galtung's conception of positive peace calls for a constant process of reflecting on what constitutes peace and justice, and what the most peaceful and nonviolent means of direct, cultural and structural change can get us there. There are many terms in circulation that share many of the values and vision of positive peace, for example "earth democracy" (Shiva 2006), "ecozoic age" (Swimme/Berry 1992) and "sustainable development" (Brundtland et al. 1987). Another term that is growing in interdisciplinary use is "Ecological Civilization" (Gare 2010).

The term ecological civilization envisions a new world system and a harmonious relationship with nature that provides the conditions for life and humanity to flourish. Process philosopher Gare (2010: 10) explains that ecological civilization brings together notions of ecology with that of civilization, which "originally was defined in opposition to barbarity as both a process and an achieved condition of social order and refinement." The term was first used by environmentalists in the Soviet Union, referring to "a further development of humanity to take into account the ecological conditions of our existence" (Gare 2010: 10). While since then the term civilization has been used in the plural, referring to "Western civilization", "Roman civilization", "Chinese civilization" and so on, Gare points out that the term ecological civilization is not using the word civilization in this way. Instead it calls for a "more dramatic sense of transformation", as in in the transition from "agricultural civilization" to "industrial civilization", and now to an ecological civilization. Ecological civilization moves away from the aim of seeking ways that nature can sustain economic growth (as may be considered encompassed by the term sustainable development), instead to consider the global economic system to be embedded in the global ecosystem (Gare 2010: 31). Gare (2010) points out to a number of reasons for choosing to use this term, one being its alignment with the Chinese government's commitment to ecological civilization (made in 2007). The term ecological civilization captures a vision of positive peace in the world, aiming to bring about an orderly, harmonious civil society that lives within the ecosystems of which humanity is a part.

Violence, peace and actions toward one or the other at direct, cultural and structural levels are all interconnected. Exploring context draws attention to the multi-directional nature of causation: people's actions (be they violent or peaceful) are significantly influenced by their culture and structures (including the laws and policies their society insists upon, their family's position in the economy, the intellectual and political happenings of a time etc.); at the same time, cultures and structures are created, maintained and changed by people's actions (from inventors to civilians, activists, governments, academics, journalists and so on). For example, today's techno-centric culture is a consequence of a line of inventors including Johannes Gutenberg (the printing press, in the West), Alexander Graham Bell (the telephone), Charles Babbage (the computer), Tim Berners-Lee (the internet), Mark Zuckerberg (Facebook), as well as the people who adopted these technologies and helped them spread. Yet each of these inventors and early adopters was simultaneously influenced by their culture, the intellectual and economic movements of the time, for example in the case of Gutenberg it was a time that people wanted to read more books) and the structures (for example each of these inventors and early adopters would have been in a financial position that enabled the education to be able to invent or invest in that technology.

The assessment of future scenario desirability encompassed by terms such as ecological civilization may be conducted according to the values that peace research makes explicit: respect for the rights of all human beings, social justice, ecological harmony and the resolution of conflict through nonviolent means. With these principles in mind, this chapter turns now to consider some initiatives that share these values and put them into action. Each of these initiatives aligns with the values of positive peace and contributes to the larger aim of ecological civilization, by encouraging an expanding public awareness and reflection on the context in which they make sense of themselves and the world, and in encouraging awareness of their participation in creating environmental and social harmony.

9.3 A Sampling of Initiatives

There are countless initiatives at global and regional levels that align with and work toward the aims of positive peace and ecological civilization. This section introduces a selection of such initiatives that the author finds most exciting. These include initiatives aimed at deep cultural change, deep structural change, and personal and group direct actions. The author believes that each of these initiatives can contribute substantially to moving toward ecological civilization.

9.4 Cultural Change Toward Ecological Civilization

On a deep cultural level, peace educator Reardon (1989) describes the search for a "paradigm of peace". Reardon envisages a shift away from "war-systems thinking" that is 'dualistic' and thinks "in terms of ends and goals". Instead, "peace-systems thinking" combines "both unity and multiplicity", and thinks "in terms of means and processes." It is a shift away from reductionism and "analysis, pulling things apart to understand them," instead building knowledge through "synthesis, putting things together in positive relationships" and "holism, asserting that you cannot understand the part unless you see it in the context of the whole" (Reardon 1988: 51). This call for deep cultural change is found in a number of interdisciplinary fields, including process philosophy, ecofeminism, and religion and ecology. It is reflected in The Earth Charter[2] and movements by indigenous people to "change the dream" of western societies.[3]

1. *Process thinking.*[4] Process philosophy explicitly shares many of the aims of peace studies, and essentially substantiates the worldview and metaphysic of Reardon's paradigm for peace. Crossing the disciplines of philosophy and theology, ecology, sociology and economics, process philosophy not only locates a peace paradigm in the history of thought, it explores the implications of this worldview for building ecological civilization. Process philosophy articulates a worldview that emphasizes relationships, connection and process. This stands in contrast to mechanistic materialist worldviews that define human beings as individuals, separate from and above nature. Such a substance-based metaphysic arguably helps to justify the exploitation of nature, other animals and other people, in order to meet the needs and wants of people in the world with the most money and power. Many of the chapters in these volumes can be seen to explore forms of violence with a deep cultural roots tied to such a materialist and mechanistic worldview. Mechanistic materialist thinking dominates Western understandings of one's self and work, and underlies many Western institutions (e.g. see Gare 1996).

The world's leading process philosophy institute, the Center for Process Studies in Claremont CA, states that process studies "offers an approach to the social, political, and economic order that brings issues of human justice together with a concern for ecology."[5] It does this by challenging dominant western analytical philosophy and its mechanistic and reductionistic metaphysics that it claims underlie the ecological crisis. In place of mechanistic materialism process thought provides a comprehensive holistic, ecological, process-based alternative based on the work of Alfred North Whitehead. This holistic process-oriented worldview helps to "harmonize moral, aesthetic, and religious intuitions with scientific

---

[2]Earth Charter Initiative, at: http://www.earthcharterinaction.org/content/pages/Read-the-Charter.html (5 May 2013).

[3]Pachamama Alliance, at: http://www.pachamama.org/ (19 September 2015).

[4]What does it mean and who are the main authors of this school of thought?

[5]Center for Process Studies, at: http://www.ctr4process.org/about/general.shtml (27 May 2014).

insights" and that it "also grounds discussion between Eastern and Western religious and cultural traditions."[6] The application of this process metaphysic is a lively field of research and collaboration.[7] More holistic approaches to science, for example those emerging from Einstein's theory of relativity, quantum theory, complex systems theory, neuroscience, and ecology, shed light on the ways in which a whole is more than the sum of its parts, as well as the interconnections between subjectivity and objectivity (e.g. see Urry 2005; Thrift 1999; Davies 1984). These scientific understandings provide a foundation for process thinking, which can be reconciled with the central insights of the world's major religious, understood in their historical and cultural contexts (e.g. see Griffin 2014). Deep cultural change toward peaceful and ecological civilization can be furthered through deepening the discussion, collaboration and support between peace studies and process studies. Together these research fields and communities could help to promote a shift to a paradigm of peace, as well as the application of a process metaphysic in developing and implementing structural and direct change toward ecological civilization.

2. *Ecofeminism.* The ecofeminist movement is a related example to process studies.[8] Ecofeminism connects the exploitation of Earth with the exploitation of women, linking the dominant western mechanistic materialist worldview with patriarchy and men's values. Led by ecofeminists such as Maria Mies, Vandana Shiva, Charlene Spretnak, Sallie McFague, Rosemary Radford Ruether, and our co-editor Úrsula Oswald Spring, ecofeminism is an exciting area for furthering ecological civilization. Like process philosophy, ecofeminism directly critiques what Mies and Shiva (1993: 2) call the "capitalist patriarchal world system," which they believe "emerged, is built upon and maintains itself through the colonization of women, of 'foreign' peoples and their lands; and of nature, which it is gradually destroying." An ecofeminist approach to research emphasizes the need for researchers to recognize their subjective influences, to commit to connecting research with action, to connecting science and responsibility, and to the importance of both individuals and groups coming to understand themselves-in-context and take action against oppressive elements of their reality (Mies 1993a: 38–50). Connecting social issues with ecological issues, ecofeminism encourages a multi-dimensional approach to problem-solving, positing that "social problems

[6]Ibid.

[7]For example, as seen in the 2015 conference hosted by the Center for Process Studies in Claremont, bringing together Bill McKibben (creator of 350.org) with Vandana Shiva, Mary Tucker Evans, Herman Daly and the world's leading process thinkers including John Cobb Jr., David Ray Griffin, Catherine Keller and Phillip Clayton.

[8]Leading process thinker John Cobb Jr. judges that "the most promising single movement today working for ecological civilization is eco-feminism." He observes the alignment of the movement's rethinking of the world-system and of the views of the world are "hardly distinguishable" from process thought "except in its addition of reflection about gender." See: Centre for Process Studies, "Seizing an Alternative: Towards an Ecological Civilization" Conference Program 2015, at: https://www.ctr4process.org/whitehead2015/wp-content/uploads/2015/05/WH2015_online-program.pdf (21 September 2015) p. 46.

(patriarchal relations, inequality, alienation, poverty) must be solved together with ecological problems" (Mies 1993b: 320). Arising from these principles, when applied to the world system, is a "subsistence perspective" that encourages local communities "to regain self-reliance and subsistence security" so that they can "become ecologically, socially and economically more independent from external market forces" (Mies 1993b: 312).

3. *Learning from indigenous peoples.* Groups of indigenous people from across the world are working to protect their land and are also looking to teach the modern industrial world more ecological ways of being. For example, the Pachamama Alliance are actively working to "change the dream" of Western people, encouraging a shift from the desire to own houses, cars, boats and fancy clothes, to "living well" by sharing the holistic nature-centered understandings that are often intrinsic to indigenous ways of seeing and being in the world.[9] Another example is the Ngarrindjeri people, who have set up a teaching center Camp Coorong, inviting non-Aboriginal people to learn about their culture and ways of living and caring for the land.[10] This may be enacted in 'localization' movements (as opposed to globalization), which create pockets of ecological civilizations that grow their own food, maintain local culture and flourish without needing to join the global mass production and consumption systems (e.g. see Norberg-Hodge et al. 2002).

4. *Global statements for positive peace.* The principles of deep cultural change toward ecological civilization are summed up in a statement called *The Earth Charter.*[11] This charter was developed by an independent Earth Charter Commission, consists of contributions from over five thousand people, and was "formally endorsed by thousands of organizations, including UNESCO and the IUCN (World Conservation Union)." The Preamble states: "We must join together to bring forth a sustainable global society founded on respect for nature, universal human rights, economic justice, and a culture of peace." The Charter articulates a holistic vision of peace, stating: "peace is the wholeness created by right relationships with oneself, other persons, other cultures, other life, Earth, and the larger whole of which all are a part" (Principle 16(f)). *The Earth Charter* continues on to provide an outline of the ultimate aims of peace between humanity and Earth. It captures an ecological narrative that overlaps with narratives of positive peace, as well as a process understanding of the self, other, our planet and our purpose. *The Earth Charter* is a watershed document that stands as a foundation for new thought and value. It reflects the principles of ecology and peace in a call to action.

Another more recent global statement, with broad celebrity and corporate support is the United Nations' *Sustainable Development Goals* (SDGs), which was ratified on 25 September 2015 at the United Nations Sustainable Development Summit. These seventeen goals build on the Millennium Development Goals,

[9]Pachamama Alliance, at: http://www.pachamama.org/ (19 September 2015).

[10]Camp Coorong, at: http://peaceliberation.tripod.com/pages/nlpaWebPage/ (12 October 2015).

[11]Earth Charter Initiative, at: http://www.earthcharterinaction.org/content/pages/Read-the-Charter.html (5 May 2013).

aiming to by 2030: end hunger and extreme poverty, fight social injustice including addressing gender inequality, improving infrastructure, ensuring access to clean water, sanitation and renewable energy for all; taking care of our environment including life in the seas, on land, creating sustainable cities, mitigating climate change; and peace and justice.[12] The goals also include economic growth and decent jobs for all, observing the need for this to involve "decoupl[ing] economic growth from environmental degradation." It is not surprising, however, that this statement of goals has been met with criticism. This is primarily due to the SDGs, beyond their admirable titles, are promoting neoliberal assumptions that it is global economic growth, privatization, free trade, aid to trade, and so on, will eradicate poverty.[13] So while these setting out of these global goals appear to express the values of a culture working toward ecological civilization, there is a disconnection between the values and the structural change and actions proposed. They are not questioning the cultural assumptions such as who should determine how another country develops, that producing cash crops and joining the free market is the best way out of poverty. Regardless of the failure of 'trickle down' economics, assuming that economic growth eventually trickles down to the bottom of the pyramid, the SDGs continue to make this assumption. This brings the chapter to the next section, in considering structural change toward ecological civilization.

9.5 Structural Change Toward Ecological Civilization

Concerns for ecological and social justice must include not only an inquiry into their relationships with culture, but also their connection to economics, politics and related institutions and structures. Structural change extends from changes in policies, e.g. implementing a tax on carbon; to changing the basis of the entire world economy. These structural changes and visions tie in with the examples and perspectives of cultural change considered above.

1. *Change in economic systems*. In 1891 John Stuart Mill wrote that in the future the economy would become stationary. In a stationary economy, Mill believed that many aspects of life including "education, art, religion, fundamental research, sports and human relations" would flourish. The consumption of irreplaceable and environmentally damaging products must be replaced with consumption of non-damaging products and enjoyment of human activities that can be "developed indefinitely" (Latouche 2006).[14] Visions of more sustainable global economic systems have been presented by various scholars of economics and political

---

[12]Global Goals, at: http://www.globalgoals.org/ (12 October 2015).

[13]E.g. see The Rules' "Open Letter to the United Nations", signed by Noam Chomsky, Naomi Klein, Chris Hedges and others, at: http://therules.org/petition/sdg-open-letter/ (21 October 2015).

[14]Latouche, Serge, 2006: "The Globe Downshifted: How Do We Learn to Want Less?", in: *Le Monde Diplomatique* (January): https://mondediplo.com/2006/01/13degrowth (31 October 2015).

science, such as the circular economy of Kenneth Boulding's *The Economics of the Coming Spaceship Earth* (1966), Herman Daly's "ecological economics" and "steady economy" (2008), and Serge Latouche's 'de-growth' economics (2004).[15] This kind of thinking contains economic growth within ecological boundaries.

2. *Change in technology.* Ecological economics aligns with 'cradle-to-cradle' thinking, which recognizes that Earth fundamentally operates as a closed system, where "the Earth's major nutrients—carbon, hydrogen, oxygen, nitrogen—are cycled and recycled. Waste equals food" (McDonough/Braungart 2002: 76). Cradle-to-cradle or birth-to-birth, is a play on the lifecycle phrase 'cradle to the grave', meaning birth until death. These regenerative design principles follows Earth's example, striving for production and consumption processes to involve *zero waste*. The cherry blossom tree is an example of a cradle-to-cradle process, where blossoms fall, decompose, feed various organisms and microorganisms, and enrich the soil. Cradle-to-cradle thinking suggests that "material flows can be divided into two categories: biological mass and technical—that is, industrial—mass" (McDonough/Braungart 2002: 92–93). It will take ingenuity to transform the "monstrous hybrids" of the two types of materials, and engineer products in ways that allow both the biological and industrial metabolisms to function (McDonough/Braungart 2002: 98–99). Buildings can be designed so that "like trees," they "produce more energy than they consume and purify their own waste water" (McDonough/Braungart 2002: 90). This ecological innovation is possible. Signs of a transition to ecological technologies can be seen in biodegradable plastic bags and detergent, as well as in new architectural developments such as Chicago City Hall.

Tim Flannery (2015) points out that the technology is there, it is vested interests—people making money from fossil fuels—that is getting in the way of its implementation. Furthermore research into technologies to help to mitigate climate change in the long term, such as seaweed farms, biochar and carbon-negative cement, all need significant investment in order to be developed, tested and implemented (Flannery 2015).[16] Solar, wind, geothermal energy is now affordable. Sweden, for example, has reduced its reliance on oil from 70 % in 1970, to 30 % in 2010, and it hopes to completely eliminate their use of fossil fuels by 2020 (Senge 2010: 4, 57). Denmark uses wind energy for 39.1 % of its electricity power, and nearly 26 % of Germany's electricity is also from clean sources.[17] Eventually, humans can design ways of consuming that leave Earth better off for it. Yet such innovation does require investment and contending with vested interests.

---

[15]Latouche, Serge, 2004: "Degrowth Economics: Why Less Should Be So Much More", in: *Le Monde Diplomatique* (November): https://mondediplo.com/2004/11/14latouche (31 October 2015).

[16]Tim Flannery distinguishes techniques like these, which follow examples from nature, from the radical proposals of geoengineering to inject sulfur into the stratosphere to reflect the sun into space and cool Earth's climate which he does not support.

[17]Ecowatch, at: http://ecowatch.com/2015/01/09/countries-leading-way-renewable-energy/ (21 September 2015).

3. *Change in business.* The primary objective of capitalism is to "realize the maximum profit" and hence production expands where "further production is profitable" (Wallerstein 1974: 398). Often this production is expanded with little consideration for the social or environmental costs. One of the reasons for this is the legal status of private corporations as separate entities, with a purpose to maximize profit for shareholders, and a stock market that allows short-term trading, hedging, options and other paper economy functions that do little more than to draw quick profits out of the real economy (Stanford 2008). This creates a disconnection between shareholders who invest for profit, CEOs who are rewarded for profit, and the interests of stakeholders to live in a healthy and socially just environment. The irony of the situation is that shareholders and CEOs are also stakeholders in the broader system, so the clash of interests can be found right through to the different roles a person plays and the values these roles encompass.

There are, however, movements toward 'purpose driven business', and in this vein an initiative worth mentioning is that of social business enterprises. Social business enterprises are businesses drive by social objectives rather than monetary profit. Yunus (2007) suggests that social businesses could work alongside the profit enterprises that we are so familiar with. Yunus theorizes that accompanying SBEs there will come a *Social Stock Exchange and Social Venture Capitalists*, trading stocks whereby the return on one's economic investment comes in the form of social profits rather than economic profits.[18] Along with social business enterprises, the *Dow Jones Sustainability Index*, "Fair trade" approval stamps, triple bottom line are increasing popularity and entering the mainstream, demonstrating how a refocus in the processes and priorities of business can also make a difference.

Whilst not wanting to discourage businesses from following through on these seemingly well-intended proposals, it may be problematic to imagine that without structural constraints (i.e. laws and policies) business will voluntarily avoid negative environmental and social impacts if it will reduce their profits. While social businesses may rise, it is unlikely that they will replace for-profit organisations. In the case that profits and helping people or the planet align, one can assume that CEOs of for-profit business might be content to take that path. Where profit and ethics conflict, it may be better to have laws and policies in place to ensure the choices in the interests of the common good are the ones that are made.

4. *Change in laws, policies and institutions.* There are many laws or policies that could be created and implemented to shift the world system toward ecological civilization. One example of an organization working to change the laws, policies and institutions that create poverty and environmental destruction is The Rules. The Rules is a "worldwide network of activists, artists, writers, farmers, peasants, students, workers, designers, hackers, spiritualists and dreamers, linking up, pushing the global narrative in a new direction." The Rules focuses on five areas they claim to be "in desperate need of radical reform: Money, Power, Secrecy, Ideas and The

[18]For example an annual statement of how many children one's financial investment has saved from malnutrition.

Commons."[19] The Rules point out that money systems need to no longer be based on debt, promoting a stable economy as suggested above. They point to the need to shift power from corporations to civilians, and bring about a return to participatory democracy. They desire to turn secrecy policies upside-down so that rather than governments and corporations having access to civilian information, civilians should have far more access to government and corporate information. The Rules also emphasize the need to 'free our mind-space' from the constant bombardment of advertising and promotions encouraging people to buy this and that; instead The Rules encourages people to engage in critical thought, questioning the stories they have been told about growth being good and the need to continually accumulate more stuff. Finally, they encourage The Commons such as water, air, rainforests, and so on to be appreciated as common goods, protected from privatization, and for corporations that pollute them to pay the price.

Attempts to regulate transnational corporations have been made, yet they have not yet been successful. Boulding (2000: 202) explains that in 1974 the United Nations Commission of Transnational Corporations was set up to 'draft a UN Code on transnational corporations that was to protect both the rights of states to regulate corporations within their borders and the rights of transnational corporations against arbitrary seizure of property by states.' The draft was circulated twelve years later, but was never implemented. Institutionalizing a transnational regulatory code, and reversing transnational free trade agreements (including the newly agreed upon Trans-Pacific Partnership Agreement, that further secures corporation's power over governments and civilians) would be an example of structural change toward ecological civilization.

9.6 Action Toward Ecological Civilization

Direct action for ecological civilization can be taken at individual, group, national and international levels. It spans personal investment in solar power and hybrid cards, signing petitions and protesting on the streets, joining advocacy groups for social and ecological justice. It includes using one's personal power in their everyday decisions at work, at home, when shopping, investing, voting, boycotting, etc. and joining with others to collectively show civilian support for governments to enact ecologically- and socially-just policies, corporations to act ethically, and states to sign binding international agreements that promote a collaborative global effort toward an ecological world system.

1. *Investment of money and time.* Fracking, building obsolescence into products, putting money in offshore tax havens, and using sweatshops for cheap labour, are all examples of decisions made by people with power and money. In place of such unethical decision-making, such persons could invest their personal or business

[19]The Rules, at: http://therules.org/about/ (19 October 2015).

accounts in green energy and in making better quality and longer lasting products (even if it means a decline in profits). These persons could choose to pay their factory employees higher wages and enforcing maximum work hours, as well as campaigning for governments to institute minimum wages and working conditions across the board. These people could also choose not to avoid tax by making use of tax havens and tax breaks, but to see their tax as an investment in their society. Within the academy, an increase in investment could be made in interdisciplinary studies that have not yet received the prestige and funding of disciplinary studies (Leiserowitz/Fernandez 2008: 21). These social and economic factors can limit or facilitate the achievements of research in peace studies, process philosophy, ecofeminism, etc., engaging in collaborations with other disciplines and hence increasing their impact.

2. *Cosmic education and big history.* In the field of education, a curriculum that goes by the name 'big history' is spreading and making an impact in schools and universities across the world. Big history takes a macro-historical approach to tell the story of the universe, connecting present understandings of the 'big bang' through cosmological and biological evolution, through human history and industrialization to the global ecological crisis (Christian 2004). This course resonates with the macro history taught in Montessori schools' 'cosmic education' curriculum, which has been promoted in UNESCO's curriculum for peace education for decades. It aligns with "The New Story" promoted by Thomas Berry, inspired by the work of Pierre Teilhard de Chardin, and told as "The Journey of the Universe" (Swimme/Tucker 2011). Big history is spreading across the world thanks to Bill Gates, who listened to *The Great Courses'* audio file of Christian's (2008) *Big History*, and set forth to put billions of dollars behind it in order to develop the curriculum (available for free) and promote it internationally. While still in its early stages, studies thus far have found that big history has the power to foster personal empowerment and care for collective action in the direction of ecological civilization (e.g. see Blundell 2015). People working in education systems could ensure big history is a part of the curriculum, and invest in teaching it in ways that bring about such experience and action.

3. *Social movements and advocacy.* One of the most practical and successful global campaigns is the 350.org's[20] campaign to for the divestment of fossil fuels and their replacement with green energy alternatives. Social movements and advocacy groups abound with focuses on specific social justice issues, for example refugees, through to those aiming to make structural change such as The Rules introduced above. From engineers to lawyers to artists, environmentalists, philosophers, and even some leaders in corporate, media and governmental worlds, people are contributing in myriad ways to the aim of ecological civilization. There is power in numbers. It is pivotal that these efforts support each other, bridging

[20]350.org is an online-based climate change movement that seeks to reduce the amount of $CO2$ in earth's atmosphere to 350 parts per million (ppm), which is the estimated number required for earth to remain habitable for humans into the future. It is currently at 400 ppm.

disciplines and movements in order to strengthen the collective effort toward a shared aim. Naomi Klein's landmark book *This Changes Everything: Capitalism vs The Climate* emphasizes the need for such collaboration, if there is any chance of evolving the capitalist world system into a system that will not destroy humanity's source of life.

4. *Bringing together religion and ecology.* A lively initiative applying a similar lineage of interdisciplinary thinking to process philosophy and peace studies, is the Religion and Ecology Forum at Yale University. Directed by John Grim and Mary Evelyn Tucker this Forum explores ecological values and solutions to environmental problems via a dialogue between religions and other academic disciplines.[21] This interreligious approach interprets religious texts in their historical contexts, reevaluating and reconstructing them in light of current issues (Grim/Tucker 2014: 8). They provide information about such thinking, as well as a list of statements from leaders of the world's major religions, encouraging the links between their religion, ecology and peace to be made.

Perhaps the most significant statement by a religious leader is Pope Francis' Encyclical (2015) *Laudato Si': On care for our common home*. In this Encyclical, Pope Francis opens up a dialogue with all the people on Earth about the intertwining issues of ecological and social justice, and their roots in the world system and culture. Pope Francis, who named himself after Saint Francis of Assisi (the patron saint of ecology), proposes a model of "integral ecology" in which all human beings see themselves as a part of the world and appreciates each living organism and ecosystem as having intrinsic worth in and of themselves. The Encyclical is a thorough, balanced and confronting piece of writing, which summarizes some key concerns that all humans should share. For example, it surveys issues of pollution, climate change, resource depletion, loss of diversity of species, clean water as a basic human right, global inequality, breakdown of society seen in the lack of employment and growing use of drugs particularly among the youth, and the unjust impact of environmental problems experienced most severely by the poor. The Encyclical draws connections between these issues and the lifestyles of people in developed countries, to corporate power and greed, to the primacy of economic growth and legal systems that enable even governments to be controlled by people with the most money. The Encyclical is having a significant impact on Catholics across the world, which represent more than one-seventh of the global population. Within three months of the Encyclical's publication, the process philosophy and Religion and Ecology communities were already furthering the call (see Cobb/Castuera 2015).

It is with a spirit of hope that above visions and efforts can have an impact on the political leaders attending the United Nations Climate Change Conference in Paris

[21]The Forum on Religion and Ecology at Yale, at: http://fore.yale.edu//about-us/ (19 September 2015).

in December 2015, and that some kind of legally binding agreement may result, that sets in motion action for real and deep structural change toward ecological civilization.

9.7 Continuing the Conversation

Each of the initiatives above, and the many thousands of other initiatives that could be mentioned here, raise further questions for furthering their contributions to ecological civilization and positive peace. For example with regard to education: In the same way that big history points to the connections between fields historically, could a 'big ecology' curriculum (essentially Peace Education) be developed to examine the relationships between human psychology, society, economics, politics, institutions and ecosystems? How might such an initiative secure the same kind of backing and expediency that big history has achieved? Or with regard to connecting cultural and structural change, do the SDGs contradict the goal of ecological civilization, or can they be used to engage business in the common aims articulated in the title of the goals (even if not in their fine print)? With regard to connecting structural change to direct action, what resources can be developed to empower individuals to work together to change structures? Overall how can positive peace, including structural peace, cultural peace and direct peace, be achieved?

This chapter has considered a selection of initiatives that aim to bring about cultural, structural and direct change toward ecological civilization. This framework of change (cultural, structural and direct) can be applied to regional and global issues of ecology and peace. The framework posits the question of *context* at the heart of resolving conflict in nonviolent ways. *What is the context of people's actions?* What are the cultural, structural and direct influences on actor's decisions? How can these be cultivated so that they resolve conflict nonviolently and work to bring about a more peaceful, social just, and ecologically sustainable world?

In the year that this book has been published there will be another IPRA conference. Here the EPC will explore a broad range of topics surrounding the development of a more sustainable relationship between humanity and their ecosystems. In these sessions the commission will discuss questions such as: In what ways is the wellbeing of humanity caught up in the wellbeing of the planet? How can conflict over environmental issues be resolved nonviolently and with a just outcome for all (including future generations)? How do issues such as population relate to poverty and the planet? How does gender relate to culture, food and water? How can humanity mitigate and adapt to climate change in a peaceful way? What can civilians to do encourage their governments to make policy decisions that hold the environment as a priority? What can motivate and spread the political will for this support? What would an Ecological Civilization look like? What are the roles of green energy, sustainable agriculture, holistic education and ecological economics in this pursuit? What direct and indirect action can bring this about? What are the priorities in moving in this direction?[22]

References

Blundell, Richard, 2015: "Waking up in the Anthropocene: Big History and the Biosphere" (Ph.D. dissertation, Macquarie University).

Boulding, Elise, 2000: *Cultures of Peace: The Hidden Side of History* (New York: Syracuse University Press).

Boulding, Kenneth, 1966: "The Economics of the Coming Spaceship Earth", in: Jarrett, H. (Ed.): *Environmental Quality in a Growing Economy* (Baltimore, MD: Resources for the Future/Johns Hopkins University Press): 3–14.

Brundtland, Gro Harlem, et al., 1987: *Our Common Future: Report of the 1987 World Commission on Environment and Development* (Oxford: Oxford University Press).

Christian, David, 2004: *Maps of Time: An Introduction to Big History* (Berkeley: University of California Press).

Christian, David, 2008: "Big History: The Big Bang, Life on Earth, and the Rise of Humanity", in: *The Great Courses* (Chantilly, VA: The Teaching Company); at: http://www.thegreatcourses.com/.

Cobb Jnr., John B.; Ignacio Castuera (Eds.), 2015: *For Our Common Home: Process-Relational Responses to Laudato Si'* (Claremont CA: Process Century Press).

Daly, Herman E. 2008: "On the Road to Disaster", in: *New Scientist*, 18 October, 46–47.

Davies, Paul, 1984: *Superforce: The Search for a Grand Unified Theory of Nature* (New York: Simon & Schuster).

Flannery, Tim, 2015: *Atmosphere of Hope: Searching for Solutions to the Climate Crisis* (Melbourne: The Text Publishing Company).

Francis, Pope, 2015: *Laudato Si': On Care for Our Common Home* [Encyclical Letter]. (Rome: Vatican).

Galtung, Johan, 1996: *Peace by Peaceful Means: Peace and Conflict, Development and Civilization* (London: Sage Publications Ltd).

Gare, Arran, 2010: "Toward an Ecological Civilization: The Science, Ethics and Politics of Ecopoiesis", in: *Process Studies*, 39,1: 5–38.

Griffin, David Ray, 2014: *Panentheism and Scientific Naturalism: Rethinking Evil, Morality, Religious Experience, Religious Pluralism, and the Academic Study of Religion, Toward Ecological Civilization* (Vol. 2) (Claremont: Process Century Press).

Grim, John; Mary Evelyn Tucker, 2014: *Ecology and Religion* (Washington DC: Island Press).

Latouche, Serge, 2004: "Degrowth Economics: Why Less Should Be So Much More", in: *Le Monde Diplomatique* (November); at: https://mondediplo.com/2004/11/14latouche (31 October 2015).

Latouche, Serge, 2006: "The Globe Downshifted: How Do We Learn to Want Less?", in: *Le Monde Diplomatique* (January); at: https://mondediplo.com/2006/01/13degrowth (31 October 2015).

Leiserowitz, Anthony A.; Lisa O Fernandez, 2008: *Toward a New Consciousness: Values to Sustain Human and Natural Communities* (New Haven, CT: Yale School of Forestry and Environmental Studies).

McDonough, William; Michael Braungart, 2002: *Cradle to Cradle: Remaking the Way We Make Things* (New York: North Point Press).

[22]For more on the 26th IPRA conference in 2016 please visit IPRA, at: www.iprapeace.org.

Mies, Maria, 1993a: "Feminist Research: Science, Violence and Responsibility", in: Mies, Maria; and Vandana Shiva (Eds.): *Ecofeminism* (Melbourne: Spinifex Press): 36–54.
Mies, Maria, 1993b: "The Need for a New Vision: The Subsistence Perspective", in: Mies, Maria; and Vandana Shiva (Eds.): *Ecofeminism* (Melbourne: Spinifex Press): 297–322.
Mies, Maria; Vandana Shiva, 1993: *Ecofeminism* (Melbourne: Spinifex Press).
Mill, John Stuart, 1891: *Principles of Political Economy* (London: George Routledge and Sons).
Norberg-Hodge, Helena; Merrifield, Todd; Gorelick, Steven M., 2002: *Bringing the Food Economy Home: Local Alternatives to Global Agribusiness* (London: Zed Books).
Reardon, Betty A., 1988: *Comprehensive Peace Education: Educating for Global Responsibility* (New York: Teachers College).
Reardon, Betty A., 1989: "Toward a Paradigm of Peace", in: Linda Rennie Farcey (Ed.): *Peace: Meanings, Politics, Strategies* (New York: Praeger).
Senge, Peter M., 2010: *The Necessary Revolution: How Individuals and Organizations Are Working Together to Create a Sustainable World* (London: Nicholas Brealey).
Shiva, Vandana, 2006: *Earth Democracy: Justice, Sustainability and Peace* (London: Zed).
Stanford, Jim, 2008: *Economics for Everyone: A Short Guide to the Economics of Capitalism* (London: Pluto Press).
Swimme, Brian; Berry, Thomas, 1992: *The Universe Story: From the Primordial Flaring Forth to the Ecozoic Era—a Celebration of the Unfolding of the Cosmos* (New York: Harper Collins).
Swimme, Brian Thomas; Tucker, Mary Evelyn, 2011: *Journey of the Universe* (New Haven: Yale University Press).
Thrift, Nigel, 1999: "The Place of Complexity", in: *Theory, Culture & Society*, 16,31: 31–69.
Urry, J.N., 2005: "The Complexity Turn", in: *Theory, Culture & Society*, 22,5: 1–14.
Wallerstein, I, 1974: "The Rise and Future Demise of the World-Capitalist System", in: *Comparitive Studies in Society and History*, 16,4: 387–414.
Yunus, Muhammad, 2007: *Creating a World without Poverty: Social Business and the Future of Capitalism* (New York: Public Affairs).

International Peace Research Association (IPRA)

Founded in 1964, the International Peace Research Association (IPRA) developed from a conference organized by the "Quaker International Conferences and Seminars" in Clarens, Switzerland, 16–20 August 1963. The participants decided to hold international Conferences on Research on International Peace and Security (COROIPAS), which would be organized by a Continuing Committee similar to the Pugwash Conferences. Under the leadership of John Burton, the Continuing Committee met in London, 1–3 December 1964. At that time, they took steps to broaden the original concept of holding research conferences. The decision was made to form a professional association with the principal aim of increasing the quantity of research focused on world peace and ensuring its scientific quality.

An Executive Committee including Bert V.A. Roling, Secretary General (The Netherlands), John Burton (United Kingdom), Ljubivoje Acimovic (Yugoslavia), Jerzy Sawicki (Poland), and Johan Galtung (Norway) was appointed. This group was also designated as Nominating Committee for a 15-person Advisory Council to be elected at the first general conference of IPRA, to represent various regions, disciplines, and research interests in developing the work of the Association. Since then, IPRA has held 25 biennial general conferences, the venues of which were chosen with a view to reflecting the association's global scope. IPRA, the global network of peace researchers, has just held its 25th General Conference on the occasion of its 50th anniversary in Istanbul, Turkey in August 2014 where peace researchers from all parts of the world had the opportunity to exchange actionable knowledge on the conference broad theme of 'Uniting for sustainable peace and universal values'.

Ú.Oswald Spring et al. (eds.), *Regional Ecological Challenges for Peace in Africa, the Middle East, Latin America and Asia Pacific*, The Anthropocene: Politik—Economics—Society—Science 5, DOI 10.1007/978-3-319-30560-8

The 26th IPRA General Conference will take place between November 28 and 1st December in 2016 in Freetown, Sierra Leone on the theme: AGENDA FOR PEACE AND DEVELOPMENT: Conflict prevention, post-conflict transformation, and the Conflict, Disaster and Development Debate.

On IPRA http://www.iprapeace.org/.
IPRA 2016 Conference Brochure http://www.iprapeace.org/images/newsletters/IPRA%202016%20Freetown%20%20CONFERENCE%20%20BROCHURE.pdf.

Previous IPRA Conferences

IPRA 2012 in Mie https://www.facebook.com/media/set/?set=a.321841277928978.77587.320866028026503&type=3.
IPRA 2014 in Istanbul https://www.facebook.com/ipra2014.
On the IPRA Foundation http://iprafoundation.org/.

International Peace Research Association (IPRA)
Conferences, Secretary Generals and Presidents
1964–2016

IPRA General Conferences	IPRA Secretary Generals/Presidents
1. Groningen, the Netherlands (1965)	1964–1971 Bert V.A. Roling (the Netherlands)
2. Tallberg, Sweden (1967)	1971–1975 Asbjorn Eide (Norway)
3. Karlovy Vary, Czechoslovakia (1969)	1975–1979 Raimo Väyrynen (Finland)
4. Bled, Yugoslavia (1971)	1979–1983 Yoshikazu Sakamoto (Japan)
5. Varanasi, India (1974)	1983–1987 Chadwick Alger (USA)
6. Turku, Finland (1975)	1987–1989 Clovis Brigagão (Brazil)
7. Oaxtepec, Mexico (1977)	1989–1991 Elise Bouding (USA)
8. Königstein, FRG (1979)	1991–1994 Paul Smoker (USA)
9. Orillia, Canada (1981)	1995–1997 Karlheinz Koppe (Germany)
10. Győr, Hungary (1983)	1997–2000 Bjørn Møller (Denmark)
11. Sussex, England (1986)	2000–2005 Katsuya Kodama (Japan)
12. Rio de Janeiro, Brazil (1988)	2005–2009 Luc Reychler (Belgium)
13. Groningen, the Netherlands (1990)	2009–2012 Jake Lynch (UK/Australia)
14. Kyoto, Japan (1992)	Katsuya Kodama (Japan)
15. Valletta, Malta (1994)	2012–2016 Nesrin Kenar (Turkey)
16. Brisbane, Australia (1996)	Ibrahim Shaw (Sierra Leone/UK)
17. Durban, South Africa (1998)	**Presidents**
18. Tampere, Finland (2000)	The first IPRA President was Kevin Clements
19. Suwon, Korea (2002)	(New Zealand/USA, 1994–1998).
20. Sopron, Hungary (2004)	His successor was Úrsula Oswald Spring
21. Calgary, Canada (2006)	(Mexico, 1998–2000).
22. Leuven, Belgium (2008)	
23. Sydney, Australia (2010)	
24. Mie, Japan (2012)	
25. Istanbul, Turkey (2014)	
26. Freetown, Sierra Leone (2016)	

IPRA's Ecology and Peace Commission (EPC)

IPRA's *Ecology and Peace Commission* (EPC) addresses the relationship between the Earth and human systems, and their impacts on peace. A special focus is placed on the linkages between problems of sustainable development and sustainable peace. The EPC evolved from the Food Study Group, which became *Ecology and Peace Commission* (EPC). In 2004 an *Earth Charter Working Group* was also set up. Many wars have been related to resource conflicts and therefore the EPC focused on conflict resolution related to sustainable development and processes of sustainable transition toward ecological civilization.

The conveners are elected by the participants during IPRA conferences for a two year period to prepare the publications for the past conference and to prepare the sessions for the next conference. The conveners between the IPRA conferences in Mie (2012) and Istanbul (2014) were:

- Úrsula Oswald Spring (CRIM/UNAM, Cuernavaca, Mexico), Full time Professor/Researcher at the National University of Mexico (UNAM) in the Regional Multidisciplinary Research Center (CRIM), lead author of the Intergovernmental Panel on Climate Change (IPCC); Email: uoswald@gmail.com.
- Hans Günter Brauch (Free University of Berlin (ret.), Peace Research and European Security Studies [AFES-PRESS], Mosbach, Germany); Chairman, Peace research and European Security Studies (AFES-PRESS), nonprofit scientific society, Mosbach, Germany (see biography as coeditor); Email: brauch@afes-press.de;

Ú.Oswald Spring et al. (eds.), *Regional Ecological Challenges for Peace in Africa, the Middle East, Latin America and Asia Pacific*, The Anthropocene: Politik—Economics—Society—Science 5, DOI 10.1007/978-3-319-30560-8

- Keith G. Tidball (Cornell University, Ithaca. NY, USA), Senior Extension Associate in the Department of Natural Resources where he serves as Associate Director of the Civic Ecology Lab and Program Leader for the Nature & Human Security Program. New York State Coordinator for NY Extension Disaster Education Network; Email: kgtidball@cornell.edu.

Based on the presentations of the IPRA conference in Mie (November 2012) they published this peer-reviewed book:

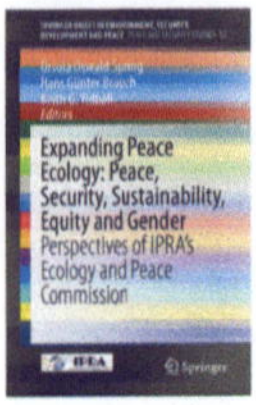

Úrsula Oswald Spring; Hans Günter Brauch; Keith G. Tidball (Eds.): *Expanding Peace Ecology: Security, Sustainability, Equity and Peace: Perspectives of IPRA's Ecology and Peace Commission 1.* SpringerBriefs in Environment, Security, Development and Peace, vol. 12. Peace and Security Studies No. 2 (Cham–Heidelberg–New York–Dordrecht–London: Springer-Verlag, 2014).
ISBN (Print): 978-3-319-00728-1
ISBN (Online/eBook): 978-3-319-00729-8
DOI: 10.1007/978-3-319-00729-8

In August 2014 in Istanbul the conveners between the IPRA conferences in Istanbul (2014) and in Freetown (2016) were elected:

- Prof. Dr. Úrsula Oswald Spring (CRIM/UNAM, Cuernavaca, Mexico)
- PD Dr. Hans Günter Brauch (Free University of Berlin (ret.), Peace Research and European Security Studies [AFES-PRESS], Mosbach, Germany)
- Juliet Bennett, Ph.D. candidate (Centre for Peace and Conflict Studies, The University of Sydney Australia); *Email*: juliet.bennett@sydney.edu.au.

Based on the presentations of the IPRA conference in Istanbul (August 2014) they published these two peer-reviewed books:

- Hans Günter Brauch, Úrsula Oswald Spring, Juliet Bennett, Serena Eréndira Serrano Oswald (Eds.): *Addressing Global Environmental Challenges from a Peace Ecology Perspective.*
- Úrsula Oswald Spring, Hans Günter Brauch, Serena Eréndira Serrano Oswald, Juliet Bennett (Eds.): *Regional Ecological Challenges for Peace in Africa, the Middle East, Latin America and Asia Pacific.*

Antiwar Day, 1 September 2015
Cuernavaca (Mexico), Mosbach (Germany), Sydney (Australia)
Úrsula Oswald Spring–Hans Günter Brauch–Juliet Bennett

About the Editors

Juliet Bennett (Australia) is a Ph.D. Candidate at the Centre for Peace and Conflict Studies, the University of Sydney. Her research explores an interface between ecology, religion and peace. Juliet has presented her research at international conferences and published papers in academic journals and edited books. She has taught at Lenoir Rhyne University, North Carolina as well as at The University of Sydney. Juliet has been the Executive Officer of the Sydney Peace Foundation since 2012, and in 2014 she became a co-convener of the Peace and Ecology Commission of the International Peace Research Association.

Address: Ms. Juliet Bennett, Centre for Peace and Conflict Studies, Mackie Building K01, The University of Sydney NSW 2006.
Email: juliet.bennett@sydney.edu.au.
Website: http://www.julietbennett.com.

Hans Günter Brauch (Germany), Dr., Adj. Prof. (Privatdozent) at the Faculty of Political and Social Sciences, Free University of Berlin; since 1987 chairman of *Peace Research and European Security Studies* (AFES-PRESS). He is editor of the *Hexagon Book Series on Human and Environmental Security and Peace* (HESP), and of *SpringerBriefs in Environment, Security, Development and Peace* (ESDP), of the *SpringerBriefs of Pioneeres in Science and Practice of the Pioneers in Arts, Humanities, Science, Engineering, and Practice* with Springer International Publishing. He was guest professor of international relations at the universities of Frankfurt on Main, Leipzig, Greifswald, and Erfurt; research associate at Heidelberg and Stuttgart universities, and a research fellow at Harvard and Stanford Universities. In fall and winter 2013/2014 he was a guest professor at

Ú.Oswald Spring et al. (eds.), *Regional Ecological Challenges for Peace in Africa, the Middle East, Latin America and Asia Pacific*, The Anthropocene: Politik—Economics—Society—Science 5, DOI 10.1007/978-3-319-30560-8

Chulanlongkorn University in Bangkok. He published on security, armament, climate, energy, and migration, and on Mediterranean issues in English and German, was translated into Spanish, Greek, French, Danish, Finnish, Russian, Japanese, Portuguese, Serbo-Croatian, and Turkish. Recent books in English: (co-ed. with Liotta, Marquina, Rogers, Selim): *Security and Environment in the Mediterranean. Conceptualising Security and Environmental Conflicts*, 2003; (co-ed. with Oswald Spring, Mesjasz, Grin, Dunay, Chadha Behera, Chourou, Kameri-Mbote, Liotta): *Globalization and Environmental Challenges: Reconceptualizing Security in the 21st Century, 2008;* (co-ed. with Oswald Spring, Grin, Mesjasz, Kameri-Mbote, Chadha Behera, Chourou, Krummenacher): *Facing Global Environmental Change: Environmental, Human, Energy, Food, Health and Water Security Concepts* (2009); (co-ed. with Oswald Spring): *Reconceptualizar la Seguridad en el Siglo XXI* (2009); (co-ed. with Oswald Spring, Mesjasz, Grin, Kameri-Mbote, Chourou, Dunay, Birkmann): *Coping with Global Environmental Change, Disasters and Security—Threats, Challenges, Vulnerabilities and Risks* (2011); (co-ed with Scheffran, Brzoska, Link, Schilling): *Climate Change, Human Security and Violent Conflict* (2012), and (co-ed with Oswald Spring, Grin, Scheffran): *Handbook on Sustainability Transition and Sustainable Peace* (2016).
Address: PD Dr. Hans Günter Brauch, Alte Bergsteige 47, 74821 Mosbach, Germany.
Email: brauch@afes-press.de.
Website: http://www.afes-press.de and http://www.afes-press-books.de/.

Úrsula Oswald Spring (Mexico), full time Professor and Researcher at the National University of Mexico (UNAM) in the Regional Multidisciplinary Research Center (CRIM), she was national coordinator of water research for the National Council of Science and Technology (RETAC-CONACYT), first Chair on Social Vulnerability at the United National University Institute for Environment and Human Security (UNU-EHS); founding Secretary-General of El Colegio de Tlaxcala; General Attorney of Ecology in the State of Morelos (1992–1994), National Delegate of the Federal General Attorney of Environment (1994–1995); Minister of Ecological Development in the State of Morelos (1994–1998). She was President of the International Peace Research Association (IPRA, 1998–2000), and General Secretary of the Latin-American Council for Peace Research (2002–2006).

She studied medicine, clinical psychology, anthropology, ecology, classical and modern languages. She obtained her Ph.D. from University of Zürich (1978). For her scientific work she received the Price Sor Juana Inés de la Cruz (2005), the Environmental Merit in Tlaxcala, Mexico (2005, 2006), UN Development Prize. She was recognized as Women Academic in UNAM (1990 and 2000); and Women of the Year (2000). She works on non-violence and sustainable agriculture with groups of peasants and women and is President of the Advisory Council of the

Peasant University. She has written 46 books and more than 328 scientific articles and book chapters on sustainability, water, gender, development, poverty, drug consumption, brain damage due to under-nourishment, peasantry, social vulnerability, genetic modified organisms, bioethics, on human, gender, and environmental security, peace and conflict resolution, democracy, and conflict negotiation.

Address: Prof. Dr. Úrsula Oswald Spring, CRIM-UNAM, Av. Universidad s/n, Circuito 2, Col. Chamilpa, Cuernavaca, CP 62210, Mor., Mexico.
Email: uoswald@gmail.com.
Website: http://www.afes-press.de/html/download_oswald.html.

Serena Eréndira Serrano Oswald (Mexico) is researcher at the Regional Multidisciplinary Research Centre, National Autonomous University of Mexico (CRIM-UNAM). She holds a Ph.D. in Social Anthropology (UNAM), an MSc in Social Psychology (LSE), an MFT in Systemic Family Therapy (CRISOL), and a BA Hons in Political Studies and History (SOAS). She has a Postdoctorate in Sociology and Gender (UNAM), a professional diploma in translation and interpreting (Institute of Linguists), a specialized training in couples therapy, in psychopathology (CRISOL), and person-centred therapy (Gestalt Institute). Certified by the National Council of Researchers (SNI I), she is currently president of the Mexican Association of Regional Development (AMECIDER).

Address: Dr. Serena Eréndira Serrano Oswald, CRIM-UNAM, Av. Universidad s/n, Circuito 2, Col. Chamilpa, Cuernavaca, CP 62210, Mor., Mexico.
Email: sesohi@gmail.com.

About the Contributors

Margaret Ifeoma Abazie-Humphrey (Nigeria) is a Principal Reintegration Officer at the *Office of the Special Adviser to the President on Niger Delta* (OSAPND), former Programme Coordinator of the Nigeria Women's Trust Fund (WF) and former Community Mediator of Perth & Kinross Community Mediation, Scotland, UK on dispute resolution. She was Programme Convener of Peacebuilding Consult, Abuja Nigeria responsible for the gender advocacy design for NGOs working on women affected with conflicts and trauma, on social justice and women empowerment. She received an M.Sc. Econ in Social Development Planning & Management, University of Wales, Swansea UK, had further trainings at American University, Washington DC; Eastern Mennonite University, Va.; Bergen Summer Research School, Norway; University of the Basque Country, Spain; and the Institute of Social Studies, The Hague, the Netherlands. In April 2015, she chaired the Local Organizing Committee of the *Africa Peace Research and Education Association* (AFPREA) Conference.
Address: Ms. Margaret Ifeoma Abazie-Humphrey, Office of the Special Adviser to the Nigeria President on Nigeria Delta, Federal Government of Nigeria, Presidential Amnesty Program, No. 4 Buzi Street, Off Amazon, Maitama, Abuja, Nigeria.
Email: ifeomaime@yahoo.com.

Charles Christian (USA) works at a DC-based non-profit to support efforts for sustainable peace in the Middle East and North Africa. He received a Bachelor of History from Trinity University in San Antonio, Texas (2008) and a Master of Arts in International Peace and Conflict Resolution from American University in Washington, DC (2013). This research was carried out as a part of his graduate studies. His current independent research focuses on identity politics in the Arabian Peninsula.
Address: Mr. Charles Christian, Program Associate, Middle East and North Africa, Search for Common Ground, USA.
Email: charlesdavidchristian@gmail.com.
Website: https://www.sfcg.org/.

Ú.Oswald Spring et al. (eds.), *Regional Ecological Challenges for Peace in Africa, the Middle East, Latin America and Asia Pacific*, The Anthropocene: Politik—Economics—Society—Science 5, DOI 10.1007/978-3-319-30560-8

Feng Feng (China) is currently a professor and renowned researcher at the School of Management, University of Science and Technology of China. He received his Ph.D. from Nanjing University in 1999. Prof. Feng's current research interests include: public policy and management, and crisis management. Prof. Feng has authored more than 80 research papers, many of which have been reproduced by XinHua Digest, and two published monographs. Besides, he has presided over 11 research projects at provincial and ministerial levels and has participated in four research projects.
Address: School of Public Affairs, University of Science and Technology of China, Hefei, Anhui, 230026, China.
Email: ffeng@ustc.edu.cn.
Website: http://dsxt.ustc.edu.cn/zj_ywjs.asp?zzid=898.

Tania Galaviz (México) is a professor in the Humanities Faculty at the Autonomous University of the State of Morelos (UAEM) and coordinates the institution's civil society outreach through its Direction of Civilian Rights-Outreach Secretariat. Among her major publications are:
Address: Dr. Tania Galaviz, Edif.19 Av. Universidad 1001, Col. Chamilpa, Cuernavaca, Morelos, México, C.P. 62209
Email: tgalaviz@gmail.com.

Audil Rashid (Pakistan) is Assistant Professor and Group Leader of EcoHealth Research (since 2007) at the *Department of Environmental Sciences, PMAS Arid Agriculture University, Rawalpindi.* Trained as Environmental Biologist, he received M.Phil. and Ph.D. degrees from Quaid-i-Azam University, Islamabad followed by post-doctorate from Peking University, China. He has a wide range of research interests including health risk assessment, urban health, ecological management and peace ecology. Dr. Rashid is on review panel of many reputed journals, and has presented his work at various international conferences. He has deep understanding of regional peace ecology issues and through his research work, he is highlighting Health—Environment dimensions of conflicts resolution.
Address: Assistant Professor Dr. Audil Rashid EcoHealth Research Lab., Department of Environmental Sciences, PMAS Arid Agriculture University, Rawalpindi 46300, Pakistan.
Email: audil@uaar.edu.pk.
Website: http://www.uaar.edu.pk/frw/faculty_details.php?dept_id=12&fac_id=81.

Fakhra Rashid (Pakistan) currently holds a Ph.D Fellowship jointly offered by Chinese Academy of Sciences (CAS) and The World Academy of Sciences (TWAS). She is working in the School of Public Affairs, University of Science of Technology of China. To her credit is research experience of EcoHealth project (2011–2013) in which she worked as Research Assistant in Department of Environmental Sciences, PMAS Arid Agriculture University, Rawalpindi, Pakistan.
Address: Ms. Fakhra Rashid, School of Public Affairs, University of Science and Technology of China, Hefei, Anhui, 230026, China.
Email: fakhra99@gmail.com.
Website: http://spa.ustc.edu.cn/english.php.

Heather Speight (USA) works as a research scientist with the United States Army Corps of Engineers, Engineer Research and Development Center, Geospatial Research Laboratory in Alexandria, Virginia. She is a licensed Professional Engineer in the State of California with a Bachelor of Science in Civil Engineering from the University of Dayton in Dayton, Ohio (2002) and a Master of Arts in International Peace and Conflict Resolution from American University in Washington, DC (2013). This research was carried out as a part of her graduate studies. Her current research focuses on the nexus between the environment, peace, and climate variability.
Address: Ms. Heather Speight, Research Scientist, United States Army Corps of Engineers, Engineer Research and Development Center, USA.
Email: heather.a.speight@gmail.com.

Seiichiro Takemine (Japan) is an associate professor at Meisei University in Tokyo. Ph.D. (International Studies: Waseda University). Co-convener of a research committee on Global Hibakusha and the board members of Peace Studies Association of Japan. Conducted filed research about the nuclear issues in the Marshall Islands since 1998. His major written works is [マーシャル諸島　終わりなき核被害を生きる] [Still Living with Nuclear Fallout in the Marshall Islands] (Tokyo: Shinsen sha, 2015 in Japanese).
Address: Prof. Dr. Seiichiro Takemine, Meisei University, 2-1-1 Hodokubo, Hino, Tokyo 191-8506 Japan.
Email: seiichiro.takemine@meisei-u.ac.jp and takeminese@hotmail.com.

Michiko Yoshii (Japan), Bachelor of French Literature at Kyoto University in 1981, Master of Vietnamese Studies at Paris VII University in 1991, Ph.D. of International Studies at The University of Tokyo in 2007. Worked as French-Japanese Interpreter, Commercial Director of a Japanese trading company in HCMC, Long-term assigned expert of JICA in Vietnam and Professor of Mie University, Japan. Actually, Professor in Faculty of Humanities, Okinawa University. Her main work: Yoshii, Michiko. 2009, "Citizens and NGOs standing up in Vietnam—Case of care activities for street children", Akashi Shoten, Tokyo (in Japanese).
Address: Prof. Dr. Michiko Yoshii, Okinawa University, 555 Kokuba, Naha, Okinawa-ken, 902-8521 Japan.
Email: yoshii@okinawa-u.ac.jp.

About this Book

Regional Ecological Challenges for Peace in Africa, the Middle East, Latin America and Asia Pacific contains peer-reviewed texts from IPRA's EPC. M.I. Abazie-Humphrey (Nigeria) reviews "The Nigeria Home-Grown DDR Programme". C. Christian and H. Speight (USA) analyse "Water, Cooperation, and Peace in the Palestinian West Bank". T. Galaviz (Mexico) discusses "The Peace Process Mediation Network between the Colombian Government and the April 19th Movement". S.E. Serrano Oswald (Mexico) examines "Social Resilience and Intangible Cultural Heritage: Case Study in Mexico". A. and F. Rashid (Pakistan) and F. Feng (China) focus on "Community Perceptions of Ecological Disturbances Caused During Terrorists Invasion and Counter-insurgency Operations in Swat, Pakistan". M. Yoshii (Japan) examines "Structure of Discrimination in Japan's Nuclear Export". Finally, S. Takemine (Japan) studies "'Global Hibakusha' and the Invisible Victims of the U.S. Nuclear Testing in the Marshall Islands".

Foreword: Ibrahim Shaw, Secretary-General, IPRA.

1 Introduction (Oswald Spring, Brauch, Bennett; Serrano Oswald)—2 The Nigeria Home-Grown DDR Programme (Abazie-Humphrey)—3 Water, Cooperation, and Peace in the Palestinian West Bank (Christian, Fisher, Jackson, Kehoe, Owen, Puleo, Rosner, Speight)—4 The Peace Process Mediation Network between the Colombian Government and the April 19th Movement (Galvaniz)—5 Social Resilience and Intangible Cultural Heritage: Case Study in Mexico (Serrano Oswald)—6 Community Perceptions of Ecological Disturbances Caused During Terrorists Invasion and Counter-insurgency Operations in Swat, Pakistan (Rashid, Feng, Rashid)—7 Structure of Discrimination in Japan's Nuclear Export (Yoshii)—8 Overlooked Invisible Victims of the U.S. Nuclear Testing in the Marshall Islands (Takemine)—9 Reflections on Moving Toward Ecological Civilization and Positive Peace (Bennett).

Backmatter: IPRA and EPC—About the Editors and Contributors.

More on this book at: http://www.afes-press-books.de/html/APESS_04-05.htm.

Ú.Oswald Spring et al. (eds.), *Regional Ecological Challenges for Peace in Africa, the Middle East, Latin America and Asia Pacific*, The Anthropocene: Politik—Economics—Society—Science 5, DOI 10.1007/978-3-319-30560-8

MIX
Papier aus verantwortungsvollen Quellen
Paper from responsible sources
FSC® C105338

If you have any concerns about our products,
you can contact us on
ProductSafety@springernature.com

In case Publisher is established outside the EU,
the EU authorized representative is:
Springer Nature Customer Service Center GmbH
Europaplatz 3, 69115 Heidelberg, Germany

Printed by Libri Plureos GmbH
in Hamburg, Germany